FRANK REFLECTIONS

OF AN ACADEMIC SURGEON

Frank G. Moody, MD

iUniverse LLC
Bloomington

iUniverse books may be ordered through booksellers or by contacting:

iUniverse
1663 Liberty Drive
Bloomington, IN 47403
www.iuniverse.com
1-800-Authors (1-800-288-4677)

ISBN: 978-1-4917-1240-5 (sc)
ISBN: 978-1-4917-1239-9 (hc)
ISBN: 978-1-4917-1238-2 (e)

Library of Congress Control Number: 2013919015

Printed in the United States of America.

iUniverse rev. date: 11/27/2013

To Those Who Pursue
"Non Sibi"

CONTENTS

Many thanks to Evangelina Rangel for her invaluable help in assembling the manuscript, and to Inger Margareta Ardern for her encouragement and support during the process of recording these recollections.

INTRODUCTION

The path through life has numerous twists and turns and the final outcome is more or less a game of chance. One's personal journey relates to a complex interaction between their genes, the environment, opportunity, and their relationship to other people. The following is a view of my life's progression, both personal and professional. It is my intent to write my experiences as I recall them, therefore, this might best be considered an autobiographic novel. The task is complicated by my age of 85 and the fact that I have Parkinson's Disease. As far as I can tell, my mind is still intact, but my hands and legs are weak. These conditions keep me out of the operating room and off the tops of mountains, winter and summer. Having to give up my favorite pastimes, skiing and hiking, has been both a challenge and a blessing. This new way of life conveniently called aging gives me time to reflect on what I have received from and given to society. The progression of my professional journey has involved many students, institutions, faculty, patients, family, friends, and people in general that I have worked with over the years. The purpose of putting my reflections into print is to share with others the satisfaction and joy that I have derived from serving the sick as a surgical educator.

My professional goal after completing college and medical school has been to participate fully in the medical academic enterprise to include patient care, teaching, research, and administration to whatever extent was required to accomplish this end. A specific desire was to develop surgeons who have a special interest in solving medical problems not only in the operating room but also in the laboratory, the clinic, and at the bedside. The challenge has been to incorporate the rapid advances in our understanding of cell and organ specific biology and diagnostic and operative technology into innovative therapies for the treatment and prevention of disease. It was and remains my hope that I can with reasonable expectations continue to achieve these goals. It was for this reason that I have included in my discussion some personal challenges that arose as I traveled along my career path that at times was difficult to manage financially. My family has been especially supportive during both the good times and the bad, and for that I am very thankful. In fact, my family and close friends are the intended audience for what I plan to express in the pages that follow. A more distant hope is that the story of my life may influence young students in general to choose the path that I have taken.

When I embarked on my surgical career in 1956, diagnostic imaging was in its infancy, and the instruments we used for operative procedures had not changed substantially for several decades. My field of interest, the surgical treatment of digestive disease was wide open for major advances at a fundamental level. The opportunity to work with Dr. Frank Glenn MD, the chairman of the department of surgery at The Cornell College of Medicine, Dr. John Beal MD, professor of surgery at Cornell College of Medicine, Dr. J. Englebert Dunphy MD, chairman of the department of surgery at the University of California in San Francisco, and Dr. John Kirklin MD, chairman of the department of surgery at the University of Alabama in Birmingham provided for me the tools to achieve my goal. They and their staffs helped me train a large number of academic and community based surgeons, and to interact with even a larger number of medical students, helping them to become competent and caring physicians. My hope was then and remains now that they in turn will pass on to their students, residents, and patients what I have learned from my own experience and that of my mentors.

It has been a privilege to have been able to work as an academic surgeon for over 55 years. Please note that I consider my academic career to have started the day I became an intern at the New York Hospital-Cornell Medical Center in July, 1956. I want to emphasize what I mean by the prefix academic. It is used to identify those surgeons who in their practice primarily emphasize the generation and transmission of new knowledge through research and teaching. Most such individuals work in academic health centers. Surgeons who work in community hospitals are no less important, and provide the majority of day to day care of surgical patients in America. It was and still is my hope that I can continue to interact and make a contribution to the education of both types of surgeons. My major reason for putting forth my life's story at this time is to inform my family and myself what I have been doing over the years. Possibly others that read my musings may also learn from my experiences how to enjoy life while helping others get well from their illness.

CHAPTER I

THE BEGINNING

I was born on May 3, 1928 in Franklin, New Hampshire. Our rented flat overlooked the mills along the Winnipesaukee River that flowed through the town to join the Pemigewasset to form the Merrimack. This river in turn flowed through lower New Hampshire and northeastern Massachusetts to enter the Atlantic Ocean just north of Boston. I mention the mills since they were such an important part of our life and the economy of the area. My mother, Elsie Wilson Moody, and father Frederick George Moody were born in Lawrence. Massachusetts and both went to work in a mill on the Merrimack at age 14. My father only completed the 9th grade. My mother graduated from high school by attending night school. They had moved to Franklin to seek a better life working in the Steven's Woolen Mill. The town of Franklin, population 5000 (I use to say including cows) was surrounded by wooded hills. The woods, rivers, and hills made an ideal environment for my sister Alice Etta Moody Seaward and me to grow up. She was 2 years older than I, and a delight to have as a sibling. My father Fred was the homemaker since he had to quit work a few years prior to my birth. He was limited in his activity by the complications of morbid obesity. We were relatively poor and he was too proud to seek free medical care. Besides cooking meals, and keeping up the house, he had odd jobs working in the stores downtown.

My mother was the primary bread winner. She worked as a burler in Stevens Mill, and was fortunate to have a job, since the early thirties was the height of the great depression. Some of my most vivid memories of that time related to bringing my mother her lunch. I was 7 or 8 at the time and fascinated (and frightened) by the large weaving machines that I used to have to pass on my way to her work station. My mother's work area was equally intimidating, shrouded by large pieces of cloth hanging from floor to ceiling. Her job, along with about 20 other middle-aged women was to mend defects in the cloth. I was impressed with how happy they were. The majority were French Canadians who had migrated from Canada which was about a hundred miles away. They delighted in telling each other off color stories while working, which my mother would tell to my father at the dinner table, much to the delight of my sister and me.

My sister Alice and I were brought up by Mrs. Meisterfield, a German lady who in fact was the owner of the flat that we lived in. Our mother would drop us off each morning at 6:30 on her way to work, and pick us up at 4:30 when she returned from work. These were fun days for us even though the environment was highly disciplined. We had lessons of various types, some in German, and learned many German songs which we enjoyed. The Meisterfield's had a young daughter (possibly 30ish) who use to visit from time to time. She was especially fun for us to play with. My mother told me that she was in a mental hospital in Concord. Of course I did not know what that meant at the time, and have pondered why over the years she was there since she seemed so trouble free to me.

My father's weight and its associated diseases greatly limited his physical activities. It was difficult for him to engage in boyhood games with me such as baseball, tag, hiking, fishing etc. We enjoyed our time together listening to mystery stories on the radio. It was a treat to lie next to him and listen to the familiar strain of "the shadow knows". My father was a great guy, known and well liked by the community. He was extremely generous and kind to those he called "the down and outers". One of his side jobs was selling lottery tickets. Not infrequently he would give one or more tickets to one of his down and out street friends, and there were many of them in the 1930s. He was so well liked on the street that he served a few terms in the State Legislature as a representative of his district. His illness likely had a profound effect on the career choices of my sister and I. Alice became a nurse, and I a surgeon. My father did not seek health care for what likely was diabetes with coronary heart disease. Several of the older physicians in town were willing to see him for no compensation, but he refused to accept their kind offer. He died of a presumed coronary occlusion at age 52.

Living in Maple Square was a real treat for me. At an early age I was allowed to roam freely through the un-crowded streets and the open fields that were filled with wildflowers and birds of all types. One of my favorite haunts was an old cemetery that was close to our house. This proximity got me a spanking on at least two occasions. The first was when I brought home a bouquet of roses to my mother that I had filched off a grave. The second time was more serious. After being spanked and told never to go to the graveyard again, I did. Unfortunately as I was climbing a gravestone it fell over on my leg. I was freed up by a passerby who took me home for another spanking. These two episodes taught me great respect for grave yards and the importance of obeying orders and keeping my hands off other peoples things, no matter how well intentioned. I also imagine that these grave yard experiences stimulated my love for the sight and smell of flowers, the feel of granite, and the urge through the healing arts to keep other people out of them.

My early years were likely profoundly influenced by the great depression of the early thirties. We were very poor but so was everyone else, so poverty was just a way of life. This was great for a four year old kid. Every stick or stone was a toy. At about age six we moved to the "flats" to make it easier for my mother to go to work and my father to go downtown. It was named the "flats" because it was located in a basin that housed Sulloway's Mill, one of our large clothing mills that lie below Steven's Mill (where my mother worked). The "flats" could also be distinguished from the "hill" where the well to do people lived. I cannot recall any ill will or bigotry between the hill dwellers and the flatlanders. In fact, we all went to the same schools which were on the "flats". Most of the churches were also on the "flats". The biggest was the Catholic Church, since most of the population on the "flats", were French Canadian. All of the non-Catholic churches had small congregations, and ours, the Unitarian Church was the smallest. We occasionally went to the Methodist or Baptist Church on Sunday mornings and to the Catholic Church for midnight mass on Christmas Eve. Our primary church affiliation was with the Unitarian Church which was located down the hill across from Sulloway's Mill. The Sulloway's were members of our church and their generosity and spirit made it a lively enterprise at the time.

My mother took Alice and me to Sunday School at the Unitarian Church at 9:00 AM each Sunday morning, and then brought us to the main service at 11:00. These were both instructive and enjoyable experiences. The lessons, and in fact the entire atmosphere displayed the importance of tolerance and respect for others. The basic idea was for the audience young and old to learn and emulate the ways of Christ. Unitarians believe that Jesus was an extraordinary man. He was considered to be a prophet but not a deity. In other words, he was a child of God like the rest of us. In this construct, there was no heaven or hell, or original sin for that matter. Imagine as kids how pleased we were to learn that.

Our Sunday school was primarily taken up with reading various passages from the Bible, and learning the good deeds that Jesus performed throughout his life. The adult service was filled with music, and a sermon that dealt with the issues of the day. After the service, we would gather for cakes, cookies, and a soft drink.

My mother sang in the choir, and when Alice and I became older (around 10 years of age) we joined her in this activity. I enjoyed singing with the choir and had the opportunity one Sunday to play a violin solo after considerable coaxing. My father rarely went to church. I am sure that his physical disability was a constraint. On one occasion he said to me that he did not want to associate with "those phonies". My father was a staunch Democrat and aligned with the flat dwellers. Most of the congregation was Republican living on the hill. My sister continued with the Church throughout her life, even when she moved away. I drifted away from going to church on Sundays when skiing became a passion. I have remained a Unitarian in my basic views of life, and try to live in the way of Christ, while respecting the beliefs or non belief of others.

The apartment on Franklin Street, while spartan, provided for each of us our own resting space. Our parents slept in their own bedroom. My sister occupied during the night a place in the corner of the dining room. I was housed in the corner of the front room which unfortunately was furthest from the wood stove that we had in the kitchen as our single source of heat. In the winter, when the temperature was always hovering close to zero, my mother would prepare my bed by placing several hot water bottles between the sheets before I would jump in. It wasn't long before the cold would creep in and I would shiver most of the night. In spite of the cold, I liked the winters the best.

Fortunately I had easy access to Devil's Hill for skiing in the winter. This was a small rise within a meadow that I could access by walking down the railroad tracks. It seemed huge to me at age 6. Close by was a steep snow covered sand pit, which when covered with snow, provided even a greater challenge for downhill skiing, and access to the Franklin Country Club where I could build small jumps and run cross country.

CHAPTER 2

OFF TO SCHOOL

The Primary School for Franklin (grades 1 to 6) was named the Hancock School, and was only a few blocks from our home on Franklin Street. I entered the first grade there at age 6, and after a few visits was able to walk there by myself. This was a great experience since the school was on a bluff overlooking the downtown area, the mills, the river, and also the Unitarian Church. There was a steep banking behind the school which I fancied as a climbing and skiing hill, which in fact came to pass as the year progressed. The teachers were just great. I especially remember Miss Thunberg, who taught me how to read and write, and Miss Morse, who encouraged me to write poetry. The class sizes were small, and the learning techniques quite interactive. My mother was very pleased with my academic progress, and insisted on me always completing my homework prior to going out to play. My father had a great sense of humor. He told me in jest that I would make a great garbage man some day. He knew how to keep me humble. I believe that part of my mother's encouragement stemmed from her not wanting me to end up in the mill like so many other kids did on the "flats".

Many of my friends lived on the "hill". They also went to the Unitarian Church. The father of my best friend Brandock Lovely was our pastor. Brandy and I use to climb up the hill to his home and play ball in a grove of trees next to his house. We usually would be joined by Leo VanCort in our games. Often I would stay overnight at either home since Leo lived across the street from Brandy. Both of the homes were large and beautiful. The overnight stays reinforced my desire to have my own room someday. This wish never came to fruition while we lived in Franklin. My folks in fact never had their own home or automobile but were happy that both Alice and I achieved that goal many years later.

I progressed on without problems academically into the 7th and 8th grade at Daniel Junior High School, and pursued the 9th and 10th at the Franklin High School. These two schools were almost physically attached to each other and therefore could easily share performing arts and athletic facilities. This provided an opportunity for those of us in Junior High to interact and mingle with the older kids in high school. This was especially advantageous for those of us that liked to go to the dances, which included me. In addition, it gave aspiring athletes like me a chance to find out early in life our competitive strengths in baseball, basketball and football. I was a lot smaller than most boys my age, and this made a difference in competing successfully in these sports. After being beat up a few times in "try outs", I finally saw the handwriting on the wall. If I was going to be good at anything, it had to be skiing. More importantly, I developed a keen interest in learning under the mentorship of the schools Principle, Miss Bessie Rowell. Miss Rowell would not allow us to fail to learn the required material, and encouraged each of us to go a step beyond our daily lessons. Her favorite saying was "hitch your wagon to a star, keep your seat and there you are". This mantra has served me well over the past 50 years, and applies equally well to young and old. It is particularly well suited for medical students, since the success of their learning experience will determine the outcome of their efforts to treat their patients.

CHAPTER 3

PHILLIPS EXETER ACADEMY (1944-1946)

I continued to perform well academically, and was popular not only with the teachers but also the students. I was elected class vice- president in the 10th grade, and felt that the world was my oyster. About this time, a prominent member of our church Dr. James Woodman asked my mother whether she might have an interest in sending me to Phillips Exeter Academy, a private high school in the southeastern part of the state. His son had gone there, and he was very impressed with what he learned, Dr. Woodman and I had met several times when I was assigned to do his yard by a greenhouse that I worked for part-time in the summer. I of course was flattered by his suggestion, but I knew that Exeter was one of the premier schools in the country, and very expensive to go to. I also developed the impression that it was a school only for the most privileged in our society. This erroneous idea derived from my spending a summer picking apples in Hampton Falls which is adjacent to Exeter. I was exposed to a very negative "townie" view that Exeter students were all spoiled rich kids.

I later found out that then as now many of the students received scholarship support. One of the major donors was the great newspaper giant William Randolph Hearst who provided scholarship support for newspaper delivery boys such as myself. In fact we were told by the Director of Admissions, Hammy Bissel, that Hearst had a special interest in supporting the poorest paper boy in New Hampshire. While I was a paper delivery boy, and fit the description, I did not think that I was smart enough to pass the entrance exam. Furthermore, Exeter felt that I should either take summer school, which we could not afford, or enter as a sophomore (9th grade), rather than a junior(10th grade), an alternative that posed the risk that I would be drafted before I would graduate in 1947. For these reasons I resisted the idea of applying, but at my mother's insistence, I took the exam. As I had predicted, I did not pass. A few weeks later, however, I received an acceptance letter to enter as a junior without having to attend summer school. This was an offer that I could not refuse. I suspect that Dr. Woodman liked the way that I kept his yard, and that he had put in a good word for me. My mother was ecstatic, as was my father and sister. What I did not know at the time was that my mother borrowed three hundred dollars from the local bank to seal the deal, which was a large sum of money in 1944 for someone who was making only 20 dollars a week while supporting a sick husband and two young children. A few months later I was off to Exeter, and this has made all the difference in the direction of my life. Lest I forget to mention it, the Exeter motto, "non sibi" (not for oneself) has stuck with me throughout my life.

Exeter was as tough academically and socially as I thought it would be. I was taken aside the first day by one of my teachers, and told that I had to wear a coat and tie when attending class and going to the dining room. When I told him that I did not have either, he provided me with a note to immediately go and purchase them from a store downtown. There are too many touching stories of kindness to relate here, but one must be told. I was assigned the job of "bell ringer" for announcing the time of change of classes on the hour. Unfortunately I did not have a watch, and was too shy to tell the assigner of the task of my situation. Our classes were conducted around what is called a Harkness Table, which is a solid oval table that allowed about 15 boys (no girls yet in 1944) to sit around it, with the teacher at one end. I always positioned myself at the far end, next to someone who had a watch, and towards the end of the hour would ask the watch bearer what time it was. After a few days, this mild disruption began to irritate the teacher, and he abruptly and gruffly asked me why at this time each day I would be disrupting the class. I told him that I needed to know the time to ring the bell. His response was surprisingly pleasant. He told me to see him after class to pick up a spare watch he had to use the rest of the year.

My two years at Exeter were difficult and challenging academically, but enjoyable. The course work was tough, and the exams even tougher. Having received mainly A's at Franklin High, it took time to adjust to initially receiving D's in my Junior Year, and finally C's and a few B's in my Senior Year. At Exeter we were encouraged to participate fully in a large number of extra-curricular activities. I played violin in the orchestra, sang in the glee club and choir, played club football, ran track, and in the winter, skied the small hills that surrounded the town. Exeter was everything it was cracked up to be. In fact even my modest performance there academically earned me an acceptance at Harvard, Yale, and Princeton, but not Dartmouth where I really wanted to go. I was put on a waiting list along with the many veterans that were returning from World War II. To make life even more complicated, I was summoned to the draft about two months before graduation. Upon appeal, I was granted a two month extension with the understanding that I would report to duty the first working day after graduation. This was a good resolution of the problem of which college to attend, since I did not have enough money to attend an Ivy League School, and I could reapply to Dartmouth after I had the money from my military service.

We had a wonderful graduation week-end in Exeter with my mother, father, and sister in attendance, along with a female friend, Elvira Gertrude Rose Whitehead (Vi). Vi and I had met the previous summer at Twin Lake Villa. It was planned that we both would return to the Villa in the summer of 1946. The threat of being drafted brought an abrupt change in these plans. Rather than be drafted, I joined the Army the day after graduation. Without even returning home I was on my way to be a paratrooper in the 82cd Airborne in Fort Bragg North Carolina. As fate would have it, during basic training in August in Anniston, Alabama I received a letter from Dartmouth that I had been accepted for the class to graduate in 1950. In response to my letter that I was in the Army they replied that I could enter with the Class of 1952 in the fall of 1948. While my girlfriend Vi and my family were not pleased with this outcome, I felt that fate had solved for me the complex problem of how to pay for a first rate education. Note that this was before the age of educational loans for this purpose. Even in the intense heat and physical demands of "boot camp", I was enjoying what I was doing, and looking forward to learning how to jump out of airplanes.

CHAPTER 4

MILITARY SERVICE (1946-48, 1950-51)

My time in the military was very satisfying in many respects. I learned and adapted to the ways of the Army, and learned how to jump out of airplanes and to keep in shape for doing so. I spent a delightful year on duty in Sapporo Japan (May 1947 to May1948), six months of which were spent racing on a ski team. During this period of time I was introduced to the biology of schizophrenia. More importantly to my subsequent career development, my initial 2 years of military service combined with an additional year (1950-51) during the Korean War provided enough educational support from the GI Bill to carry myself and my family through my years in Medical School and early years of my surgical residency.

How I happened to get to Sapporo is an interesting part of my life story. After spending a few months in Fort Bragg after jump school in Columbus, Georgia, I was sent to a staging area in New Jersey on my way to join the 101st Airborne in Germany. My name was called out one morning to report to Headquarters, which I did, and to my surprise I was greeted by my old primary grade school buddy, Brandock Lovely. Brandy informed me that I was not going to Germany, but was reassigned to the 11th Airborne in Sapporo Japan since the 101st was returning home. This sounded like a great assignment and in a few weeks, I was on a train to

Seattle, and soon on a troopship to Japan. After 14 uneventful days except for being seasick, we arrived in Yokohama. During the trip, I read in a daily information sheet that a Doctor Louis Ogata was giving a course in Psychology in Sapporo for the military personnel. This sounded like an educational activity I would enjoy participating in during my tour of duty.

I fell in love with Japan during my first night in Yokohama. A light rain was falling, and I could hear outside of our makeshift barracks the tap, tap, tap of wooden shoes. The next day I was amazed at the colorful kimonos worn by the short in stature, polite and smiling men and women. The 24 hour train ride to Sapporo was equally exciting. I was especially impressed with the terraced rice fields, and the rock formations along the side of the sea. What I had not appreciated during the war years was the extensive damage that our bombings had done on the larger cities, including Sapporo. Our barracks at Camp Crawford just outside the city were newly built, and very comfortable. I was assigned the task of company clerk. In this position I was assigned a jeep to drive, and drive I did through the beautiful mountains of the area.

While in Sapporo, I was most fortunate in being able to take the course in psychology from Dr. Louis Ogata that I had read about on the trip across the Pacific Ocean. He had a most interesting history in that he was born in Lima Peru and while studying with Dr. Ernst Kretchmer (the father of body type psychiatry) in Leipzig, the 2cd World War broke out. Dr. Ogata, being a citizen of Peru, was prevented from returning home to Lima. At the end of the war he was expatriated to Sapporo where he was teaching and working in a laboratory studying the content of bound water in the brain of schizophrenics. We spent a lot of time together discussing mental illness. I also was frequently invited to dinner in his typical Japanese home. His wife was an excellent cook and a superb homemaker. Dr. Ogata was especially interested in American movie stars so in return for his kindnesses

I had my mother send over several magazines for his perusal. Of more relevance to my future work, he arranged for me to watch several operations performed in the library of the professor of surgery at the University of Hokkaido. This was my first exposure to surgery, and I was very impressed with the precision involved in removing the stomach of a patient with gastric cancer. I had no inclination for becoming a surgeon at the time. Through my interactions with Dr. Ogata, I became convinced that I wanted to be a psychiatrist with an emphasis on neurophysiology. This was not too far different than my ambition to be a sociologist when I graduated from Exeter.

The year in Sapporo went by very fast. The snow came early and by the middle of November we were skiing on a regular basis at a site that in the future would house the Winter Olympics. The ski area had a small chair lift, a warming hut, a ski jump, and wonderful steep slopes that once climbed, were excellent sites for slalom and downhill. One day on the bulletin board I noticed a request for skiers to sign up for a ski team. I immediately signed up and was accepted with the idea that I would compete in four events, downhill, slalom, cross country, and jumping. I qualified for the first three, but never became proficient in jumping. We had excellent instruction in all four areas from former members of the 1932 Japanese Olympic ski team. My status on the ski team excused me from my normal duties for 6 months except for an occasional parachute jump. To top things off, in the spring, my skiing buddies and I went out to the countryside to a large inactive volcano where the snow was terrific. Our holiday was interrupted by a rather terse letter to return to Camp Crawford for immediate discharge. Reluctantly, we obeyed.

There was one incident that warrants recording. One afternoon, while riding in a personnel carrier on our way for an evening on the town, a bus full of young and old people ahead of us veered off a bridge into a rapidly running mountain stream. We jumped out of our vehicle and started to pull people out of the water as rapidly as we could. We administered first aid to several, and tried to calm the others until the local authorities arrived. We then jumped back into our truck and went on our way. A few weeks later we were instructed to put on our dress uniforms for a photo op during a ceremony that recognized our rescue effort. Much to my surprise, a month or so later, I received a copy of a photograph which had been published in the New York Times Newspaper describing our rescue efforts. This was my first exposure to civilian trauma in which quick action had saved numerous lives.

Our trip back to the States was also pleasant and for some reason I was not sea sick. After 12 days on the pitch black Pacific Ocean, we all gave out a cheer as we saw the lights of San Francisco. Once discharged, I took a train down to Los Angeles to visit my uncle Frank. This was fun. He and his girlfriend at the time took me down south of LA for a lunch on the beach. It was cloudy and cold. There were many others having lunch on a beautiful beach, but none were swimming. A few days later, I headed East on a bus to Chicago, and a train to Charlottesville to visit Vi, my summer sweetheart at Twin Lake Villa with whom I had been communicating with by mail. I had a wonderful time with her and her family, but was disappointed but not unhappy when she told me she was going to marry an old boyfriend called "Monk". This came as no surprise to me since she had mentioned him several times in her letters.

I was not ready to settle down at the time, and was glad to return home without any commitments. When I finally got home a few weeks after discharge, my mother was wondering what took me so long. I explained to her my side trips, and she was very understanding. It was fortunate that I had visited my uncle since a few years later he had a devastating stroke.

CHAPTER 5

ON TO DARTMOUTH

I returned home in May of 1948 with no fixed commitments until the fall when I was to start my freshman year at Dartmouth College. I signed up for unemployment insurance, bought a touring bike, and spent several days climbing in the White Mountains. I worked several other odd jobs, and took long bike rides on the week-ends. It was great fun just being at home with my parents. I ran, went swimming, played tennis and started to read, in order to be up to speed when I entered Dartmouth. My reading list was skewed toward Freud, Jung, and Adler since by then I was convinced that I wanted to do psychiatry with a focus on neuroscience.

I have forgotten how I got to Hanover in the fall of 1948, but I imagine I hitched a ride from a friend. I can remember however registering, and receiving a bright green hat labeled 1952, which was my year to graduate. I was to wear this "beany" at all times in my first year since it identified me as a "greeny beany", the lowest level on the student hierarchy. It did not take long to get into the routine of the study program which was fairly rigorous for those of us taking the five year Premed-Med Program. This program consisted of three years of liberal arts that focused on math, science, and social studies. I handled my course work quite well, and had time for singing in the choir, and running cross country. Much to my surprise, I ran well enough to get a big D lettered sweater in the sport.

I also joined the ski team in the first year. This required doing well in a time trial with the first snow fall. One early November day over two hundred students turned out on a hill on the edge of town. We shoveled snow into the middle of the hill, and set up some gates in order to run a time trial. The event was somewhat intimidating since the race was watched by the famous ski coach Walter Prager. I had a good run on the slalom course, and was selected for further training. My year in Sapporo had served me well in this regard. I was impressed with the caliber of young skiers that had been attracted to Dartmouth. I also realized that I would never qualify for the first team, since most were four event skiers in those days, and for some reason, I was not skilled as a jumper. There still was room however for slalom and downhill racers, which is the area I chose to concentrate on.

In the summer of 1949 at the completion of my first year at Dartmouth I returned to Twin Lake Villa in New London New Hampshire, a summer resort where I had worked in my teens as a cook, salad man, dishwasher, and other jobs in the kitchen. The staff was mostly young college kids like myself, trying to make some money for the fall while having fun. I was pleased to see that one of my old friends Victor Daub had also returned to the Villa as a bell hop. Our close friendship was quickly re-established even to the point where he consistently beat me in tennis. Vic went to College at Lehigh where he received a degree in math and engineering, married Janet, and produced and intellectually nourished a very successful family. Vic has spent most of his professional life in Tucson. Inger and I have had an opportunity to visit with Vic and Janet in Tucson, and they have recently spent a few days with us in Sandy. Vic is my oldest and dearest childhood friend.

The time went by fast, and I returned to Dartmouth as a sophomore in September of 1949. The sophomore year also went well at Dartmouth and it was not long before I was back at the Villa doing odd jobs. This was the summer of 1950 when the Korean War broke out. I did not take notice of this event since I had already done my time. You can imagine my surprise when I opened a letter in early August ordering me to report in two weeks to Manchester, NH to join a National Guard Reserve Unit. I had forgotten that I had signed a paper at the time of discharge in 1948 indicating that I would like to join the Guard since it provided a small stipend each month for a week-end of training. I had never been contacted by the Army that my request had been granted. I thought that there was some type of mistake, but on inquiry, the officer in charge made it very clear that either I report or they would come and get me. Needless to say, I reported for duty, and informed Dartmouth of my dilemma.

The situation was further complicated by the fact that I had just met Barbara Schmelzer, a person who I had become very attracted to. In fact, the attraction was mutual, and it appeared that we were heading towards a long term relationship. We had enjoyed each other's company, and were both concerned about the separation that was about to occur when I reported for duty. Fortunately I was going to be stationed at Cape Cod, not far from where Barbara lived. We saw each other on week-ends, and our interest in each other grew at a rapid pace.

In the fall, I was transferred to a Medical Unit within the 82cd Airborne in Fort Bragg, North Carolina. The unit was on "ready alert", and I was sure that within a few months I would be called to duty in Korea. We decided to get married in spite of the likelihood that I soon would be off to Korea. The marriage in Billerica was attended by our families and many of our friends. It was a traditional wedding with no signs to portend the difficult times that lie ahead for Barbara and I. Soon we were off to Fort Bragg as man and wife to start a new life together. I enjoyed my work as a medic, learning how to establish an advanced surgical unit. Barbara also enjoyed her life as secretary for an up and coming lawyer, Terry Sanford. Again, chance went my way, and in August of 1951, I was called into the Commander's office. He said that I did not belong in the Army, and that he had arranged an honorable discharge so that I could return to Dartmouth.

Entering the 3rd year of a highly competitive 5 year program after a year in an Army field hospital was a challenge. Barbara and I established a home in an old Army barracks just off the main campus of Dartmouth called Wigwam Village. Barbara was able to get a job as a secretary, and I knuckled down for an intense period of study. The usual pattern would be that I would go to class at 8 and return home for dinner at 6. I then would go to the library at 8 and study until 12 or 1 AM. The work was interesting, and my grades were good enough to gain me a position in the medical school component of the curriculum for the coming year. I was unaware at the time that this schedule took its toll on Barbara emotionally. It started subtly with Barbara experiencing panic attacks with each creak of the old barracks in the cold of winter. She was afraid to stay alone for long periods at night. I was only partly successful in modifying a work habit that I have continued throughout my life. As a function of time, Barbara started to make friends in the complex, and we developed a social life that at least kept me home most week-ends. We enjoyed our time together. There were a lot of activities on campus, which we participated in, and the year was over before we knew it.

The fourth year of the liberal arts curriculum was in fact the first year of medical school that was combined with a special year long class called Great Issues. We studied anatomy, physiology, biochemistry, and histology in the Medical School Building. Our class size was small, about 22 students as I recall. It seems like the size of the Medical Faculty was also small, but very dedicated to teaching their subject. I especially remember our sessions with Dr. Rolf Syvertsen, the Dean, and his associate Dr. Harry Savage. They were constantly by our side, cheering us on.

I still remember the difficult time that my group of 4 had in dissecting the abdomen of our cadaver. It took us a few sessions just to get into the abdomen, and another few days sorting things out. It turns out that what we thought was the stomach was in fact the large bowel. The patient had died of a volvulus of the right colon. I looked up the medical consequences of this type of event, and realized that the patient should not have died from it. On further review or our patient's history, I learned that he had been in prison at the time of the event. I wondered if the circumstances were different whether he might have survived.

My interest in the possibility that this patient's tragic death was a consequence of his imprisonment likely was the reason that I was invited to a burial ceremony at the completion of the course. This was a much sought after honor, since it included a lobster dinner at the Exeter Inn with Dr. Syvertsen. Unfortunately Sy, as he was affectionately called, died several years later in an automobile accident. We all felt that this would happen someday since Dr. Syvertsen would always drive fast wherever he went. His passing left a big hole in the heart of all those who knew him. His dedication to medical education made a profound influence on me and probably was a major factor in my subsequent deep interest in the educational experience of medical students and residents.

I was fortunate in my fourth year to obtain a part-time job as an orderly in the operating room of the Mary Hitchcock Clinic. This provided for me some additional money, but also a chance to watch world class surgeons in action. I found myself enjoying the operating room environment, and my interest in Psychiatry began to bend a bit. I was especially interested in the emerging field of Psychosomatic Medicine as it related to diseases that had a background of mind-gut interaction. Since it was necessary to transfer at the end of my fifth year to complete my last two years of Medical School (years 6 and 7), I began to research this topic. It did not take long to long to identify the exciting work being conducted in this area at the Cornell University Medical College in New York City. Dr. Harold Wolf, a neurologist, and Drs Thomas

Almy and Marvin Sleisenger, gastroenterologists, were publishing their work on the effects of stress on diseases of the stomach and the intestines. I decided that I wanted to transfer to Cornell for my last two years of medical school. This required discussion with my advisor, since most students automatically transferred to Harvard. Once outlining my career plan to be a psychiatrist, my advisor agreed that is where I should go.

Graduation from Dartmouth was a wonderful experience for my wife Barbara, my mother Elsie, my sister Alice as well as myself. I was the first one on either side of the family to graduate from college. To make it even more interesting, the President to be, Dwight Eisenhower was our graduation speaker. Unfortunately my father did not live to celebrate the event. He had died of a heart attack the previous year.

CHAPTER 6

CORNELL UNIVERSITY MEDICAL COLLEGE (1954-1956)

Barbara was pleased with the fact that we were moving to New York where she would have more opportunity for professional development. One of her brothers helped us move our belongings in a rented trailer that today would not be allowed on the road. We did not have a car, and neither Barbara nor I had a driver's license. We had rented a walk up flat on 79th street on the East Side of Manhattan where many of the married medical students lived. It was called "Ma Friedman's" in recognition of the owner and caretaker. She was most helpful in getting us settled. During the first night in the apartment we heard a lot of noise and when we turned on the light, there were hundreds of cockroaches marching along the wall. We were forewarned, but not for this. We soon learned that they were a way of life, and harmless. The rent was cheap and the location was perfect for walking to school. It was at Ma Friedman's that Barbara and I met Nancy and Gil Diethelm, with whom we became lifelong friends as I will expand upon when I describe the Birmingham years.

It did not take me long to get actively involved in the last two clinical years of the medical school. The New York Hospital was physically attached to the Cornell Medical College. This was convenient since we could visit the clinics, the wards, the laboratories, and the lecture halls without moving outside into the hustle and bustle of the East Side of New York. The level of instruction was superb, and soon I was swept along at a rapid pace learning clinical medicine. I sought out Dr. Almy and Dr. Wolf, and told them of my interest in their work. Dr. Wolf directed my attention to a conference that he and the world famous neurosurgeon Dr. Bronson Ray had each week. It was a great conference for a budding psychiatrist, since it dealt with a large variety of illnesses related to aberrations in brain function. I enrolled in a brain modeling elective under Dr. Ray's indirect supervision. Dr. Almy referred me to Dr. Marvin Sleisenger, a junior faculty member at the time that was interested in inflammatory bowel disease. He assigned me the pleasant task of helping to assess patients who were being treated by steroids for ulcerative colitis. I did not realize at the time that this was pioneering work. As you might imagine, I was very busy keeping up with the clinical rotations and pursuing my special areas of interest in mind-gut interactions.

I also had an opportunity to participate in a study of the quality of health care given to recent immigrants to New York from Puerto Rico carried out by Dr. Helena Gilder, the Director of our Surgical Laboratories. Early in the study I became impressed with the effects of lack of access to medical care on the burden of disease in this population. I was impressed with how resourceful these people were in sharing what little they had to the new comers to the community. It was not unusual to encounter ten or more people living in a single room, cooking their meals on the fire escape, and storing their food in the entry way. I was almost overwhelmed by the idea that I as a fourth year student was their primary care physician.

During the middle of my fourth year I secured a position as an intern in Medicine, and a resident in Psychiatry at the New York Hospital after my graduation from Cornell. Towards the end of my fourth year, I did a month as an extern at the Westchester Division of the New York Hospital, a private psychiatric hospital north of New York City. I was assigned two patients to study and treat. The first was a 16 year old boy who could not or would not speak because of presumed severe schizophrenia. During the first session with him I told him that I was a medical student, and that my teachers had asked me to speak with him. He smiled, but over several days of trying to get him to talk, I had failed. On the last day however he motioned for me to follow him outside to a basketball court, which I did. He then started to shoot baskets flawlessly and then threw me the ball, and seemed pleased that I could not put the ball through the basket. I now realize that he was trying to communicate with me through the basketball, and likely suffered from an extreme form of autism rather than schizophrenia.

I was assigned a second most unusual case of a young male recently admitted from New Haven. He was a freshman at Yale. He seemed quite normal to me as we greeted each other. I asked him why he was here and he explained that he had been arrested by the police because he was walking around nude in Central Park. He explained that it was part of an initiation stunt. We both had a laugh, and then got involved in a serious discussion which revealed a lot of deep lying pathology which required hospital treatment.

My experience at the mental hospital convinced me that I would not be happy being a psychiatrist. Fortunately I had just completed a rotation on a general surgical service at Cornell where the staff and Chief Resident George Wantz, encouraged me to go into surgery. They laughed when I earlier had said that I wanted to be a psychiatrist, and laughed even louder when I went back to them and told them I wanted to be a surgeon. They suggested that I talk to Dr. Frank Glenn, the Lewis Atterbury Professor of Surgery and the Surgeon-in-Chief of the New York Hospital. I told Dr. Glenn of my interest in surgery. He said report on July 1st, pick up your uniform (the house staff were always dressed in well starched white shirts, pants, and coats), and go to work. There was no matching program in those days (1956). After the interview, I informed Dr. Hugh Luckey, the Chief of Medicine, and Dr. Oscar Diethelm, the Chief of Psychiatry that I would not be joining them. They were quite understanding of my change of heart, and not concerned about filling the slots that I was vacating.

CHAPTER 7

SURGICAL RESIDENT, CORNELL-NEW YORK HOSPITAL (1956-1963)

The residency training program at the New York Hospital-Cornell Medical Center in 1956 was similar to the one that was successfully introduced at Johns Hopkins University by Dr. William Halsted in the early years of the 20th century. The Cornell program consisted of a graduated surgical experience over a seven year period. There were 12 interns at the beginning in our program, and only 3 chief residents finished at the end. The lineage was easy to trace. Frank Glenn had trained at the Brigham Hospital in Boston under Harvey Cushing. Cushing had trained at John's Hopkins under Halsted. George Heuer, the first chair of surgery and surgeon-in-chief of the new New York Hospital on 70th street and York Avenue had also trained at Hopkins, and was Halsted's last chief resident.

The program at the New York Hospital had a reputation of being quite demanding in terms of time and effort. There was little time off, and even in more recent times, residents were required to live in the hospital. When I joined the program, marriage was not encouraged (and in fact discouraged in subtle ways), and if married, the house staff in surgery was expected to live close to the Hospital. The Hospital and later the Medical School both provided low cost living for residents and their families. Barbara and I moved down to an apartment building owned by the Hospital on 70th and York. It took me only 5 minutes to get to the Emergency Room, and 8 or 9 minutes to the wards and the operating room. The long working days and large volume of patients requiring surgery was like manna in heaven to the type of surgeons attracted to this pyramidal program. Barbara and I had discussed the rigorous nature of the program, and decided to give it a try.

We were pleased by the arrival of our first child, Anne Elizabeth during November of my last year in Medical School. Anne was an active, robust child who during the early months of my internship developed an acute episode of Hemophilus Influenza (croup) that required a tube to be placed into her wind pipe (tracheostomy). This allowed her to breathe more easily, as the inflammatory process in her throat was treated by antibiotics. Within a few weeks the tube that had been placed within the trachea in her neck was removed. Anne not only survived, but thrived, and life gradually returned to normal. It was a reminder however that we were living pretty close to the edge. Barbara handled this crisis very well, and soon she was able to return to work. I was impressed with her ability to manage the household affairs and take care of a young child in the middle of New York City. While I was just across the street, and could get home for short periods of time, I don't think that I was very useful around the home. My workload was all consuming, and I often would fall asleep as soon as I sat down to eat dinner.

The educational programs for the general surgical services were well set up for surgical training. The city/borough or institutionally sponsored public patients were housed on two services of about 35 beds each. Private and government sponsored health care plans were not yet generally available. The staffing consisted of a Faculty Director, a Chief Resident, a Senior Resident, and several junior residents and interns, plus four or five medical students per service, The Chief and Senior Resident remained on the service for a year. Dr. John Beal and Dr. Samuel Moore were the Directors of the resident services. They were assisted in their supervisory tasks by several geographic full time clinical faculty who the chief resident could call upon if desired because of their special expertise. The chief residents in this system were quite autonomous in managing their service in a pure Halstedian manner. A third teaching service housed semi-private patients that were also cared for by a full time house staff. The attending of record was responsible for supervising the care of the patients that was carried out by a senior and junior resident. Private patients were housed on the higher floors of the hospital, and were cared for by junior residents that were supervised by the private surgeon.

There was ample operating time since each service had its own operating room that could be utilized each day until the work was done. Each service performed about eighty to a hundred cases a month. Emergencies were usually taken care of at night by the on-call team. These very active clinical services cared for a wide variety of problems to include pulmonary, gastric, liver, pancreatic, bowel, breast, vascular, and endocrine cases. John Beal was interested in foregut problems, Dr. Moore was developing peripheral vascular surgery, and Dr. Glenn was interested in gallbladder disease and the emerging fields of endocrine and heart surgery.

As a junior resident, I became interested in peptic ulcer disease of the stomach and duodenum, and diseases of the bile ducts and the gallbladder. For reasons still unknown to me, I decided to become an academic surgeon, and recognized that the path to success in this endeavor was to develop a better understanding of the diseases we were trying to treat. Keep in mind that we had very primitive diagnostic tools at the time. A barium swallow, rigid esophagoscopy, and an oral cholecystogram were the only tools available for diagnosing esophagogastric and biliary problems. Rigid proctoscopy and a barium enema were the essential tools for diagnosing large bowel abnormalities. We relied heavily upon plain xrays of the chest and abdomen for the diagnosis and treatment of many of our cases. Flexible endoscopy was not even on the horizon. Imagine managing complex pulmonary and gastrointestinal disease without ultrasound, computed tomography (CT Scan), Magnetic Resonance Imaging (MRI), Visceral Angiography, or Positron Emission Tomography (Pet Scan) to help detect and stage abnormalities within the chest or abdominal cavity.

I had appreciated during my student days at the New York Hospital that it had a large staff devoted to keeping good records. The Hospital also provided large, well staffed clinics to ensure a very careful follow up of each patient cared for there. Whenever I encountered an unusual case, I would go to the record room to see if others of like kind had been recorded. The staff was very helpful in "pulling charts" and setting them aside for my perusal. I made it part of my routine to drop by the record room a few hours three or four times a week. In this way I was able to put together papers and presentations on unusual gastrointestinal, hepatobiliary, and pancreatic conditions during the course of my residency.

I was especially interested in documenting our results with the surgical treatment of peptic ulcer disease of the stomach and the duodenum. Because of this interest, I was assigned by Dr. Beal to supervise the management of a well established post-gastrectomy follow-up system. This experience stimulated my interest in gastric acid secretion, which in turn led to the development of a research proposal to examine the role of gastric blood flow in the development of acute gastric erosions.

The Department of Surgery had a well supplied and staffed large animal research laboratory that we rotated through for four months in the 2cd year of our surgical residency. I was anxious to get started early on learning the methodology and techniques of research, so I started hanging out in the lab during slow times on the ward during my internship. In this way, I had an opportunity to participate in some of the ongoing projects and to get to know the residents and staff involved. The resident in the lab at the time, Dr. Okinaka, was studying the essential role of gastric acid secretion in the pathogenesis of duodenal ulcer. He was using a Heidenhain Pouch of the dog for this purpose, which is an innervated segment of the greater curvature of the stomach that secretes hydrochloric acid. I became interested in studying how gastric acid and ulcerations developed in this part of the stomach. In order to pursue this idea, I had to develop a way to house the stomach wall with its blood supply and nerves intact in a water tight chamber so that I could collect its secretions and observe its surface during exposure to noxious agents. This turned out to be a major undertaking that consumed most of my spare time during the remainder of my residency. The success of this approach provided a lot of opportunities for me to prosper academically which I will describe later. In retrospect, this was the key to my future success in establishing a well funded laboratory for my students and myself throughout the remainder of my academic career.

The seven years of surgical residency went by very fast and as the years rolled on I got busier and busier. I became involved in the surgical treatment of ever more complicated diseases, and developed an increasing interest in finding a way to prevent them. Working nights and weekends to keep up with the work load, the teaching, the laboratory and the clinical research did not leave much time for the family. Our son Frank Wilson was born on April 30, 1961, just at the time that I was starting the Senior Year of the residency. Fortunately I now had more control over my time, and could spend more time with the family.

Barbara was doing a remarkable job balancing out our finances, and caring for the home and the children. I very much enjoyed taking the children to the park with Barbara on the week-ends.

Anne was now of the age in which she could walk and run on her own. It was not long before Frank could do likewise. The senior years of the residency also went by very fast, and the time was approaching to find a faculty position either at Cornell or elsewhere.

It was my good fortune to have been part of several presentations and publications during my residency. Drs Glenn and Beal knew of my academic potential and interests. I imagine it was one of them that recommended me to Dr. William H (Harry) Muller Jr, The Chairman of Surgery at the University of Virginia. I received a call one day in my Chief's Year from Dr. Muller inviting me down to visit the University of Virginia to see if I would be interested in joining his faculty as an Assistant Professor of Surgery. The idea would be that I would replace Dr. Dean Warren who was on his way to be the Chair of Surgery at the University of Miami. I, with considerable enthusiasm, accepted his offer, and within a few days, Barbara and I were off to visit Charlottesville. We had a lovely visit, and the job that Dr. Muller had in mind for me had ample time for research. Dr. Warren had established a very active research laboratory studying portal hypertension. It was fully equipped and ready for my type of research. He did not plan to take any of the equipment with him. Barbara liked Charlottesville, so by the end of the visit I accepted the job offer with great anticipation and enthusiasm.

Life is never simple. Shortly after I accepted the job in Virginia, I was invited to give a Grand Rounds at Harvard to the department of surgery at the Peter Bent Brigham Hospital in Boston. After my presentation I was invited to the office of Professor Francis D Moore, Chairman of the Department for a cup of coffee and a chat. He, in a very kindly way, said that he enjoyed my talk but that I needed more scientific training. I am sure he was surprised when I agreed with him. He made several suggestions including joining his lab, but the one that caught my interest was to spend time learning how water moves through biologic membranes. This was an appropriate choice since hydrochloric acid was primarily water with an admixture of electrolytes and hydrogen ions.

This discussion turned out to be a life changing event. Upon return to New York I went directly to the library to review what was known about the movement of water through biologic membranes. The list was small. I wrote letters to five very distinguished scientists requesting an opportunity to work in their laboratory. They included Dr. Horace Davenport, Chair of Physiology at Michigan, Dr. Robert Berliner, Chair of Biophysics at Yale, Dr. Charles Code, Chair of Physiology at the Mayo Clinic, Dr Frank Brooks, Chair of Gastroenterology at the University of Pennsylvania, and Dr. Richard Durbin, a scientist working in the Cardiovascular Research Institute at the University of California in San Francisco. Dr. Durbin was a biophysicist who had worked in Professor A K Solomon's lab at Harvard, who was the acknowledged leader in the field. It was my good fortune that Dr. Durbin accepted me into his laboratory for one year as a Cardiovascular Research Fellow. I did not realize at the time how important this opportunity would be for my future development as an academic surgeon. I called Dr, Muller about my chat with Dr, Moore, and my need for a year of pure science, and he agreed, and placed me on a leave of absence. Barbara was as pleased as I with the move since we as well as Anne and Frank had the feeling that spending a year in San Francisco would be exciting.

CHAPTER 8

CARDIOVASCULAR RESEARCH INSTITUTE, SAN FRANCISCO (1963-1965)

I finished the residency at the New York Hospital on May 1st, 1963, and Barbara, Anne, and Frank and I were on our way to San Francisco the next day. We planned to take the train to Chicago, and then journey on to San Francisco through Salt Lake to visit our long time neighbors at 70th and York, Jim and Marilyn Warenski. As we entered the Yellow Cab on our way to the train station, I felt a great sense of relief since now I would have time to spend with the family. I was surprised when Barbara said that she was going to divorce me when we got to San Francisco. I said, "don't be silly", and never gave it a second thought. The trip was exciting for all of us, and without incident. We especially enjoyed visiting with the Warenski family in the Salt Lake railway station. The train ride through the mountains and valleys of California was spectacular, and quite a contrast to the concrete canyons of New York.

The Durbins' picked us up at the train station in San Francisco and took us to a small, well furnished house facing the Pacific Ocean which we immediately rented. It was like being in heaven. I went and took a drivers license test which I passed and a few days later bought a car. Within a short period of time, I was ready to go to work.

Dick's laboratory was in the middle of a large scientific enterprise called the Cardiovascular Research Institute founded and headed by Dr. Julius Conroe, a famous pulmonary physiologist. I did not know until I arrived that I was designated (and paid) as a research fellow of the Institute. This gave me the privilege of attending all of their weekly laboratory sessions, and to later in the year present my work to a distinguished group of scientists. Dick's laboratory was in the cell membrane transport section of the Institute adjacent to a very inspiring clinician-scientist, Izzy Edelman. Dr. Dinkar Kasbaker, a PhD postdoctoral fellow, was also working in Dick's laboratory studying various aspects of the energetics of membrane transport.

I was anxious to get started on some experiments, but Dick was a clever teacher with a strong interest in the needs of the learner. He pointed out that we first must find an important question to try to answer, and he suggested that I spend several weeks in the library searching out what this question might be. Along the way, we would enter into discussions of what was known about water movement in general, and its movement through a lipid rich membrane of an epithelial cell more specifically. My learning curve was steep, because I had to start at the beginning and learn about kinetic energy of water molecules, and the characteristics of cell surfaces, and the influence of hydrostatic and osmotic forces that allowed the movement of water through them. I quickly picked up on the intellectual challenge of the pursuit of knowledge, and lost my longing for being back in the operating room. I have employed Dr. Durbin's mentoring style in introducing future surgeons to the joy of basic research as a component of their surgical practice.

My first experiment was the challenge of characterizing the forces that allowed water molecules to move through the viscous interface of mesityl oxide from an area of lower to higher concentration. This was a fun exercise, which with a lot of help from Dick, I accomplished. Dick taught me how to keep good scientific records. I started out by writing down numbers and observations on scraps of paper and the back of envelopes. It was not long before he had me using hard bound lab books within which I would record legible data points.

Later in the fall, I was able to receive a very junior appointment in the department of surgery at the University of California in San Francisco (UCSF) which at the time was headed by Dr. Leon Goldman. This gave me access to the surgical conferences and the surgical laboratories. One day as I was waiting for an elevator at the Moffitt Hospital, the major teaching hospital at UCSF, the door opened and out walked Dr J. Englebert Dunphy, the Chairman of Surgery at Oregon. We greeted each other because we had met previously at a meeting in Florida. I thought that he likely was a visiting professor, but actually he was being recruited to be the chair of surgery at UCSF. In fact, this is what happened a few months later.

A few months after arriving in San Francisco Barbara announced that she was pregnant. This was a pleasant and welcomed surprise which came at a convenient time in my career. Barbara, as well as I, and the children were very happy in San Francisco. I was home every night for dinner. On the week-ends we would visit the many sites to enjoy on the West Coast ranging from Crater Lake Oregon to Ensenada Mexico, and the Yosemite and Sequoia National Parks, and even a visit to Salt Lake City for a ski vacation. Barbara's pregnancy went well, and she delivered Jane Abbott Moody on December 5th, 1963 without incident. Barbara seemed somewhat depressed to me and also to her obstetrician who referred her to a psychiatrist. She was diagnosed as having postpartum depression and was placed on a mood elevator, to which she responded. I did notice that she was paying less attention to her household duties and the children. In addition, she started taking an increasing number of acting lessons for bit parts in television.

A few months later she informed me that she would not return with me to Virginia. One evening when I returned home from the lab, I found a book that she had placed on my pillow on how to get a quick divorce in Nevada. I asked her what this was all about and she explained that she loved me and was going to get a divorce to free me to pursue my academic career. She had already secured a lawyer, and stated that there were no conditions under which she would change her mind. I could tell from her tone of voice and demeanor that she was serious. I pleaded with her to reconsider her decision, but she insisted that this was the best thing for the family. We had a few sessions with her lawyer. He also strongly encouraged her not to divorce me since in his words "you are killing a goose that was about to lay a golden egg". Her mind was made up, and in the spring of 1964, she asked me to move out of the home. I was reluctant to do so, but did on the advice of our lawyer. She retained the car. All I had was a suitcase full of clothes, my skis, and a broken heart. Fortunately Anne had matured to where she could care for Frank and Jane, and help to manage the home.

I clearly was faced with a serious dilemma. I called Harry Muller and told him of my problem. He was most kind in extending my leave of absence for another year. The major problem of how to care for the children was more difficult to solve. I didn't believe that Barbara was up to the task. Obviously I needed a job in San Francisco. Fortunately by this time Dr. Dunphy had assumed the chair at UCSF. I told him my tale of woe. It seems like it was a story that he heard several times before. He immediately offered me a junior faculty position and said that he could give me a lot of opportunity but little money. He offered $6,000 a year to start with, which I gladly accepted. I was fortunate in having received a research award from the American Heart Association which provided support for the laboratory, supplies, and personnel required to carry out the experiments. It included a small stipend for myself. Furthermore, I had an opportunity to supplement my salary through clinical practice.

My research activity in Dick's lab had slowed down a bit during this difficult period in my personal life, but being alone provided time for opening up new avenues of inquiry. I was anxious to bring my work back to the animal laboratory, and Dick encouraged me to do so. Dr. John Najarian, the Director of the surgical laboratories at UCSF (soon to be the chair of surgery at Minnesota) provided me with the facilities to perform experiments that involved the use of the chambered segment of the acid secreting portion of the dog stomach that I had developed at Cornell during my residency. The CVRI had an excellent shop facility for fashioning the chambers that I used in this type of experiment, and soon we were studying water movement during acid secretion in dog stomach. Fortunately Dick was also interested in examining the mechanism of water movement from the parietal cell in the dog during histamine stimulated acid secretion. The osmotic and hydraulic forces that account for the volume flow of gastric juice had not been systematically studied before. We designed a double lumen chamber which allowed the precise measurement of the effects of exposure of the mucosal surface of one side of the chamber to osmotic or hydrostatic challenge while using the other lumen of the chamber as a control. This approach became the major thrust of my work.

Life, when it hits a rough spot in the road, has a way of correcting itself. In June of 1964, Barbara moved with the children to Carson City Nevada in order to obtain a divorce after six weeks of residence. During the third week of this pre-divorce residence of my family in Nevada, I was invited to a going away party for Dr. Gunnar Wallin and his wife Kickan who were about to return to Uppsala Sweden where Gunnar was a member the faculty of neurology. Barbara had become quite friendly with Kickan, and I with Gunnar since we worked in adjacent laboratories at the

CVRI. When I arrived at the home of Dr. Strickland, Dr. Wallin's mentor, everyone inquired where Barbara was. I told them that she and the children were on holiday in Nevada. They did not know about the impending divorce. As I entered the room, which contained a rather large gathering of friends that I knew, my eyes were attracted to a beautiful Swedish friend of the Wallin's, Miss Maria Charlotta Stolpe (Maja). It never entered my mind that she would soon be my wife of forty years, and the surrogate mother of my children.

Maja was the life of the party. As the night progressed we got closer and closer together, until finally we had an opportunity to talk to each other. The chemistry between us was electrifying. My interest was further heightened when she began to entertain the group with Swedish ballads, while playing the guitar. After about an hour of singing, she then excused herself. As she prepared to leave, I started washing dishes, which was unusual behavior for me. As she started to leave, I shook the soap off my hands and bid her good-by. On impulse, I left several minutes later. Fortunately I knew the general area where she lived, and caught up with her just as she drove up to her parking garage. She at first was frightened until she saw that it was me. After parking her car, she invited me in for a nightcap. I noticed that she had not been drinking any alcohol at the party therefore was surprised when I opened the cupboard in her kitchen to fetch a glass and encountered a rather complete bar that included my favorite brand of scotch. She explained that she had just returned from Sweden and had picked them up at the duty free shop on the ship.

By now it was about 2 AM on a Sunday morning. She prepared a wonderful breakfast that included the best Swedish pancakes I had ever eaten. It was surprisingly easy for us to talk about our life situation. I invited her to join me on a trip to Stinson Beach later in the morning. She had planned to go to Carmel, and invited me to join her, which I did. The day was spent telling our personal stories. Maja was 49, single, had never been married and had no children. I was 36, married with three children, but soon (within three weeks) to be divorced. She had come to America to start a new life after being disappointed by the break-up of a long standing relationship with a Swedish boyfriend. She worked north of San Francisco for a few years as a housekeeper for an elderly friend of the family from Örebro, her hometown, in Sweden. She then moved to San Francisco where she became a homemaker and cook for a very wealthy family. Several years later she went to beauty school to become a hair dresser. At the time that I met her, she had established a very successful beauty shop on Taraval Street, not far from where she and Barbara and I lived.

During the ensuing week, Maja and I saw each other frequently, and decided to drive up to Carson City to visit my children. She was immediately accepted by the children, and it was obvious that she was equally impressed with them. On the way back to San Francisco we decided to get married. We went about registering our intent and securing the wedding ring. When I told Robert Karp, my Chief Resident, and a close friend of mine of our plans he locked me in a closet of his home and told me that he would not let me out until I recovered my sanity. After a few hours of serious discussion, he understood the wisdom of our decision. In subsequent years, Bob became a very dear friend of Maja and our whole family.

My divorce was scheduled for Saturday morning the 22cd of July, and we planned to get married in the afternoon. Unfortunately I was scheduled that evening for call at the Moffitt Hospital. I only had time to participate in the divorce proceedings before returning to San Francisco, and therefore we delayed our marriage until the following day. The divorce was personally very traumatic for myself and the children, and probably also for Barbara. I did not inform them of my pending marriage. Barbara had planned to take the children that evening to Los Angeles where she planned to pursue an acting career. After a quite emotional good bye to the kids, I headed back to San Francisco.

The patient flow through the emergency room at the Moffitt was quite light during the night, giving me an opportunity to sleep for several hours. Maja and I drove back to Carson City the next morning, our marriage being only delayed by a day. It was a beautiful Sunday morning. We stopped at a home designed as a wedding chapel. A lovely middle aged lady answered the door, and explained to us that the Justice of the Peace that performed the marrying ritual was over at the City Hall on Sundays, and that we could be married there. When we signed the marriage register, we were the 347th couple to do so on the week-end. We were in rather informal attire, and inquired whether we should change our clothes. The clerk at the desk said that we looked just fine in our shorts and T-shirts. Within a few minutes we were brought into a lovely room that was decorated as a Wedding Chapel, and introduced to a Justice of the Peace. He asked us "where is your witness"? We told him that we did not know that we were supposed to have one. He said, "don't worry, most of my clients do not bring one either". Next thing we know he calls out "Hey Joe, we have a young couple that needs your services". Joe was a delightful middle aged man who only charged us $25 for being a witness to our marriage. The marriage service was beautifully delivered by the Justice who also happened to be an ordained minister. Maja and I exchanged vows, rings, and a kiss, and that was it. We were both pleased with the beauty and brevity of the service, and took off immediately for what would be a one day honeymoon at Emerald Bay on Lake Tahoe. Maja had prepared a wonderful lunch, the weather was perfect, and we were very happy to be man and wife. Most of our conversation centered on how to relate to the children.

I moved in with Maja since my room was too small to house even one person comfortably. Just as we were settling in, I received a call from the Los Angeles General Hospital that they had admitted my former wife Barbara to the psychiatric unit there with an acute schizophrenic crisis. They requested that I come down and pick up our children, which I did, and brought them back to Maja's apartment. Maja was very effective in calming their fears and assuming the role of a surrogate mother. This was the first of many challenges in dealing with Barbara and her relationships with the children. A few days after she was discharged from the hospital, she contacted me, demanding that I return the children which I did on the advice of my lawyer. Barbara rented an apartment only a few doors from where we lived, which made it convenient for me to see them each day, but created other problems until she moved several blocks away.

CHAPTER 9

MY DUNPHY YEARS AT UCSF (1964 -1966)

Shortly after Dr. Dunphy arrived at UCSF, he was appointed acting Chancellor of the campus. He called me into his office one day after I had joined the full time faculty and asked me to run his surgical service while he was the Chancellor. I was flattered that he had that much confidence in me, and immediately accepted the privilege. There were several very accomplished surgeons on the service whom of course I treated with respect and deference when sensitive issues arose. Being director of the service gave me an opportunity to work directly with some outstanding interns and residents to include Larry Way, Donald Morton, Ronald Stoney, Robert Karp, George Sheldon, Orlo Clark, Ted Schrock and a long list of others. I also had an opportunity to interact directly with some outstanding students such as David Fromm and Robert Albo for example. The surgical faculty included several outstanding clinical surgeons to include Glenn Bell, Leon Goldman, Horace McCorkle, Maurice Galante, Jack Wylie, Orville Grimes, William Silen, John Najarian, Al DeLorimer, Al Hall, and William Blaisdel. My major surgical experience related to my role as a teaching assistant to residents assigned to the Dunphy Service. This was fine with me, since I still had a major interest in pursuing my work in the laboratory. The volume of resident cases on the service and the few personal referrals that I received each month seemed to satisfy my clinical needs.

Fortunately, Dr. Dunphy returned to reclaim his service in 6 months, and I returned to the lab and assumed only a secondary role in running the service. This was a plus for my own education because I became a close observer of how Dr. Dunphy ran the Department, and interacted with the students and residents. Dr. Dunphy was very popular with surgical leaders both at home and abroad. He had attracted a remarkable number of young academic scholars at my level of development. These included such household names in American Surgery as Frederick Belzer (transplantation and future Chair at Wisconsin), Thomas Hunt (wound healing and Distinguished Professor of Surgery at UCSF), Donald Trunkey (a world class trauma surgeon and Chairman of Surgery at Oregon), John Skillman, a famous trauma surgeon who has spent most of his academic career at Harvard, to name just a few. The International Scholars included, Bengt Zetterfeldt, from Gothenberg at the time, but soon to be the Chair of Surgery at Malmo, Sweden, Frank Ellis from Guy's Hospital in London, James Watts and James May, both of whom subsequently went on to play prominent roles in surgery in Australia. An opportunity for all of us to interact with outstanding surgeons from around the world on almost a daily basis provided an exciting learning environment. I was fortunate to be at UCSF at a time that it was emerging as one of the top medical schools in the country, especially in the area of molecular genetics. Being located in San Francisco of course was a big plus for my hiking and skiing addiction. I was proud to be considered one of "Dunphy's Boys".

John Najarian, soon to become the chairman of surgery at the University of Minnesota was the chief of transplantation at UCSF and director of the surgical laboratories. We became instant friends on first meeting. I guess our major attraction to each other was our serious interest in the science of our respective fields. He assigned to my research team a superb laboratory facility sitting on the side of the hill above the main campus which provided a magnificent view of the city and the Golden Gate Bridge. We called it the "The Tea House of the August Moon". The only short coming was that my associates and I each day would have to transport our experimental subjects up and down the hill. My team and I did not consider this to be a negative since we were away from the main laboratory, and we could work well into the night on the long experiments we were conducting at the time. We were able to obtain a grant from the NIH which allowed us to have generous support for our research. Since I was still a Fellow of the CVRI, we also had full access to its expertise and facilities.

I continued my investigations with Dick Durbin on the osmotic regulation of water flow during acid secretion, and started a separate group of experiments designed to elucidate the relationship between gastric blood flow and acid secretion. The chambered segment offered an excellent way to measure total blood flow from the pouch, and a way to stimulate acid secretion by the direct intra-arterial delivery of histamine. This was thought not to be possible, since it had been attempted previously by Borne and Vane, two giants in gastric physiology, without success. When the distinguished gastric physiologist Dr. Mortimer Grossman heard me present my positive results on this issue, he sent his associate in Los Angeles, Eugene Jacobson to San Francisco to check us out. We set up a chambered segment preparation for him and I was as amazed as Gene was with the result. When we started to administer the histamine into the single artery to the pedicle of the wedge, the mucosa lit up like a light bulb, and highly acid juice started to rapidly accumulate in the chamber. The total blood flow increased several fold. The explanation of why others had failed to stimulate acid secretion by the direct intra-arterial administration of histamine related to the fact that they had not prepared the pedicle so that histamine could not by-pass the mucosa of the stomach through collaterals. His visit and the success of the experiment was a good experience for me because in the eyes of two important people who would subsequently review my work I had achieved a level of credibility.

My work with Dick Durbin continued at an appropriate pace considering the difficulty of the question we were trying to answer. We learned that the gastric mucosa was relatively non responsive as regards water movement across its mucosal surface to even large increments in osmotic pressure. It was sensitive however to hydrostatic pressure, but we were not certain as to whether this was at the level of cellular transport or due to an effect of pressure on the flow of blood through the microcirculation of the stomach on the test side of the dual chamber used in the experiments.

In a separate group of experiments we demonstrated with certainty that inhibition of acid secretion by thiocyanate was not due to a change in total blood flow through the chambered segment. The maintenance of a high level of oxygen consumption associated with acid secretion suggested that mucosal blood flow was also sustained. We employed an infrared scanning device to precisely measure the temperature of the surface of the stomach during histamine stimulation of acid secretion and its inhibition by thiocyanate. These experiments confirmed that the increment in total blood flow was mirrored by the several fold change in mucosal temperature presumably accompanied by a comparable increment in mucosal blood flow. I mention these two groups of experiments since they were a reflection of ideas and experiments that I carried out independently, and was able to get published in two well established journals, Gastroenterology and American Journal of Physiology. I also learned from Dick how to be a good mentor. He helped me to prepare the manuscripts, but did not want to be a co-author since he was not involved in the conceptualization or conductance of the work. Dick felt that it was very important for me to develop independence as an investigator. He also invited me to the Sixth Symposium of the Society for Experimental Biology held in England in 1964. The topic, "The Movement of Water in Living Organisms", was discussed in depth. This was a very exciting experience for me to hear the ideas and work of the best biologists of the time being expressed in rather heated tones. I also had an opportunity to meet the then young Jared Diamond whose work on epithelial function and books on human cultural evolution I have admired over the years. He arrived just as the reception was starting, still dressed in his jungle garb. I was impressed with his relating his experiences in the jungles of New Guinea.

I spent an additional two weeks in England, feeling a bit guilty since I had just been married to Maja. She was remarkably understanding of my interest in visiting several other units as long as I was travelling such a long distance. As I subsequently learned, this was the nature of her character. She was totally supportive of my work (and play in the mountains) ethic. My major side visit was to Sir Andrew Kay's Unit in Glasgow where Tom Hunt was studying at the time. I was impressed with the work being done there on oxygen physiology at the cellular level, and the intensity of Tom's interest in the topic. There is no mystery why he subsequently became a leader in the field.

This was a very special time to be in the Department of Surgery at UCSF. Dunphy was a dynamic and charismatic leader. He and his wife Nancy sure enjoyed a party. I have described several of them in an article I wrote for the journal Surgery titled "Dunphy Stories". One comes to mind here which I never will forget. On the occasion of having Dr. Jonathan Rhodes, Chairman of the Department of Surgery at the University of Pennsylvania, as a Visiting Professor at UCSF, Dr. Dunphy arranged a large stag dinner party at a restaurant downtown to which all the staff and residents were invited. Dr. Dunphy had also invited the famous malpractice trial lawyer Melvin Belli to be the after dinner speaker. This was the time in which Carol Doda was very much in the news since she was the first one to popularize silicone breast augmentation, and Belli had defended her in a court case. We all were very interested in what he was going to say. After a few complimentary remarks about Dr. Dunphy and his Department, he turned to a curtain behind him and asked Miss Doda to please join him since he wanted to examine her. She stepped forward and after sitting down took off her blouse and bra to display the largest breasts most of us had ever seen. He put a stethoscope to his ears and began to listen to her heart. Of course in this activity he could not avoid fondling her breasts. There was a lot of cat calling and laughter from the audience. At the end of about 15 minutes of this activity, he told her that she was healthy and could leave. He then asked us to be quiet since he wanted to inform us that he would be visiting our Department in order to obtain material for writing a book titled "Scalpel, Sponge, Subpoena". It was so quiet you could hear a pin drop, except for the laughter of Bert Dunphy. This was one of the funniest gags I had ever seen. It was a stunt that even Dunphy would not be able to pull off today without serious retribution.

By my second year on the surgical faculty at UCSF, my laboratory was running full bore, and my practice had attracted an increasing number of interesting cases. Maja and I had just moved into a new home across the Golden Gate Bridge in Mill Valley. Maja had left her beauty shop to spend full time caring for the children. Barbara had left the children with us with a small note that she had been remarried, and was on her way to honeymoon in Hawaii. We did not know how to interpret this new information, but did feel that things were going our way in terms of stabilizing our family situation.

It was at about this time that I was invited by George Hallenbeck to visit the Mayo Clinic in Rochester, Minnesota. I had been recommended to him by Dr. John Kirklin, chairman of the department of surgery at the Clinic. The job description was interesting. They were looking for an individual who could perform clinically in the management of complex general surgical cases and be a productive basic science investigator. I looked at the job since it provided what I was interested in, an active surgical practice and resources and time to maintain an active research program. I turned the job down because I was not ready to leave San Francisco. In fact, I planned to spend the rest of my life there.

A few months later I received a call from Dr. Kirklin, informing me that he had accepted the chairmanship of surgery at the University of Alabama in Birmingham. This was big news for the surgical community worldwide since he was one of the leading cardiac surgeons in the world, and had developed an outstanding cardiothoracic training program at the Mayo Clinic. I had no interest in moving to Birmingham, and told him that my plan was to spend my professional career in San Francisco. He asked me why, and I explained that I liked the lifestyle in the department of surgery at UCSF. I thought that that would put him off, but he kept calling me on almost a weekly basis. I asked why he was so interested in me, and he related that he had read my research grant proposal for studying acid secretion that I had sent to the NIH which he thought was superb. Furthermore, he had asked about my clinical skills from my previous professors. I guess I passed muster. Out of respect for Dr. Kirklin, I agreed to fly into O'Hare Airport in Chicago, and listen to his plans for Alabama.

Dr. Kirklin outlined a very ambitious proposal for the development of a first rate medical program. He articulated his vision with enthusiasm, precision, and commitment to excellence. He asked me what I was doing at UCSF, which he wrote down on a napkin, and then proceeded to convince me that I had a non job. He told me that he would share the indigent services with me, and provide me with an opportunity for a private practice, and resources for pursing my research. I said I would accept the offer if he designated me as the Director of the Division of Gastrointestinal Surgery. He said that there was no such entity, but understood that this area of surgery needed to have a boost since the morbidity and survival statistics were not good in complex diseases of this organ system. I told him that I would be happy to visit Birmingham with my wife Maja, and give careful consideration to his proposal.

Keep in mind that 1966 was a remarkably restless period in Alabama, and Birmingham was a focal point for racial violence. Four black children had just been killed in the bombing of a church. This did not dissuade Maja and I from visiting Birmingham since we thought it would be unlikely that we would or could move there because of the uncertainty of the status of our children. We had not heard from their biologic mother Barbara for over a year. Our visit to Birmingham was surprisingly pleasant and productive. Peggy Kirklin, John's wife, showed Maja the town while John took me immediately to the Jefferson Hospital to show me around a very active surgical facility. I was introduced to the faculty and residents, and had an opportunity to visit with the President of the University of Alabama Medical Center In Birmingham, Dr. Joseph Volker, a Dentist and world class educator. He had big plans for the Medical Center to include the development of an undergraduate campus. I could immediately grasp why John was moving there. I also met with Paul Brand, an administrator in the president's office which included responsibility for of the Medical and Dental Schools which in fact were organized as a single educational entity. Mr. Brand was very helpful in facilitating our move to Birmingham.

It did not take us (the family) long to accept John's offer. I was to be chief of one of the two charity services, John being chief of the other. I was also to be chief of gastrointestinal surgery, a gratuitous title to facilitate the future development of this field. Of special interest to me was that the division of gastroenterology was directed by Dr. Basil Hirschowitz, the inventor of the flexible gastroscope. He had recruited several outstanding basic science investigators to include Gabriel Makhlouf, George Sachs, Andrew Blum, and Edward Moore. Dr. Warren Rehm, a gastric physiologist was the chairman of physiology. This concentration of talent in my field of interest insured that I would continue to learn about the origins of gastrointestinal disease. I accepted Dr. Kirklin's kind offer, and joined him a few months later as an Associate Professor of Surgery.

CHAPTER 10

THE ALABAMA YEARS WITH JOHN KIRKLIN (1966-1971)

Dr. Dunphy was less than pleased when I told him of my decision to move to Alabama. He thought that this would not be a good environment for my budding career. What he did not know was that my opportunities to get clinically immersed in complex surgery would increase by at least ten fold. Over the next two months, I closed the lab, sold our house, packed up two cars, and headed for Alabama with Maja and our three children. The trip was uneventful until we entered the room of a randomly selected motel in Birmingham, and I picked up the telephone which was ringing rather ominously. At the other end was a San Francisco police officer that told me that they had just removed the body of my former wife from San Francisco Bay. They had positive identification that it was her, including a birthmark on her right thigh, which they had learned by contacting her family in Massachusetts. He extended his condolences to me, and hung up. We decided not to tell the children of this tragic event at that time.

Paul Brand, an administrative assistant to President Volker helped us rent a beautiful apartment in Vestavia. To the children's delight it had a large swimming pool which they quickly jumped into.

As was my custom, I immediately went to work. Dr. Kirklin had decided that he and I would staff the two charity services, and that we would be the only faculty members that the residents on the service would relate to. In the past, the residents would more or less manage the patients without direct supervision from the surgical faculty. There was a separate private service for the faculty members to admit their patients and manage them with the help of a more junior resident staff. This meant that Dr. Kirklin and I would be the responsible surgeons on the teaching services, and would alternate emergency call every other day. The resident's were bright, hard working, and technically adept, but in need of further instruction in critical decision making.

Dr. Kirklin was well prepared to undertake this assignment since he had detailed protocols of how to manage most general surgical procedures. I was less organized in my approach, and used more of a Socratic approach to surgical decision making in that I engaged the residents in a consideration of a number of options for each surgical encounter. Dr Kirklin in the early days used to come in and watch us do our surgical procedures, a large number of which were for peptic ulcer disease. He once asked me why we did so many different types of operations for ulcer disease. He obviously was trying to encourage me to use the Mayo Clinic approach where most surgical interventions were performed by protocol. I stood my ground by explaining that times were changing, and that vagotomy along with a lesser resection of the stomach was replacing the standard subtotal gastric resection that was being done on his service. He seemed to be satisfied with this answer and never mentioned the subject again. This conversation stimulated me however to start to accumulate the evidence that the procedures we selected to do were substantiated by objective outcomes data.

The charity services that John and I managed, John the Red and mine the Blue had their own geographic area in the Jefferson Davis Hospital. The charity units consisted of about 25 beds each.

Each service had two operating rooms every other day. John within several months had a very large cardiovascular service, and I had a relatively small gastrointestinal surgical service for referral patients. This was staffed with one junior resident and an intern. These two services provided more than enough cases to keep our two operating rooms working well into the night.

Patients with acute traumatic injury were managed in a separate wing of the hospital called the "Old Hillman". The volume of trauma cases was sometimes overwhelming, especially on Friday and Saturday nights. Birmingham had a very active "knife and gun club". There were many times when we had to prioritize the patients for their operative intervention by lining their stretchers up along the wall until it was their time to be taken into the operating. One of my first cases to manage was that of a 76 year old lady who had been stabbed in the back as she rocked forward in her rocking chair. The residents handled this case extremely well. Later in the evening, I was called about my opinion on how to manage a stab wound into the orifice of the vagina. I told the resident to proceed with caution and that I would be right in. The resident's were surprised to see that Dr. Kirklin and I were interested in helping with these cases since they were accustomed to operating on them without staff supervision. The Hillman had a large amphitheater that was filled on Saturday nights with students who wanted to watch the mayhem.

Dr. Kirklin and I were able to cover our busy services by taking call every other night. Our resident's were so good at emergency care that they could manage most of the routine cases without our help. If they were unsure of how to proceed, they would consult us by telephone. Occasionally, there would be a mistake made. For example, early one morning I was called by a very fine resident surgeon Bill Shadburn who had just seen in the emergency room a young man with a stab wound of the heart who presumably had bled to death. Gruffly I said, why are you calling me, you should be calling an undertaker. As we were making rounds the next morning in the intensive care unit, Bill took me to the bedside of the patient that he called me about the night before. After we had completed the call, the patient was found to have an electrical signal on his electrocardiogram. They continued with their resuscitation and took him emergently to the operating room. Upon opening the chest they found a large penetrating wound of the base of his aorta, which they closed. The patient improved rapidly, and was returned to the Intensive Care unit.

On rounds the next morning, I congratulated Dr. Shadburn and his staff on a remarkable, life saving intervention. As I placed my stethoscope on the patient's anterior chest, I heard a very loud continuous murmur (like the whirring of a machine), and turned to Shadburn and said "you screwed up". Take a listen. He heard what I heard, but was not sure what it meant. I explained to him that it likely was a laceration of the septum between the aorta and the pulmonary artery. Dr. Robert Karp, one of Dr. Kirklin's senior cardiovascular fellows and my former resident at UCSF was making rounds on his cardiac patients in the same unit, and I asked him to take a listen. He agreed, and explained to us that this acute aortic-pulmonary window required urgent repair, which he did with a successful outcome. Bob stayed on the faculty at UAB for several years before assuming the Chair of Cardiothoracic Surgery at the University of Chicago. He retired somewhat early to his home in Aspen, Colorado. It was with a saddened heart that I learned from my daughter Jane several years ago that Bob and his wife Sony had died in an automobile accident in Southern France.

The Gastroenterology Service under the direction of Dr. Basil Hirshowitz was very busy. By the time I arrived on the scene he had started to actively use the flexible endoscope that he had developed. His Division included Dr. Marshall Garrett and Jerry Luketic. Marshall had trained at the Mayo Clinic, and was expert in esophageal manometry. Jerry was trained as a gastroenterologist, and had a very broad and active clinical practice with a clinical interest in inflammatory bowel disease. The availability of the flexible gastroscope attracted a large flow of patients with foregut disease. I quickly let my interest in reflux esophagitis, peptic ulcer, hepatobiliary, pancreatic, and colon disease be known, and it was not long before I began to see each week more cases than I saw each year in San Francisco. I use to enjoy watching Dr. Hirschowitz endoscope his patients. He kept me so busy that it never occurred to me that surgeons could also master this technology. I believe that I missed a unique opportunity to introduce at an early date (1967) flexible endoscopy into the surgical armamentarium. On the other hand, if I had, my referral practice would likely have come to an abrupt halt.

With the help of three excellent secretaries, I was able to develop a data base for a prospective tabulation of our experience with the surgical treatment of digestive disease. This fit in with the thrust of Dr, Kirklin's interest in computerizing the care of patients in the cardiovascular intensive care units, and to actively pursue other applications of the emerging field of information technology. This work was carried out under the leadership of Lewis Sheppard, a pioneer in this area. I was envious of the cardiac surgeon's computer program which required a very large room filled with complex equipment since the desk top computer had not as yet been designed. We resorted to the old fashion punch card/ice pick technique, hoping that soon we would have a digital way of storing and assessing our data.

In collaboration with Dr. Garrett, I was able to very quickly initiate a prospective study on the efficacy of treating well established reflux esophagitis by a Nissen Fundoplication. This was the era where we tried to control symptoms with antacids, small frequent feedings, and elevation of the head of the bed. H2 receptor blockade and proton pump inhibitors were not available, but on the horizon. This lack of effective therapy provided a wealth of surgical material. Dr. Garrett's expertise in evaluating esophageal anatomy and function before and after surgery brought us an increasing number of patients with esophageal disorders. We evaluated and treated several patients with unusual motility disturbances of the esophagus such as mega-esophagus in advanced achalasia, hypercontracting sphincter in esophageal spasm, and an achalasia like manometric pattern in patients with lye injury of the esophagus.

Shortly after my arrival, Dr. Hirshowitz and his colleagues referred a variety of unusual cases to include a patient with Menetrier's Disease associated with a protein losing enteropathy. This occurred in a teen age boy who was cured with a total gastrectomy. One of the most unusual cases I was asked to consult on was a 24 year old male who had episodes of severe abdominal pain with vomiting. Plain films (xrays) of the abdomen revealed an image of half of a skull with a jaw and teeth attached. Upon exploration of the abdomen, I found a large fluid filled mass at the base of the mesentery of the small bowel. Fortunately I was able with care to mobilize the mass from the vessels in the area, and safely remove it. When I opened the mass on the back table it revealed an intact hemi skull with hair on it, and a hemi-jaw with teeth. There were no malignant elements in the tumor when subjected to pathologic examination. The boy made an uneventful recovery. And so it went during my entire time in Alabama. Each day and night was associated with several challenging surgical cases.

I had established myself, probably without merit, to be a thinking surgeon in the eyes of the internists. Early in my tenure at UAB I was asked to see a middle aged lady with unexplained weight loss. She had been extensively worked up by the medical service under the supervision of Cliff Meador, a highly respected endocrinologist. Keep in mind that this was in 1967, long before the availability of precise imaging. The working diagnosis was cachexia from Addison's Disease. I was accompanied by Cliff and his entourage of junior faculty, residents, and students to the patient's bedside. After the resident presented the history, I asked a few questions, examined the patient, and told her that she had a partial blockage of the major blood vessel to her small intestine.

Of course making this diagnosis and suggesting how to treat it was not because I was smarter than the internists caring for her, I just listened carefully to her upper abdomen for a bruit, which was there. At operation, I found an atheromatous plaque at the origin of her superior mesenteric artery which I removed without complications. She regained her ability to eat, gained weight, and made a full recovery.

I had failed to realize how important it was for me to have a big dose of complex surgery when I completed my residency training. My intense interest in laboratory research had compromised my clinical skills and the boldness required to take on new challenges. I remedied this in part by watching Dr. Kirklin and his fellows do the cardiac and vascular cases. One thing that I observed was that they always used a headlight, and frequently wore magnifying glasses when performing their procedures. I therefore started to do the same thing, and greatly improved the view I had in the dark recesses of the abdomen. My associates thought that I was cozying up to the Chief, but I noticed that they soon began to appreciate the advantages of seeing what they were doing, and followed my example.

The second thing I learned was not to assume that a trainee "de novo" knew all the tricks of the trade. One day while scrubbing with Dr. Kirklin, as he prepared to do a total correction of a Tetrology of Fallot, a complex surgical procedure, I naively said, you must have done close to a hundred of these. He tersely replied, over 500. He was a master surgeon who paid attention to every detail of preparation and execution of a procedure. In fact, he had cue cards to remind himself and the anesthesiologist of the sequence in coming off cardiopulmonary by-pass. He was equally intense in whatever he did. Because of this characteristic, he was nicknamed "The Wire". Because of my animated way of explaining things, they called me the "Dancing Bear"

John called me into his office one day to discuss what we were going to do about the remarkably high mortality we were having with our surgery for portal hypertension. I knew that this was coming since we often found ourselves helping the resident do an end to side portacaval shunt in the middle of the night only to see the patient die within a week or two. I thought that he was going to recommend that his cardiovascular fellows start doing the procedures. But that was not the case. He clearly said, "Frank, you are personally going to manage these cases including the operative intervention". I said yes sir, and immediately got to work reviewing what was known about shunt surgery.

I had only performed three portacaval shunts during my residency. Fortunately, my instructor was George Wantz, an expert in the field. I vaguely remembered his admonition that we should avoid doing shunts in the middle of the night. What I decided was that we would control the acute hemorrhage by balloon tamponade and provide for each patient intense medical management for several weeks before operating upon them. I made it clear to the resident's much to their chagrin that I would be doing the shunt procedures from skin to skin on an elective basis as I had been instructed to do by my boss. In addition, I provided the residents with a very detailed protocol of how we were to manage them. I had learned rather early that it was important to standardize the approach to complicated operative procedures if you wanted to consistently obtain excellent results.

Towards the end of my second year at Alabama, John recognized that my plate was getting full. On the way to a football game one evening in Tuscaloosa, he recommended that I recruit one of his trainees at Mayo, Dr. Joaquin Aldrete. This was a superb recommendation for two reasons. Joaquin was an outstanding clinical surgeon and a wonderful human being. He also was an ideal recruitment for my purposes of developing academic surgeons since he had a need for training in research, and we had a need for a junior faculty member in gastrointestinal surgery.

There was funding available through an Academic Training Grant at the Birmingham Veterans Administration Hospital. In order to get a quick start in the laboratory, he joined our group in our studies of the permeability of the gastric mucosa to acid during the development of acute erosions. This work taught Joaquin the techniques involved in large animal research. In addition, he participated in the presentation of the work at the Thirty Second Annual Meeting of the Society of University of Surgeons at Yale which he attended with me in 1970. The work was subsequently published in Surgery in July of 1971 and Joaquin's academic career took off like a rocket.

Joaquin's assignment at the VA was fortuitous since it gave him access to a large number of patients with cirrhosis. I had developed an interest in finding a way to assess hepatic functional reserve. I learned during a review of our prior experience with portacaval shunts that the high death rate was due to liver failure after the shunt. I also learned that most of the patients with bleeding varices that presented to our emergency room were Child's Class C, the sickest of the sick. We decided to pursue a rigorous study protocol designed to raise each patient up a notch in the Child Classification, A being best, and C being worst. That is, if they came in a Class C, we tried to improve their status to Class B, and if a B to A. Child's Class A patients would undergo a portacaval shunt electively by Joachim or me, usually within a week. We documented the changes in liver blood flow by measuring the clearance of indocyanine green dye as was advocated by Joseph Levy in Miami. By pursuing this conservative approach, we were able to lower the death rate from over 80% to below 10%. I believe that we had confirmed John's opinion that if you are going to try to improve the therapy of a complex and potentially lethal disease you had best immerse yourself in its treatment.

John Kirklin had many talents but one of his strongest was administration. He looked far into the future, and in spite of institutional roadblocks, found solutions to the creation of the first rate Medical Center that exists at the University of Alabama in Birmingham. I appreciated his sharing many of his plans with me. In fact I was involved directly in helping to solve one. There was no renal transplant unit in the State of Alabama. He called me into his office one day and assigned me the task of finding someone that could develop a transplant unit within the Department. I told him that I knew a person that I had trained with at the Cornell—New York Hospital Medical Center, Dr. Arnold G. Diethelm (Gil), who was currently pursuing a research fellowship in Dr. Francis D. Moore's Lab at the Brigham. He actually was working on the suppression of the immune response with Roy Calne who in the future would be the Regius Professor of Surgery at Oxford and be knighted by the Queen for the outstanding work that he did there. I knew that Gil was being recruited to Michigan and told John so. This did not dissuade John from instructing me to fly up to Boston and convince Gil to visit with us first before finalizing his appointment at Michigan.

Upon meeting Gil in his lab at the Brigham, I was surprised that he was deeply jaundiced. He was recovering from a severe bout of hepatitis, but otherwise was well. I told him of our need for someone to develop transplantation at UAB. I explained to him in enthusiastic and realistic terms what a great opportunity it was for him to join us in Alabama. I knew that if I brought him in contact with John, that he would come south rather than going west. I must have given a good pitch since he came down and the rest is history. He not only joined our faculty and developed the largest renal transplant program in the United States but also subsequently replaced John as the Chairman of Surgery when John retired. Gil also retired several years ago and subsequently has had a liver transplant, and a renal transplant. I recently chatted with him on the phone (March, 2013) and both transplanted organs are serving him well.

The University of Alabama Medical School had and still has a strong interest in the teaching of medical students. I would be remiss not to mention three that I had close relationship with during their clinical years. The first is Kirby Bland, the current Chairman of the Department of Surgery at UAB. It was obvious when I first met Kirby that he was destined for greatness. His trajectory through Hiram Polk's program in Louisville, as a faculty member with Ted Copeland at the University of Florida in Gainesville, Chairman at Brown University in Rhode Island, and now Chair at The University of Alabama has been phenomenal. He is one of the foremost surgical oncologist in the country, and deserving of all the accolades he has received.

The second student that I worked with at Alabama was Dr. Ronald Merrill, who trained in general surgery at the Barnes Hospital of the Washington University in St. Louis. Ron, upon completion of his residency joined the faculty at Stanford University in Palo Alto. I tracked Ron for years before I finally was able to recruit him to Houston to develop an islet transplant laboratory and to share his extraordinary teaching skills with us. He was recognized for his educational skills by being appointed as an Associate Dean of Medical Education. We had a wonderful time together until he took the Chairmanship at Yale, then the Chair at the Medical College of Virginia before retiring last year to his home State of Alabama.

The third student that I got to know real well was Michael Torma, who worked with me in the lab when he was a medical student at UAB. He grew up in a military family, and had a strong desire to pursue his professional career in the military. He spent year in my laboratory in Salt Lake during his residency, and subsequently rose to the rank of General in the Medical Core before retiring to civilian life in Shreveport, Louisiana. This is not to imply that a year in my lab made a difference in this achievement, but I would like to think that the research he did with us made him a better doctor.

I was very involved with curriculum development at Alabama, and enjoyed my interactions with Al Farmer, an internist in the Department of Medicine who subsequently left to be the President of the Medical School at the University of Maryland. He was an outstanding educator, and set a standard that I have tried to emulate. John Kirklin was also a very inspiring teacher, at least for his first full academic year at UAB for which he received the best teaching award. He became somewhat distracted with his clinical and administrative work load the following year, and at the student banquet he received the toilet seat award for being the worst teacher in surgery. This consisted of having his portrait framed by a toilet seat. I almost laughed but I could see that he was not pleased with what I considered to be a joke. This was the last time that he attended the award ceremonies. Possibly this cute but true story should not be told.

It goes without saying that the Alabama football team was judged to be the Number One football team in the nation for three of the five years that I was there. Who would expect differently with Bear Bryant as their coach. John had two seats assigned to him next to the President of the University on the 50 yard line. He asked me to represent him at the games when they occurred in Birmingham, and I was delighted to do so. My wife Maja, being a Swede, had never seen an American style football game. The first one she attended, she sat next to Dr. Verner Von Braun, the famous World War II rocket scientist. He was most kind in explaining to Maja how the game was played. I was amused, since he was not too sure about the rules himself.

My professional and personal life was going very well at Alabama, without a worry in the world except for the welfare of my patients. That is until one day on arriving home, I opened a letter from Barbara Moody. Recall that she was supposed to have drowned in San Francisco Bay a few years previously. Subsequent investigation revealed that the letter was authentic and she was alive and therefore I paid the back alimony that she had requested. Several months later, my secretary opened my office door and said that my wife was there to see me. I wondered, why the formality, and soon learned why when Barbara entered my office dressed like a bird. I could hear the giggles from the girls in the office, and immediately began to consider how I could get out of a rather difficult predicament. I invited Barbara to have a seat, and we engaged in a very friendly conversation. It turns out that she had hitch hiked to Birmingham from San Francisco without a change of clothes. That explained why the bird feathers on her red dress were soiled. I called Maja and informed her that we had a visitor. Maja had never met Barbara, and was pleased that I was bringing her home to visit with her children. I then walked out of the office arm and arm with Barbara as if we were the best of friends, as we were.

Once getting home, Maja helped Barbara bathe, and provided her with a new set of clothes. This all seemed very natural. When the children returned home in the late afternoon they were surprised and somewhat apprehensive when they first saw their mother. Barbara was very pleased to see them, and soon the warmth of their relationship emerged as we enjoyed a family style dinner. It was obvious to Barbara that Maja was an extraordinary mother. In fact, Barbara thanked her for taking such good care of the children. There was throughout the evening no behavior to suggest that Barbara had chronic schizophrenia. We did not discuss why she had hitch hiked across the country dressed like a bird.

After the children went to bed, we engaged in a conversation about the future, and I suggested that it might be in their best interest for us to adopt them. Barbara liked this idea. Fortunately I had already approached a lawyer of how to formally adopt the children since Barbara was supposed to be dead. The next day, we visited the lawyer's office, and Barbara signed the adoption papers without a tear being shed at the time. And that was it. Maja and I were legally the parents of the children.

Barbara was very pleasant and displayed normal behavior throughout the visit. She was anxious to return home so we made arrangements for her to take a bus back to San Francisco the next day. We all went to the bus station to see her off. It was a festive occasion. Two nights later I received a call from a policeman just outside of Orlando, Florida. He said that he was just checking on a female hitch hiker who gave him my number, and said that she was my wife. I told him that she was likely my former wife Barbara. On this recognition he let her go on her way. While as fate would have it, over the next several years, I would not see Barbara again, but there were several unusual encounters which I will relate at an appropriate time. We never did address the issue of who the person was that was found in the San Francisco Bay, but one thing for sure, it was not Barbara.

CHAPTER 11

CHAIRMAN AT THE UNIVERSITY OF UTAH (1971-1982)

Things continued to go well in Birmingham, both at work and at home. I had only one problem, John would not let me go the next step in developing an identity for gastrointestinal surgery. What I wanted to do was to train a limited number of academically inclined gastrointestinal surgeons who could handle the complex problems in this organ system. I went to John one day with a proposal to develop a fellowship in gastrointestinal surgery to be supported by an NIH sponsored academic training grant. He praised me for the good work that I was doing, and politely said no to my proposal. He was concerned, as I, that such an approach had the potential of fragmenting general surgery. I politely said thank you, and left, realizing that I had to go elsewhere if I was to achieve my goal in this area. I understood his reason for denial, but was concerned at the time about the morbidity and mortality of patients undergoing surgery for advanced diseases of gastrointestinal tract, liver, and the pancreas. I knew that I had to assume a chair of surgery elsewhere to achieve this goal. There was not much in the way of incentive to leave UAB. The program was expanding, my own work was progressing well, and the family liked Birmingham.

Apparently the word was out that I wanted to leave Birmingham. My old friend Gene Jacobson from my California days called to see if I would be interested in the new chair of surgery at the University of Texas in Houston. He had just accepted the chair in physiology there. I thanked him for thinking of me, but told him that I was not up to the challenge of starting from scratch. Dr. Stanley Dudrick of total parenteral nutrition fame from the University of Pennsylvania was the initial chairman at UT Houston Medical School, and did a good job of getting the program off the ground. Little did I know that 12 years later I would be the 2nd chair of surgery at University of Texas Medical School in Houston. Several months after the Texas inquiry in 1970, I was approached by Dean Harrell of the new Medical School in Hersey, Pennsylvania, that was recently established by Penn State University. Not only was it a startup, but the University Hospital was only half completed, and the School's commitment was to develop family physicians. I sensed that this was a non-starter for me. John Waldhausen, a cardiac surgeon from the University of Pennsylvania subsequently took the job, and developed a superb academic department there.

What I particularly liked about my job in Birmingham was the opportunity to meet the many distinguished surgeons that came to visit John. I was especially impressed with a visit by Dr. Bryan Barrett Boyes, a cardiac surgeon from Tasmania and one of John's favorites. A visit from Chris Barnard of Cape Town South Africa just before he returned home to do his first human transplant was very exciting. Maja especially enjoyed hosting Clarence Craaford from Stockholm, Sweden who had performed the first resection of a coarctation of the aorta. One of my favorite visitors was Dr. John Goligher, the Chairman at Leeds University who wrote the book on colorectal surgery. These visitors to include many others contributed breadth to the educational program at Alabama.

I felt a special loyalty to John, not only for the remarkable opportunity that he was providing for me professionally, but also for his concern about my family. During my third year at Alabama, he gave me a financial bonus so that I could take Maja and the children to Sweden to visit Maja's family and friends. This was offered without solicitation. It was on this visit that I met the 20 year old daughter of Maja's closest friend, Holger Ekstrand. Little did I know at that time that Inger Margareta would forty years later become my wife a year after Maja's death.

John and I, and our wives Peggy and Maja became close friends and most months we had dinner together at some nice restaurant before going to the symphony. It was always a standing joke to see which one of us would doze off first. John won most times, although I was not very far behind.

Keith Reemstma, the chairman of surgery at the University of Utah called one day in the early spring of 1971 to see if I had any interest in moving to Salt Lake City. He had just accepted the Bard Chair and Professorship at Columbia University in New York City. As I mentioned earlier, Barbara and I had visited Jim and Marilyn Warenski one Christmas in Salt Lake City, and I was impressed with the quality of the snow at Alta. I told Keith that I would be very interested in the Chair at Utah even though I knew nothing about the place. Within a few days I received a call from Dr. David Bragg, the chairman of radiology at Utah, and chairman of the search committee for the chair of surgery. He wanted me to make an early brief visit to see if I had an interest, and I said that I could only do it soon for a day within a few days since I was on my way to Germany to give a talk. I flew up on my way to Europe, and was amazed at what Keith had put together with almost no state financial support. A small 300 bed University Hospital had just been completed. All of surgery was in one Department of Surgery, including Ophthalmology.

The residency program in general surgery with the help of the local hospitals finished three chief residents a year. The basic sciences and departments of medicine and pediatrics were highly academic. The department of surgery was relatively devoid of research except for the division of artificial organs directed by Willem Kolff of renal dialysis fame. The committee appeared to be very interested in my vision for the development of a highly academic department of surgery. Arrangements were made for me to revisit in about 2 weeks with my wife.

As we approached the Salt Lake valley in June of 1971, Maja commented on how dry everything looked. She had never seen high desert country before. What I saw was the granite of the mountain tops and patches of snow. We were picked up by Dave Bragg, who explained that the committee and Dean Ebaugh were really interested in me coming to Utah. My visit was very informative, and I became interested in the job. I thought it would be an ideal place to develop academic surgeons.

Maja, who had been introduced to a real estate agent called me later that day to tell me she had found an A-frame home which she would like to live in if we moved to Salt Lake. I arranged for a quick visit at lunch time to see the property and shared Maja's attraction to the home. I made an honest offer, which was only a thousand dollars in those days, in order to put a hold on the property for three months. I informed Dr. Bragg what I had done. The search committee apparently were disturbed by my action, and called an urgent meeting to inform me that they had other candidates to consider. I acknowledged that they should complete their search but explained that we wanted to live in that home if they should give me the job.

It was not by chance that the home that we wanted to buy was very close to the mouth of Little Cotton Wood Canyon which was the road to Alta, and the soon to be built Snowbird, one of the finest skiing resorts in the world. I am sure that the location of the University of Utah in proximity to such beautiful mountains played a role in my enthusiasm for the job. But I also figured that if such greats as Max Weintrobe, George Cartwright, Louis Goodman,

Leo Samuelson, Willem (Pim) Kolff, and Keith Reemstma to name only a few of the individuals who had achieved their academic goals there, so should I.

I returned to Birmingham, and told John that I was very impressed with Utah. He related to me that he hoped that I would stay in Alabama. We reviewed the pros and cons of a move at that time. It seemed to John that it was the wrong time to make a move because Dean Ebaugh had returned to Stanford. Utah was without a Dean. I thought that this might be a plus.

A few months went by with no news from Utah. Then in late summer, Dr. Thomas King, a thoracic surgeon, and Provost of the University called and asked me if I was still interested in the chair of surgery at Utah. I said yes, and he said that the chair of surgery is yours. He then inquired how much of a financial package would it take to get me there. I said whatever you can give me because I know that you want me to succeed. My only request was for moving expenses for my family and my laboratory, which was granted.

Things then moved very rapidly and by mid-October we had sold our home, shut down my practice and the laboratory, and was ready to head west. Fortunately by this time, the Division of Gastrointestinal Surgery was very active. Dr. Aldrete had a busy practice and was happy to take over the Blue Service. We had a few years earlier been joined by another senior Master Surgeon from the Mayo Clinic, Dr. George Hallenbeck. George was a wonderful addition to the Department. Recall, that Dr. Hallenbeck a few years earlier had offered me a job at the Mayo Clinic. He not only was a first rate surgeon, and an imaginative clinical researcher, but also a very delightful guy to be around because of his sense of humor In addition he was a celebrity since he had removed Lyndon Johnson's gallbladder while he was still President of the United States. He had over a two year period at the UAB developed a large referral practice, and had introduced highly selective vagotomy into our surgical treatment of peptic ulcer. Joaquin had developed a very active hepato-biliary and pancreatic practice. The program at Alabama was developing rapidly in all dimensions, including gastrointestinal surgery. It was with reluctance that we said good bye to Alabama.

On a warm, sunny fall day in Birmingham, we supervised the final loading of the moving van, packed our personal belongings and children into two cars, and headed to Utah. We stayed the first night in Oklahoma, and only once did we become separated and I had to have the State Police locate Maja. We stayed the second night in Cheyenne, and as the evening progressed we were warned of a storm that was moving towards the Wasatch Mountains that lie between us and Salt Lake. In the morning the weather was fine where we were, so we headed West on I- 80. It started to snow by the time we reached Rock Springs, but the road was clear, and the snowflakes melted as soon as they reached the pavement. We all were fascinated by the snowflakes, since we saw them rarely in Alabama. It never occurred to us that we did not have snow tires. The further West we went, the harder it snowed, so that by the time we reached the high pass at Parley's Summit that led into Salt Lake, we were engulfed in a blizzard. Maja, who was ahead of us with Anne and Jane in her car, disappeared into the swirling snow. I promptly slid off the side of the road, and had to be pushed back onto the road and up over the pass by a police car that had chains. I was very concerned about Maja and the other children but pressed on until I reached the bottom of the pass and pulled into a Holiday Inn. Much to my delight, I saw Maja's car, and soon was having a hot drink with them, no worse for the experience.

This was only the beginning of our adverse events upon entering what the natives call "Happy Valley". When we called the real estate agent to pick up the key to the house on Kingshill Drive that we had put a down payment on, she told us that the builder/ occupants were not ready to leave and were reconsidering their offer to sell. Fortunately we had a legal bill of sale, and upon threat of legal action they said that they would move in a week. This in a way was fortuitous since our moving van had become snowbound in Rock Springs. Much to the delight of the children, we spent a week in the motel.

The moving van with the research laboratory transported from Birmingham arrived the next day at the Medical School. I now was confronted with even a bigger challenge. When I went to the Dean's Office to pick up the key for the lab space which had been shown to me on my recruitment visit, I was told that it had been reassigned and that there was no space immediately available for my lab. I kept my cool, and said in no uncertain terms that I was going to turn the van around and head back to Alabama. Within a few hours, I was reassigned even better space than originally assigned for my purposes. The new space was larger than the old, and had a magnificent view of the snow clad mountains. Within a few weeks, we had organized the lab, and moved into our new home. I was ready to go to work.

CHAPTER 12

ESTABLISHING AN ACADEMIC PROGRAM

The Medical School, the University Hospital, the School of Pharmacy, the Nursing School, and the Medical Library were at the East end of the University of Utah Main Campus separated from it by a lovely 9 hole golf course. Surrounded by very impressive mountains, and its location at the edge of a dynamic city, made it an ideal place to attract anyone who liked a year around active outdoor life. The department of surgery in addition to general surgery included all of the surgical disciplines including ophthalmology. These specialties were designated as divisions, and were administered by directors who had the responsibility for both the clinical and academic programs in their disciplines. I held three titles on the organizational chart; Chairman of the Department of Surgery, Surgeon-in Chief of the University Hospital, and Director of the Division of General Surgery. All of the department chairs had similar lines of responsibility. The divisions of surgery had, from my point of view, more than adequate leadership. Dr. Russell Nelson, the Director of the Division of Cardiovascular Surgery was the only one that was not full time. He was an excellent cardiac surgeon, and well known nationally. I saw no reason for replacing him but at the time I was under pressure to do so since his practice was primarily at the LDS Hospital. I resolved the problem by designating Dr. Richard Hughes, an experienced cardiac surgeon as the Chief of Cardiothoracic Surgery at the University Hospital.

The program in general surgery was directed by the interim Chair of Surgery, Dr. Ralph Richards. Ralph was an accomplished general surgeon with a relatively large referral practice. He had been trained by Dr. Philip Price, the first Chair of Surgery who preceded Walter Burdette and in turn Keith Reemstma. Dr. Price had trained at Hopkins, and had spent several years at the then Peking Medical College in Beijing as a Missionary Doctor. He had established at Utah a program with a strong emphasis on the details of patient care. I assumed the position of Director of General Surgery and its educational programs since it offered the best way to get to know the staff, the residents, and the students. Ralph was most gracious in supporting me as the chief of general surgery. He was concerned whether my external involvement in NIH and VA study sections, surgical organization work, visiting professorships plus the administrative load of running the department would allow me enough time to do a good job at running the division. I thought that with his support, which he generously gave, that we could get the job done.

The administrative aspects (space, salary, academic program etc) were managed by an executive committee that consisted of the directors of the various divisions, with the surgeon in chief as the chair of the committee. We handled the affairs of the department through a process of consensus building. Our stated goal (consensus statement) was to create an environment where surgical innovation and knowledge could be developed through research, and transmitted through its educational programs to the care of patients at the University, the Veterans Administration, and the LDS Hospitals. These hospitals formed the core for the student teaching and the residency training program, which for general surgery was five years in length. Three additional hospitals, the Holy Cross, St. Marks, and the Ogden Mckay Dee Hospitals also were involved in resident and student teaching. These very active affiliated clinical hospitals provided a large number and variety of operative cases for resident education. A very dedicated and skillful clinical and full time faculty utilized these hospitals for their clinical work. They took pride in participating in the teaching of surgery. With this coordinated multi-hospital clinical program, we were able to finish about 5 or 6 chief residents per year. I often would visit the teaching hospitals when invited to make teaching rounds or consult. I considered this to be one of the unique features of the program in Utah. Keep in mind that the University served the entire Intermountain West to include parts of Idaho, Nevada, Wyoming, Arizona, and Colorado. This was a large surgical catchment area.

I immediately went to work evaluating the strengths and weaknesses of the faculty and was impressed with the quality of their clinical work. Dr. Ralph Richards was an excellent clinical surgeon and teacher. He conducted a very broad surgical practice which he unselfishly shared with his residents. The other members of the full time general surgical faculty included Dr. Gary Maxwell, Dr. Brian Rasmussen, Dr. Frederick Chang, and Dr. Jan Freeman. Dr Mark Wolcott served as a superb Chief of Surgery at the Salt Lake City Veteran's Administration Hospital. The faculty was appropriately sized for the number of beds allotted to surgery (about 25). There were only five operating rooms at the University Hospital, one of which was dedicated to urology for cystoscopic procedures. The emergency room was also small, but adequate for resuscitating the few trauma cases that we saw each month. The clinic space was also appropriately sized for the relatively few private patients that we initially cared for. It was obvious that we would need an expansion of clinical as well laboratory and teaching space over time if we were to achieve our goal of developing a highly academic clinical faculty. I felt confident that I was up to the task with the background that I had acquired at The Cornell-New York Hospital Medical Center (Glenn), The University of California in San Francisco (Dunphy), and the University of Alabama in Birmingham (Kirklin).

Chance again went my way. I was placed on the search committee for a new Dean. We recognized within a few months that he was already amongst us, currently serving as a senior member of the administrative staff of the University of Utah. His name was John Dixon, a highly respected surgeon who had been head of the surgical unit at the McKay Dee Hospital in Ogden before assuming the role of Vice President for Buildings and Grounds at the University of Utah years earlier. He was well known throughout the State since he had been quite involved in the activities of the church, as well as the State Medical Society. John was an excellent surgeon, and an even better administrator. He and I were both confident that we could move the institution forward.

The next order of business was to strengthen the residency, and make it more academically oriented. I recognized quite early that I had to establish myself as a clinical surgeon. This was enhanced by the fact that the division of gastroenterology directed by Dr. James Freston was very active in my areas of clinical interest. He was assisted by Dr. Malcolm Berenson, who had an interest in Barrett's esophagitis, and Keith Tolman, who had an interest in inflammatory and neoplastic lesions of the colon. It was not long before we had a constant flow of complex gastrointestinal problems that required a surgical intervention.

I initially spent most of my time developing the Surgical Laboratories around gastroesophageal, hepatic, biliary, and pancreatic diseases and their pathogenesis. This was facilitated by the fact that I had brought a complete laboratory setup from Alabama to deal with such problems to include research protocols, and an NIH Grant to support the studies. I also utilized money that I received as compensation for my surgical services to hire a technical staff. Within a few months, we were able to start screening the existing house staff for potential trainees to join us in our research activities.

CHAPTER 13

THE SURGICAL LABORATORIES AT UTAH

As mentioned previously, there was little laboratory based research activities in the division of general surgery at Utah. The fact that Dr. Kirklin had let me bring my laboratory intact to Utah, and that the School provided me with prime space to use it, was a godsend to our aspirations to be an academic training center. This was a time in academic surgery when the ability to do bench research was considered to be an essential requirement in the development of an academic surgeon. We proceeded with the critical task of finding trainees who were willing to extend their surgical education for hopefully two years to achieve this goal.

I will describe below the career paths of eight of our residents who over a short period of time after completing their extended academic training (about ten to fifteen years) went on to achieve the designation of Chairman of a major Department of Surgery. Most of them were, as others in the residency, interested in pursuing the clinical practice of surgery, or one of its sub-specialties. I related to the residents and faculty that the development of academic surgeons was one of the primary goals of our program, and that training in research was a privilege to be offered to only a few who were interested and qualified to pursue an academic track. In other words, time in a research laboratory was not mandatory but strongly recommended for those who wanted to pursue an academic career.

The first person that I interviewed for a year or two in the laboratory was **Dr. Laurence Cheung, MD** (Larry). Larry had spent his formative years in mainland China, and Hong Kong. He was a graduate of the Military Medical School in Taiwan. As I recall, he entered the Residency at the University of Utah after a year as an Intern at the Holy Cross Hospital in Salt Lake City. The faculty gave him high marks on his clinical rotations. I was very impressed with his breadth of knowledge, but noticed that he had no research experience. When I asked him what he wanted to do in the future, he said "I want to be an academic surgeon like you". I immediately offered Larry a two year Fellowship in my lab, which he accepted, and the rest is history. Upon completion of his Fellowship and the Residency, he joined our faculty and within a few years he was recruited by Dr. Samuel Wells to the faculty at Washington University. A few years later he became the Chairman of Surgery at the University of Kansas in Kansas City where he had a very distinguished career. As evidence of respect for his scholarly work, he was made President of the Association of Academic Surgeons and received numerous accolades from his peers to include the Outstanding Scholar Award at the University of Kansas. He currently is the Director of the surgical residency at the Providence Hospital in Detroit, Michigan.

I again had a stroke of good luck. The Academic Training Grant in Digestive Surgery that I was preparing for UAB was approved for our program in Utah. The Grant provided support for a Fellow and research monies for a two year period within a laboratory of their choice. This was an ideal mechanism for developing our Department at Utah from within into areas where we lacked expertise. I immediately recognized that one of our second year residents **Dr. Layton F. Rikkers, MD (**Bing**)** was an ideal candidate for this program. He was a graduate of the accelerated Medical School Program at Stanford, and I believe he was sent to Dr. Reemstma by Dr. Shumway, Chief of Cardiovascular Surgery at Stanford, for the purposes of exposing him to a few years of general surgery prior to returning to Stanford to train in Cardiovascular Surgery. Dr. Shumway felt that more than two years in general surgery was a waste of time for the training of a cardiovascular surgeon. I was on the American Board of Surgery when Dr. Shumway a few years later argued this point for one of his outstanding associates who was trying to take the examination of the Board but had only a few years of general surgery but three years of cardiovascular training. His candidate was so superior to the others taking the examination at the time that I sort of agreed with Dr Shumway that maybe a few years in general surgery were sufficient for preparing an individual to pursue a career in cardiovascular surgery. Whether such an individual should also be certified in General Surgery is another issue that still is being heavily debated.

I convinced Bing that at least a year of research would be of benefit to him. This turned into three years, one in my lab, one with Dame Sheila Sherlock at the Royal Free Hospital in London, and a year with Dean Warren who at that time was the Chairman of the Department of Surgery at Emory in Atlanta. These were very eventful years. During his year with me he showed conclusively that the quantitative measurement of ICG clearance could precisely measure the regenerating mass of the liver after a three segment hepatectomy in the dog and rat. He tried to apply this technique to Dame Sherlock's patient population with diseased livers with only marginal success, but along the way he learned a lot about human liver disease.

His year with Dean Warren was more successful and relevant to his career. He analyzed and reported on the results of a prospective randomized trial comparing the selective Warren splenorenal shunt to a standard portacaval shunt. The trial clearly demonstrated the superiority of the Warren Shunt. We were most fortunate in having him return to Utah for several years before assuming the Chair of Surgery at Nebraska. After developing a very fine Department there he moved on to Wisconsin where again he developed another outstanding Department of Surgery. He was editor of the premier Annals of Surgery journal for 17 years. As I write this section he is editor of the Weekly News of the American College of Surgeons, and is retired from the Annals and the Chair at Wisconsin. He richly deserves his recent election (2013) to the Presidency of the American Surgical Association.

Both Larry and Bing were equally comfortable in the operating room and in the laboratory. In addition, they were prolific writers. They put our academic training program in Utah on the map, along with several others from our training program that I will mention below, not necessarily in temporal order. **Dr. Byers Shaw** only spent a short time with us in the laboratory pursuing studies on papilla of Vater motility. He was not very interested in this field of research. Bud was a very gifted technical surgeon, and I thought somewhat bored with some aspects of the residency. This was also the impression that he gave to the rest of the faculty. I therefore wrote him a letter stating that if he did not start working up to his potential, he would have to leave. This got his attention. I knew that he was energized when one day while hiking with me up the back side of Timpanogos (about a 12,000 foot mountain and 4000 foot vertical climb), he took off like a greyhound, reaching the top hours before me. He had a big smile on his face, possibly gaining some solace for the stern letter I had sent to him earlier.

Towards the end of the residency he told me that he wanted to be a liver transplant surgeon. I told him that he should train with Dr. Thomas Starzl in Denver which actually was the only option at the time. He was accepted into the Starzl training program. Soon thereafter he came by the office to inform me that Starzl was moving to UCLA. I said great, stick with Starzl. A few weeks later in comes Bud again appearing somewhat dejected. He explained to me that something went wrong at UCLA and Starzl was moving to

Pittsburg. Again I emphatically said go with Starzl and he did. He subsequently became one of the premier liver transplant surgeons in the world. Bud moved to Nebraska, where he developed an outstanding liver transplant center, and also helped Bing Rikkers develop a strong Department of Surgery. He then succeeded Bing as the Chairman of the Department there when Bing moved to Wisconsin. Bud has now retired from the Chair and is devoting much of his time to creative writing.

Dr. James Becker MD was recommended to us by his father Dr. Norman Becker from Fond De Lac Wisconsin. Norm was visiting our Department of Surgery in Salt Lake one day with the Wisconsin Traveling Surgeons Club. He proudly told me about the talents of his son Jim who was soon to graduate from the Western Reserve School of Medicine in Cleveland. I told Norm that we would be very interested in his son joining us with the possibility of recruiting him into the Academic Training Program. Jim joined us, and was every bit as talented as his father had said that he was. Jim became interested in some of the work that we were doing clinically on the role of the papilla of Vater in the pathogenesis of gallstone pancreatitis.

He and Dr. Michael Duff MD, another imaginative resident in the program, thought that we ought to study the myoelectric potentials of the sphincter of Oddi. The diagnosis of biliary dyskinesia at the time was invoked as a reason for doing a transduodenal sphincteroplasty in patients with biliary like pain without gallstones. I liked the idea of pursuing this questionable diagnosis in the laboratory, but I did not like the rat, mouse, or dog as an animal model for the study. Jim and Mike then came up with the idea of studying the opossum, since it had a large biliary sphincter that was located outside of the duodenal wall. Jim joined us in the lab to study this problem. Unfortunately we had no experience or knowledge of how to study gastrointestinal motility. This is where the Grant came in handy. We approached Keith Kelly, an academic surgeon, and an expert in such matters, to accept Jim into his laboratory at the Mayo Clinic. During his year there, Jim became interested in the reconstruction of the hind gut after total coloproctectomy by an ileo-anal J-Pouch, and this became his primary area of interest.

Jim Becker was also a great help in mentoring Dr. Kong Ti MD, a Senior Lecturer from the University of Malaysia. They showed rather convincingly that the feeding of a meal to an executive monkey (a Rhesus trained to sit quietly in a chair) was associated with free reflux of bile during the digestive process. This required the establishment of a jejunal conduit from the outside of the abdominal wall to the tail of the pancreas for purposes of sampling the content of refluxed bile in the pancreatic duct during feeding and between meals. The hypothesis to be tested was that under normal conditions there was free reflux of bile into the main pancreatic duct that was cleared by the secretion of pancreatic juice following ingestion of a meal. Further studies were planned to explore whether smoking or chronic pancreatitis, risk factors for pancreatic cancer, would restrict this stripping or clearance factor of the flow of pancreatic juice. It took so long to develop a reliable way to study pancreatic secretion and clearance in the controls that money from our three year grant ran out.

The idea that there may be something in the bile that is oncogenic, and that if it bathes the pancreatic duct for a prolonged period of time it may lead to neoplastic changes in its epithelium is yet to be studied. I think that this is still an idea worthy of study since it is based on the observation that pancreatic cancer most often occurs in the proximal segment of the gland. A word of caution—the monkeys did not like their role in the study. I was reminded of this fact some years ago when Inger and I visited Dr. Ti and his family in Singapore where he is a Professor of Surgery. We had fun reminiscing upon these studies, and the time that we spent together in Salt Lake in general.

Dr. James Becker MD (Jim) completed his chief's year in 1980 and joined our faculty as an Assistant Professor of Surgery. His research years had prepared him to immediately take on the responsibilities of a junior faculty member. It was a delight to see how efficiently he, on his own, organized a program to study the function of a J Pouch ileo-anal reconstruction in patients with ulcerative colitis and familial polyposis. It turns out that there was a large population of patients with the latter disease in Utah because of the work of Dr. Gardner, a PhD developmental biologist at Utah State. Jim Becker organized a clinical research program to determine the cause of inflammation in the J-Pouch reconstruction called pouchitis, a relatively common complication of the procedure. He and his group demonstrated that a disturbance in the motor function of the pouch was a prominent feature of the disease.

The success of his work led to his recruitment to Washington University in Saint Louis by Sam Wells, chair of surgery there. He remained on the faculty for a few years before being recruited to the Brigham Hospital in Boston. A few years later, after developing a large referral practice in Boston, he assumed the chairmanship of the department of surgery at Boston University, and moved his practice to the Boston Medical Center. I understand that he has retired recently after a very successful career as the chairman of surgery at Boston University and plans to continue his surgical practice in the Boston area.

As for Michael Duff, he resisted my offer to join us in the lab. Upon completion of his residency, he moved back to Duffsville, Arkansas where he has developed a very busy practice. He contacted me recently to exchange a few exciting ideas, just like the old days.

Dr. Steve Lowry approached me one day in his second year of the residency asking if he could go to the NIH to study oncology under the mentorship of Dr. Murray Brennan. I thought that this was a great idea. He spent two years with Murray and then returned to the program for three years to finish his residency. By then, Dr, Brennan had moved to the Memorial-Sloan Kettering Cancer Center. Steve accepted a faculty position at the Cornell-New York Hospital Medical Center. He also had a joint appointment at the Memorial Cancer Center. Steve was a pioneer in identifying the role of cytokines in inflammation and neoplasia. His work in New York led to his being recruited to the Chair of Surgery at the Rutgers-New Jersey Medical Center where his academic star continued to shine brightly. He was rewarded for his pioneering work in cytokines by receiving the Karl-Flancz Award for outstanding research by the American Surgical Association. Unfortunately he died last year of a ruptured thoracic aneurysm.

A second well known resident from Utah of that vintage, Dr. James Seeger MD, died a few years ago from a heart attack. Jim was at the time the Chief of Vascular Surgery at the University of Florida in Gainesville, and had by the time of his death made many seminal contributions to the field of vascular surgery. Both of these former students will be deeply missed, and were role models for what academic surgery is all about.

Dr. James Goodnight MD entered our surgical program in Utah after serving two years in the Public Health Service on an Indian Reservation. He was in a way a fully minted academic surgeon from the "get go". His unique strength was in teaching, and it was of interest to me that he always received from the students the "best teacher" award. The same was true when he undertook an oncologic fellowship and subsequently a faculty position with Dr Donald Morton in UCLA. Jim was not only a superb teacher, but also a gifted surgeon. It was not long before he was recruited to the chair of surgery at the University of California in Sacramento. After a very successful career as chairman, he moved up another notch in the system, and became a Vice President for Health Affairs with his primary assignment being the management of the clinical activities of the Sacramento General Hospital.

Dr. Edward Nelson MD was also one of our outstanding clinician-teacher residents. I wanted him to stay on the faculty at the time, but did not have a position for him. What I did have was an opportunity for someone to join an HMO in Guam for a year, and recruited Ed for the job with the understanding that we would bring him back the following year to become a full time faculty member. He went to Guam, and found the experience to be relatively unrewarding. I did appoint him to the faculty for the following year, but I feel that he has not as yet forgiven me for sending him off to Guam. He did a magnificent job as a clinician-teacher, and subsequently became interim chairman when I left for Texas a few years later. He has emerged as one of the top general surgeons in the Intermountain West.

Through the publications and presentations of the work derived from the Surgical Laboratories, we caught the attention of the Chairs of Surgery across the country. Utah became a place where those programs without such a resource considered sending their promising residents to us for a research experience. **Dr. John Potts III MD**, who was referred to us by the late Dr. Rainey Williams, the Chairman of the Department of Surgery at Oklahoma, is a good example of the success of this joint training model. John spent a year with us in the lab during his residency at Oklahoma. He then joined our faculty in Houston several years later after completing his residency and having spent time on the Faculty at Emory, Vanderbilt, and the Cleveland Clinic in Fort Lauderdale. We recruited John to the Faculty at the University of Texas Houston (1990) to be the Program Director of our general surgical residency, which was on probation at the time. He quickly resolved this problem, and went on to develop a highly sought after program that has produced a large number of outstanding academic as well as surgeons practicing in the private sector. Because of his interest in education, he became an Associate Dean for Graduate Education at UT-Houston, a Director of the American Board of Surgery, and more recently coordinator of Programs in Surgery for the Accrediting Council for Graduate

Medical Education (ACGME). John has moved his home to Chicago to be close to his work. He has recently married an internist, Annie, whose family home is in Houston. The fact that John and Annie have a beach house in Galveston suggests that we will still see them frequently, especially during the cold, windy, winter months in Chicago. It will be interesting to see how he helps to resolve the manpower and funding problems that lie ahead for Graduate Medical Education.

Dr, Henry Bahnson MD (deceased), the Chairman of the Department of Surgery at Pittsburg at the time, and a world renowned cardiac surgeon called me one day and brought to my attention **Dr. James McGreevy MD**, one of his residents that wanted to be an academic surgeon. I subsequently talked with Jim at an American College of Surgeons meeting, and was impressed with his commitment to learning the ways of science, and invited him to join our laboratory. During a period of two years, he made many contributions to our understanding of the pathogenesis of stress erosive gastritis. We had an opportunity to present his work in Uppsala, Sweden at the 500th Anniversary of its founding. As an aside, he and his partner decided to get married in a small church that Maja and I had at our summer house in Klässbol, Värmland Sweden. They had to get permission from the King of Sweden to do so, which was done, and we had a wonderful time at the wedding.

I was very impressed with Jim's ability to solve experimental problems, and to ask important questions. Following the completion of his residency with Dr. Bahnson, he joined our full time faculty to continue work on the mechanism of chloride transport through the gastric epithelium. He was stimulated to take on this tough question by Dr Stanley Schultz, who was the Chairman of Physiology at Pittsburg at the time. Unfortunately, just as Jim was getting his laboratory work off the ground, I was on my way to the Chair of Surgery at the University of Texas in Houston. Jim had a few setbacks in his academic career. He was unable to get his research funded by the NIH, and was turned down for membership in the Society of University of Surgeons. He became disenchanted with academic surgery and clinician-scientists like myself. He told me one day that he thought we were a bunch of fakes. I just listened. Jim was a well trained surgeon, and very much revered by the residents. He worked his way up the academic ladder at Utah to become a Professor of Surgery and the Program Director of its very successful surgical residency. He subsequently was designated Chief of Surgery at the Salt Lake VA. Jim had a right to be disappointed in me, since I did leave the Chair at Utah at a critical point in his academic career for reasons that I will explain later.

There are two additional surgical residents that I worked with at Utah who have become leaders in American Surgery and hold prominent Chairs. I did then and continue now to have a significant interaction with **Dr. John Hunter MD,** and **Dr. Nathaniel Soper MD**.

John joined our residency program after graduating from the University of Pennsylvania School of Medicine. I noticed that he was from Hanover, New Hampshire and wondered whether he knew Dr. John Hunter, a neurologist at the Mary Hitchcock Clinic. He said that he knew him very well since he was his father. I related to John that his father had cured my mother of her depression after my father had died. We quickly established that he was an excellent skier and hiker. I also learned that he was not interested in chasing molecules but was more attracted to the emerging technologies of laser and endoscopic surgery.

Dr. John Dixon MD had just completed a 3 year term as Dean, and a three year term as Vice President for Health Affairs when John Hunter was searching for a mentor. Under John Dixon's leadership, a new University Hospital had been completed in record time. This is to name only one of the numerous things that had occurred while he was at the helm. John Dixon and I had a very exciting discussion one day about his future plans. Basically what he wanted to do was to become a surgical endoscopist, and simultaneously establish a laser lab for ablation of superficial tumors of the foregut, and vascular lesions of the skin to include superficial varicose veins. He also was very interested in finding a way of enhancing the sensitivity of neoplastic cells for laser ablation.

John Hunter joined John Dixon in pursuing these novel ideas. They also spent a lot of time together fishing, since they were both avid fishermen. I imagine that this is where a lot of their innovative ideas came from. John Hunter went on to finish his residency to include a year in Boston at the Massachusetts General Hospital formally learning how to do diagnostic and operative endoscopy. He returned to Utah just at the time that lapascopic cholecystectomy was being developed in the States in the early part of the 1990's. At the suggestion of Dr. George Berci, an accomplished laparoscopist working at Cedars- Sinai hospital in Los Angeles, John developed a very popular course in how to do the procedure of "Lap Chole" which I took somewhat belatedly. John and several of my former residents watched expectantly as I started to take out the gallbladder from a very large pig. I sense that they were waiting for me to fail, but I disappointed them by accomplishing the task without too much prompting.

I have followed John Hunter's career with great interest, as he helped to develop a wide variety of minimally invasive techniques to include laparoscopic bile duct exploration and Nissen Fundoplication. He moved on to Emory University in Atlanta, and continued to do pioneering work in the field. By chance, I was asked to consult by the Dean of the University of Oregon Health Science Center on the choice of a Chairman of Surgery. I thought that John was the best man for the job and was delighted when he got it. When he had settled into the job a few years later, he invited me to give Grand Rounds. I told him that I would like to talk about the pathogenesis of acute necrotizing pancreatitis. He said I could talk about that at a separate research conference, but that he would like me to talk about The Mentoring of Academic Surgeons at Grand Rounds. In preparing for this talk, it suddenly dawned on me that that was what I was doing for most of my professional life. John has been very successful in all of his endeavors to include Editor of the World Journal of Surgery, President of SAGES and the SSAT, and other leadership roles that are too numerous to mention. Unfortunately his mentor John Dixon died of a heart attack many years ago, but can bask in the light of the success of his mentee from his perch in heaven.

The talents of **Dr. Nathaniel Soper MD** were brought to my attention by his father Dr. Robert Soper, the former head of Pediatric Surgery at Iowa. Bob and I used to play tennis together when we would attend the Western Surgical Association Meeting. On one occasion he mentioned that he had a son that was interested in training at Utah in General Surgery. I said send him along, and he did. I was very impressed with Nat's problem solving ability and surgical skills. In addition to the work, we had fun playing. Our favorite act at parties was to do headstands. Nat was much better than I because he was a former wrestler. I am not sure how he decided that he wanted to spend his lab time at the Mayo Clinic, which he did, and focused his work on gut endocrinology. In fact he participated in the investigations that led to the discovery of the ileal break. I had left Utah by that time, and lost the thread of how he like Larry Cheung and Jim Becker before him ended up on the Faculty at Washington University.

Our paths crossed again when he joined me in a study of the role of lithotripsy and bile salt dissolution in the treatment of cholesterol gallstones. He called me one day and said that he could not participate any longer in the study, and that he was working with a pig model on how to remove the gallbladder laparoscopically like they do in humans in France. I understood his reason, since as the Principle Investigator on the trial I could see that the lithotripsy/bile salt dissolution was not working. This was fortuitous for it provided he, as well as I later, many patients that needed a laparoscopic cholecystectomy. Nat wrote a very popular Handbook for surgeons young and old on how to do the procedure safely. His academic star has risen very quickly. He followed in John Hunters footsteps as President of Sages, and soon thereafter became the Chairman of the Department of Surgery at Northwestern Medical School in Chicago where he resides today.

CHAPTER 14

THE SURGICAL RESIDENCY AT UTAH (1971-1983)

I have reviewed in some detail above the accomplishments of several residents that trained with us at Utah, and have gone on to Chair Departments of Surgery. I have mentioned two others who had trained elsewhere, but entered my life through their time in the lab at Utah. There are numerous others who have assumed leadership roles in their community or other academic medical centers. Possibly through the publication of this book we can renew our relationship.

During the years 1972 to 1983, we graduated 68 Chief Residents in General Surgery from the University of Utah Affiliated Program. At least 21 have entered into the practice of academic surgery; 8 have held major Chairs. The other 47, the majority, have gone on to play a leadership role in the practice of general surgery in their community or have pursued further training in a surgical specialty.

The first group to greet me on my arrival to Salt Lake included Drs Halverson, Hogle, Depp, Pickens, and Galbraith, the Chief Residents in the **Class of 1972.** I will never forget the picnic in Big Cottonwood Canyon, and the train ride to Saltaire on the Hogle Express. They were memorable occasions that set the tone for what was ahead. Hugh Hogle pursued a Fellowship in Plastic

Surgery, and developed a successful career in this discipline that was unfortunately interrupted by illness. He is alive and active (he shoots ducks with Loren Helfrich each year). I am aware of Chad Halverson's successful practice in general surgery in Salt Lake, and Jim Pickens success as a plastic surgeon in Salt Lake. I have no information on Drs Depp and Galbraith, although I assume that the latter returned to his home town in Amarillo since he always spoke so highly of the quality of life there.

The **Class of 1973** included Drs Cheung, Helfrich, Matolo, and Snyder, an excellent group of residents. I since have visited with Loren Helfrich in Missouri where he is Chief of Surgery at the Missouri Valley Medical Center. I enjoyed my time with him and his staff as the 31st Annual Warren Cole Lecturer. Loren and I have also shared a few hikes with the Timpanogos Surgical Society. I had an opportunity to chat with Nat Matolo at a recent (2013) meeting of the Southwestern Surgical Congress in Santa Barbara and was pleased to learn that he still is actively involved in the teaching of surgical residents in the Stockton area in two hospitals associated with the University of California in Davis. I assume that John Snyder is still "one upping" the lawyers in Anchorage. I have already praised the accomplishments of Larry Cheung.

The **Class of 1974** included Drs Babcock, Bucko, Byrne, Houtchens, Owens, and Swenson. I assume that Jim Babcock is still enjoying life in Southern Idaho. I have lost track of Jim Byrnes, but have located by a computer search Dennis Bucko and Milt Owens. They are enjoying busy practices in Southern California as a Plastic and Bariatric Surgeon respectively. Bruce Houtchens, after finishing the residency and joining the faculty in Utah moved with me to Houston. He continued to pursue his interest in space exploration and did some very imaginative work on a medical bay for the space station, and a telemedicine link to Russia where he met his wife Maria. They subsequently moved back to Salt Lake, had a son a few years after he had reestablished his practice there at the Veterans Administration Hospital. Bruce unfortunately died of a myocardial infarction while hiking on Black Mountain with Maria within site of the helipad at the University. I will comment more extensively on his tragic death in more detail later. I see Sven Swensen from time to time. He has had a very successful career at the Salt Lake Clinic between trips to Kilimanjaro.

The **Class of 1975** included Drs Ellertson, CD Richards, Schaeferle, Slawson and Smoot. I know that Dave Ellertson had established a very active practice in cardiac surgery in California since I had the opportunity to train his son in Houston after I had moved to Texas. Dave Richards has established a general surgical practice in Salt Lake, and has been actively involved in the development of the Society of Abdominal Surgeons. Doug Slawson also remained in the practice of surgery in Salt Lake, as did Dr. Smoot. I was not able to track down Dr. Schaeferle, but I believe that he is a Plastic Surgeon.

The **Class of 1976** (Drs Wertheimer, Archibald, Bergstrom, Goodnight, Hines, Hunter, Rikkers, and Warden) became rather large with the return of several of the people from the laboratory (Goodnight, Hunter, and Rikkers). I have lost track of Dr. Wertheimer, but have located Tom Bergstrom. He is practicing vascular surgery in Iowa City according to Google. Many years ago I bumped into Andy Hines in a lawyer's office on a very festive occasion in which his Plastic Surgery Group had been given a favorable award. Lyle Archibald and I worked closely in the lab for a year during his residency figuring out how to measure gastric mucosal blood flow with microspheres. Following graduation from the residency, he has established a very successful practice in Ogden, Utah. It has been easy to keep track of Glenn Warden, the founding father of our burn unit at the University of Utah Hospital, and subsequently the chief of the burn Unit at the Shriner's Hospital in Cincinnati. He was at the Burn Center in San Antonio pursuing a highly sought after burn fellowship with Dr. Basil Pruitt when I arrived in Salt Lake City. I was very pleased to have him return to our program as a resident then subsequently as a faculty member since he personified what I wanted to accomplish in Utah, the incorporation of basic science into our care of the surgical patient. He retired several years ago, and returned to Salt Lake to pursue his interest in what I call artificial skin.

As can be appreciated by the narrative above, it was difficult to adjust the number of chief residents that we could finish each year to the number of senior level positions and complex surgical cases available. We attempted to be as flexible as was necessary to insure that each academic resident became as proficient in the operating room as they were in the laboratory. We were pleasantly surprised by the large number of residents that wanted to spend two years in the laboratory as part of their clinical training.

The **Class of 1977 (Drs Byrd, Hillam, Kwan-Gett, Paton, K E Richards, Tebbets, and Voorhees)** was also a large class, possibly as a reflection or our increased clinical load. I know that Byrd and Tebbetts pursued a career in plastic surgery in Dallas. Joe Hillam established a busy general surgical practice in Brigham City which included flexible endoscopy. He was well ahead of his time. Kent Richards and Hugh Voorhees have also established very busy practices in Salt Lake. Cliff Kwan-Gett returned to the practice of cardiac surgery, and developed instant fame when Barney Clark received an artificial heart that he had helped to design.

The **Class of 1978 (Coleman, Duff, Fazzio, Noyes, Robinson, Welling, and Williams)** also had two individuals who have pursued an academic career in a unique way. I had the opportunity to get to work closely with **Dave Welling** when he was a medical student at the University of Utah. At surgical meetings, Dave would relate to me his experiences in military medicine. I was very receptive to our conversations, because I was a consultant to the Surgeon General of the Air Force at the time. I enjoyed visiting the teaching hospital at Wilford Hall in San Antonio, and the famous (and nicely located) Tripler Hospital in Hawaii. I enjoyed these visits, not because the residents would answer my questions with the prefix sir, but also because they had a wonderful mix of general surgical cases for us to discuss. They set a very high standard of surgical care. Dave spent quite a bit of time at the large military base in Frankfurt Germany, and in recent years, he has joined the faculty at the Uniformed Services Medical School in Washington, DC. I was pleased to see the publication from his group on recent trends in the treatment of peptic ulcer which was well written and researched.

I also have had a chance to spend time with **Dr. Dirk Noyes**, who after completion of the residency at Utah and a fellowship at the MD Anderson Cancer Center in Houston has established an advanced surgical oncologic practice at both the LDS and the University Hospitals. He has made important contributions on how to manage malignant melanomas, and backs up his recommendations with the results of well controlled randomized trials. This is quite an accomplishment while managing a large private referral practice. I also am aware of the contributions that Bruce Williams has made to the surgical care in the St. George area. Rumor has it that he has retired. He beat me to it. I believe that Coleman is practicing general surgery in North Carolina, no worse for breaking his leg skiing during his residency. I have already identified that Michel Duff is very happy in Duffsville. In fact, he continues to share a bright idea with me from time to time.

The **Class of 1979 (Drs Black, Downing, Nelson, Spicer, and Petersen)** has several individuals whose accomplishments I am familiar with. Rich Black joined Dale Johnson in the practice of Pediatric Surgery after further training in this specialty. Ed Nelson, as described before has had a very successful career at the department of surgery in Utah to include leading it for several years. Scottie Petersen has been very active as the chief of trauma and program director of the residency in general surgery at the Saint Joseph's Hospital and Medical Center in Phoenix. I do not know the current whereabouts of Downing and Spicer, but assume that they continue to enjoy the fruits of success in their practice of surgery.

The **Class of 1980 (Drs Becker, Belnap, Levison, Perdue, Lowry, and Seeger)** Steve Lowry and Jim Seeger are hard to say good bye to, but their time on earth was well spent in service to their fellow man. Steve died a few years ago from a ruptured thoracic aneurysm on his way back from a medical meeting I was told. Jim died of a myocardial infarction at a medical meeting that I also attended a few years ago. Sounds like academic surgery may be a high risk game. Jim Becker, as I mentioned before has retired from the chairman of surgery at Boston University after a very successful career. LeGrand Belnap has had a remarkable career as a liver transplant surgeon while in private practice at the LDS Hospital. This is an extraordinary feat when one considers the resources and personnel required to secure a liver from elsewhere, and implant it within hours into a recipient. I had an opportunity to review his results several years ago, and they were quite acceptable. Marc Levinson is pursuing an academic practice in a community hospital in New England. I have lost track of Dr. Perdue, but will find him during the next phase of my research on this book.

The **Class of 1981 (Jolley, Mintz, Nelson, Sharp, and Shaw)** had to deal with my visiting several potential chairs of surgery elsewhere during their chief year. I attempted to keep up my obesity practice, which I do not believe was for the chief residents on my service their favorite type of surgical experience. I know that Steve Jolley trained in pediatric surgery, and after practicing in Las Vegas, moved to Anchorage, Alaska. He is known for his important contributions to the management of esophageal reflux in the young and the new born. Dr Sharp also went on to train in pediatric surgery with the Group in Kansas City, Missouri, and subsequently joined them in practice. Steve Mintz moved back to Houston, Texas, but our paths rarely cross. Loren Nelson has taught surgery (and possibly sailing) at St. Georges in the

Caribbean. I understand that he is currently an Associate Dean at a new medical school in Florida, but rumor has it that he may return to the better sailing in the Caribbean.

The **Class of 1982 (Drs Alldredge, Cordell, Holman, Saffle, Seiffert, and Weiss)** was a super class, and I regretted not having more time to spend with them on the clinical units and in the operating rooms. By now, we had the new hospital fully operational. I had accepted the chair of surgery at the University of Texas in Houston with the idea that I would split my time between Salt Lake and Houston for 6 months until January of 1983. This did not appear to have a negative effect on either educational program. Nor did it appear to limit the educational opportunities for the resident staff. No one has given me feedback on this issue one way or the other. Linda Cordell deserves special comment since she was the first female to finish the residency program. Linda came to us from the University of New Mexico. She was one of our top picks because of her scholastic accomplishments and enthusiasm for training in general surgery which was reflected later by her thriving on the long hours entailed in the work. I was pleased when she joined Dr. Alldredge in the practice of surgery at the Alta View Hospital in Sandy. Linda has rapidly moved up the administrative ladder of the Intermountain Health Corporation to become its Vice President for the Medical Staff. John Holman joined the transplantation team, and after several years as a kidney transplant surgeon, moved into corporate medicine. Bart Weiss established a practice with the Intermountain Health Corporation in Logan Utah where he has emerged as one of the senior surgeons there. Jeff Saffle has had a very successful academic career at the University of Utah, taking over the directorship when Glenn Warden moved to Cincinnati. He has received recognition for his unique contributions to this field by being elected to the Presidency of the American Burn Association and the Southwestern Surgical Congress. Ken Seiffert is currently practicing vascular surgery in Scottsdale, Arizona.

The **Class of 1983 (Drs Bell, Gaddy, McFarland, Rotteering, and Thorne)** worked with me during their earlier years in their residency. Their names are engraved on a lovely silver tray that I received from the residents who had spent most of their years at Utah while I was Chairman. I only know of the subsequent whereabouts of Dr. McFarland, who is a practicing general surgery in Austin, the heart of Texas.

I have spent most of this Chapter highlighting the residency training program at Utah. It was a great privilege to have worked closely with such fine young surgeons. I realized that the chair's role was changing, and that the control of resources that I enjoyed at Utah would no longer be granted to chairs of medical school departments. The specialties were pressing for administrative control of their divisions, and the institutions that we work for were becoming more interested in gaining control of the flow of clinical dollars. Unfortunately Utah had a relatively low tax base for supporting professional education. There was a limited amount of state dollars to support the expanding units within the Medical School, and even in 1982, NIH dollars were becoming more difficult to obtain. Fortunately however in surgery our finances were in good shape thanks to our external funding, and patient care income.

Below, I will discuss some issues that involved my leaving Utah, and it was not because of the quality of the snow. Nor did it relate to lack of support from the administration. In a nutshell, I had accomplished as much as I could for the school, and it was time to move on and let the department continue to grow and seek its destiny.

The success of a surgical residents experience in the Surgical Laboratories depended upon the generous sharing of knowledge and expertise of the research staff. Several of them were senior scientists themselves. Good examples are Dr. Margaret Simons MD (who went on to become a radiologist), Charlotte Zaleswski

PhD, a world class morphologist who moved with me to Houston, Dr. Kenneth Larsen PhD, who was so helpful to Kong Ti and I when we attempted to study the reflux of bile in the monkey. We were also assisted in these studies by Dr. Stellan Björk, a very gifted Surgical Fellow from Gothenberg. Stellan visited Inger and I a few years ago at our summer home in Tomta. He is currently a very successful colorectal surgeon in the Gothenberg area.

There were several other very loyal laboratory assistants such as E.K. Davis, Walt Pederson, and M.A. Allen who participated in our studies of gastric acid secretion. These studies were enhanced by the work of Dr Torme and Dr Moysaenko, both of whom were talented research fellows from the military. The activity generated by these individuals in collaboration with a large number of students and residents from our own program led to the development of a National Institutes of General Medical Sciences (NIGMS), National Institutes of Health (NIH) Sponsored Trauma Research Center at Utah. This multi-disciplinary program project involved basic and clinical scientists, and replaced the Academic Training Grant that was completed in 1975. Putting together this training grant with Dr. Harrison Lazarus and Glenn Warden was an interesting and in a way a remarkable experience since we had almost no clinical trauma at the University Hospital except for the burns cared for by Dr. Warden. We received approval on the basis of the scientific output of the Surgical Laboratories.

I guess that my presence on the NIGMS Study Section which had initiated and funded the centers helped us to be at least aware of their existence. The fact that Glenn Warden was interested in the immunology of burns, and I was interested in the pathogenesis of stress erosive gastritis was helpful since they also were timely topics. Our interaction with several basic scientists from other disciplines was also an important reason for our success in keeping the Center intact for several years of funding.

CHAPTER 15

SOME UNIQUE CLINICAL EXPERIENCES

I became interested in the unexplained upper abdominal pain that occurs months to years after cholecystectomy. My interest centered on the papilla of Vater as being a source of this pain. This was not an original thought since it had already been extensively studied by others. Prior studies had included patients with alcohol induced chronic pancreatitis. I was attracted to the idea that I might be able to remove alcohol as a confounding factor by studying a cohort of Mormons that did not drink by religious preference. Fortunately for the study, there were many patients in Utah and adjacent states that did not drink alcohol, and had a high incidence of gallstones and cholecystectomy.

We postulated that upper abdominal pain after cholecystectomy in the absence of a gallstone within the common duct could be due to stenosing papillitis from the prior chronic passage of gallstones through the papilla of Vater. We speculated that the pain was from the resistance to passage of pancreatic juice through a narrowed duct of Wirsung. Evidence for this possibility related to the fact that the pain could be reproduced by stimulation of pancreatic exocrine secretion by the exogenous administration of Secretin, the so called modified Nardi test.

Dr, Dominic Albo, the chief of our teaching service at the Holy Cross Hospital asked me to consult on a patient that he thought might have this problem. She was a middle age female with long standing episodic right upper abdominal pain coming on a few years after a cholecystectomy for presumed gallstones. She denied drinking alcohol. Attempts at treating her addiction to narcotic analgesics had not been successful, and she was in the process of being transferred for chronic care in a mental facility. Her liver chemistries and pancreatic enzymes were normal.

Dr. Albo and I felt sympathetic towards her situation, and after a careful briefing of the patient and the family, we explored her abdomen. The pancreas and other abdominal organs were normal to inspection and palpation. The cystic duct stump, bile duct, and pancreas were normal as was an operative cholangiogram. We passed a filiform catheter (a very small semi-rigid tapered tube) through the papilla, and used it as a guide as we entered the duodenum through a small anterior opening opposite to where we could feel the protruding tip of the probe. Inspection of the outside of the papilla was unrevealing. Upon opening the papilla on its anterior surface for a distance of about three centimeters (a little more than an inch), it was obvious that it was compromised by scar tissue. I initially had trouble inserting even the smallest lacrimal probe (a very small metal tube) into the duct of Wirsung, the major pancreatic duct in her case. With care, I finally was able to divide the septum that separates the bile duct from the duct of Wirsung. I have described the technique in some detail since it is the index case for three subsequent series of patients that we studied very extensively at Utah and subsequently at the University of Texas in Houston.

The patient made an uneventful recovery, and was asymptomatic until she died of a heart attack three years later. The family confided in me that their mother was actually a "closet alcoholic" in that she had explained to them that she would have a few alcoholic drinks each evening to cheer her up. If I had known this earlier, I would not have operated upon her, but learned from the experience that even alcoholics can develop gallstones and stenosing papillitis.

It was not long before I started to see a constant stream of patients with post-cholecystectomy pain. They could best be characterized as middle aged females who developed recurrent episodes of severe upper abdominal pain months to years after cholecystectomy. They all denied use of alcohol. The majority were Mormons. Their work up for the most part did not reveal the source of their pain. Endoscopic retrograde cholangiopancreatography and transpapillary manometry was not yet available. Most were addicted to prescribed narcotic analgesics.

We entered 28 such patients (five were males) into a tightly controlled, but non-randomized prospective study of the outcome following the performance of an operation we called a transduodenal sphincteroplasty with transampullary septectomy. We presumed that the removal of the septum between the bile and pancreatic duct in order to improve the flow of pancreatic juice was the key to success with this operation. I had each patient seen pre-operatively and at intervals following operation by Dr. Malcolm Berenson from the Division of Gastroenterology. The biopsies of the papilla and the septum were analyzed by Dr. Donald McClosky from the Department of Pathology. We reported our results to the annual meeting of the American Surgical Association in 1977 on 28 patients whom had been followed for a mean of 26 months. We were surprised that we had obtained total relief of pain in 16 patients, partial relief in 5, and no relief in 7. I was pleased that our paper was discussed by the leading experts in the field including Drs Marshall Bartlett from Boston, William Longmire from UCLA, Larry Carey from Ohio State, Thomas White from Seattle, and Kenneth Warren from Boston. They all had seen such cases, but were as skeptical as I to the origin of the pain. While there were no deaths and few complications, the risks of the procedure were emphasized in order to dampen its promiscuous use.

I continued to have an interest in the surgical treatment of peptic ulcer disease on arriving in Utah in 1972. By 1974, however, I realized that soon, gastric procedures for peptic ulcer would be seriously challenged by the emerging potent anti-secretory agents such as H-2 histamine blockers, and proton pump inhibitors. The warning signs that ulcer surgeons would soon be out of business was obvious.

It was at this time in the mid 70s that Dr. Edward Mason at Iowa directed our attention to treating morbid obesity by reducing the size of the stomach by gastric by-pass. As I was considering bariatric surgery as a possible way to insure that the residents would at least see and touch the stomach, a lovely somewhat plump young lady came to my clinic one day asking me to help her lose weight. She was overweight by the Metropolitan Life Insurance Tables, but not that fat in my opinion to warrant major surgery. This was before we used Body Mass Index (BMI) as a metric. Furthermore, I told her I had never done a gastric by-pass. She reminded me that I had the reputation of being a gastric surgeon, and with this flattery, I performed a gastric by-pass. Her recovery was uneventful, and she went on to lose a noticeable amount of weight in a very short period of time. It was not long before my waiting room was filled with people of various sizes. The operative case load was controlled by the fact that the operations were being done without the availability of stapling devices. However, as soon as the TA-90 Stapler was available in 1977, I opted to do the safer gastric reduction procedure of horizontal gastroplasty.

It was clear that Utah was in the forefront of an obesity epidemic, because within three years I had performed over three hundred horizontal gastric staplings. We had accumulated a multi-disciplinary team of nurses, dietitians, patient coordinators, and investigators to study the 9 or 10 patients a week that we were stapling. We learned very early that there was a strong genetic pattern to the type of obesity we were treating in Utah. We also noticed that many of the patients were on mood elevating medications. Because of this finding, our psychiatrists initiated a psychiatric audit, whose results were rather interesting. The matched controls of normal weight patients had more major psychopathology than the obese patients that we were to operate upon. Most of the latter did manifest what I termed a situational neurosis from frustration with the lack of success with medical weight management strategies.

I met Dr. Edward Mason in an airport one day in the early 1980s and told him of the success we were having with stapled horizontal gastroplasty. He told me that it would not work over the long hall, and that I should convert to the vertical banded gastroplasty that he currently was evaluating. He was right. I continued to try to perfect the horizontal stapling technique by fashioning a valve at the communication of the upper pouch to the main stomach on its greater curvature, but to no avail. Our very careful and almost 100% follow-up revealed that the failure rate was about 20% or more each year in spite of our efforts to fashion a valve. The handwriting was on the wall that many patients would soon have to be converted to a more effective procedure. But of interest to me is that many continued to have a good to excellent result, and to my delight, there were no operative deaths or major late complications in the 330 patients that I had operated upon in this way over a five year period (1977-1982). It appeared that just manipulating and stapling the upper portion of the stomach led to early satiety in all patients, and long term satiety without sequela in about half.

The best spin on my experience with bariatric surgery at that point in the mid1970s and early 80s is that I did not harm anyone, and I seemed to have helped many. The more cynical colleagues of mine held the view that the high recurrence rate in this study is why I moved to Texas, but that is not true. I continued to use this approach in Houston for a year while learning how to perform a small pouch gastric by-pass as described by Walter Pories and his colleagues at the East Carolina Medical School in North Carolina.

The residents were not very interested in bariatric surgery at the time since it was a lot of heavy lifting and long hours in the operating room. Furthermore, I did the mobilization and stapling of the stomach in most cases. There was one resident that I did assist in doing the procedure skin to skin, and that was Bud Shaw, who I had sent a warning shape up letter to. He had developed into a superb surgical technician. Furthermore he had long fingers. Recall that I described earlier how he bested me on hiking Mount Timpanogos. Fast forward 15 years when Bud was the Director of Liver Transplantation in Nebraska. He expressed an interest in developing an alumni society that involved our years together at Utah. As I recall, Scott Petersen, Dirk Noyes, Bing Rikkers, John Hunter, and Larry Cheung were involved in our first meeting held at Sundance Resort. It was named the Timpanogos Surgical Society, since Sundance, which was owned by the film star Robert Redford, was at the foot of the mountain. The idea was to have a hike up the mountain as an annual event as we met to discuss generic problems in surgery. Bud was to host a dinner at his condominium which he and his brothers had purchased at Sundance.

At the initial meeting, a relatively large group of former residents and I started up the back side of the mountain on a clear, crisp day in late September. There were two groups of hikers, those who planned to go to the top, and those who planned to only go to the lake, which was about half way up the 12,000 foot mountain. I stayed behind to chat with the slower group, but when we arrived at the lake, I decided to catch up with those going to the summit. I noticed that a thin layer of clouds had set in, and the wind was picking up. As I approached the ridge that separates the east from the west side of the mountain I could hear what I thought was a sonic boom created by the jets landing at the Salt Lake City Airport.

When I reached "the saddle", a prominent landmark that led to the summit ridge, I saw a large dark cloud approaching rapidly from the Great Salt Lake. The boom I heard was thunder, and now I could see the lightening. I had been on this mountain many times before, and judged that I could safely traverse the summit and glissade down the snowfield on the other side before the storm arrived. I was wrong. The storm moved in with rain, thunder, lightening, and snow. When I arrived at the semi-enclosed shelter on top, the storm was at its peak, and lightening was flashing horizontally from peak to peak. I briefly considered hunkering down until the storm passed, but the possibility that the shelter was a lightening rod with its tin roof made me abandon that idea. I had to get off the peak as soon as possible. The only option was to move quickly to the snow field and slide down to a lower level. While the narrow trail was covered with snow, I knew it well enough to be able to traverse it safely. I soon reached the snow field, but it had iced up, and I could not see its end. I shuddered at the thought of rapidly sliding down the snowfield, and suddenly being stopped by a pile of large rocks. I therefore went further south to the side of the snowfield, and climbed down the rocky moraine.

I finally made it to the trail below the lake, wet, cold, and likely with my hair standing on end from the vast amount of electricity now high above me. To my surprise, a group of climbers was coming up the trail. I thought to myself, how dumb can they be. As we got closer, I saw that it was a group of my former residents coming up to rescue me. We continued down the mountain, and as I recall the only serious casualty was John Hunter who had to be rushed back to the lodge with hypothermia. He warmed up quickly with a hot shower, just in time for the cocktail party.

The Club had several very successful meetings, but no hikes quite as challenging. The Shaw post-hike receptions Friday evenings were wonderful affairs. The Saturday Banquets were equally exciting, and provided an opportunity to meet with many of the former residents who practiced in the area. I recall two outstanding talks, one on a dramatic and tragic climb of Mount Everest by Barry Bishop, and a second by Robert Redford's son on how to make a movie. Many of the original Club members became too busy to attend on an annual basis and Sean Mulvihill, the Chairman of the Department of Surgery at Utah, who was very supportive of our efforts to get the alumni together wanted to develop a more formal way of doing it. Bud became more interested in creative writing, and an attempt to have this as a subject of a meeting was not well received. The club had outlived its purpose. The department of surgery at the University of Utah continues to thrive, turning out outstanding clinical surgeons who someday might want to revive a "think tank" that is physically as well as intellectually active called the Timpanogos Surgical Society.

CHAPTER 16

FAMILY AFFAIRS

My family and I were enjoying our time in Utah. In fact, by 1981, we had an "empty nest" without the anxiety that some parents have when the children leave the home. Anne, Frank, and Jane were all off doing their thing. None of the children expressed an interest in going into medicine. I think that they were influenced by my long hours of work, and my absence from many of the high points in their own lives as they were growing up. Maja had to bring them up more or less as a single mom. Basically she was in later years a taxi driver who was responsible for getting the children to their various activities. It is of interest however that all of them at some point in their lives worked in medically related fields.

Anne Elizabeth, my oldest daughter received a BA Degree from Utah State University, and a PhD in Anatomy from the Medical College of Wisconsin. Subsequently she pursued postgraduate work for several years at Johns Hopkins University in neural development and genetics. She, along with her husband, Dr. Corey Mjaatvedt, PhD, joined the Faculty of the Department of Anatomy at the Medical University of South Carolina. At age 45, Anne decided to become a lawyer, and until recently was practicing law in Charleston, South Carolina. She and Corey have a lovely daughter, Megan, who is a graduate of New York University. She currently works in Charleston South Carolina as a chef and an artist, with plans to move West in a few years. Anne, her mother has already moved to Seattle where she plans to practice law. She recently passed the Bar Exam there, and is a Certified Food Handler. She is equally proud of the latter accomplishment since it provides an opportunity to support herself by working at Starbucks while volunteering her services through legal aid. Her long term goal is to be a Public Defender. She and Corey have recently divorced for reasons not known to me.

My son Frank Wilson Moody (Frank W) showed little interest in surgery in spite of the fact that I had him work as a volunteer in the Surgical Laboratory at Utah during two summers while he was going to high school. At that time in his teens he was more interested in music and the good things in life. In fact I got so fed up with his lifestyle that I asked him to leave home after he had completed high school at Wasatch Academy and was taking classes at Utah State. We did not see him for a few years during which time he had organized a jazz band and had moved to Denver. It therefore was a surprise when I met him in the hall of University Hospital one day. I asked him what he was doing, and he told me he was working in the burn unit as a technician. He initially was hired as a janitor. Glenn Warden, the Director of the burn unit recognized him, and took him under his wing so to speak, and taught him how to take care of severely injured burn patients. He worked for several years as a burn technician with a high level of proficiency and empathy. He was loved by his patients since he became not only their caregiver but also their friend. His rehabilitation was complete. I was very proud of his accomplishments, and welcomed him back into the flock.

Frank excelled in his role as care giver. After several years he became in succession an ultrasound technician, and then a respiratory therapist. These highly specialized paramedical areas offered a challenge to his interest in information technology and transmission. His wanderlust continued, and he moved with his wife Wynne Smith, and two children, Francis and Rachel to Wasatch

Academy in Mount Pleasant, Utah, where he had completed his last two years of high school. Wynn had assumed the role of the Development Director at the school, and Frank worked as a volunteer informational technologist.

It was just by chance that I was president of the board of directors of the school at the time. I had accepted a position on the board at the request of Keith Reemstma, who was a graduate of the school and also on the board. Keith had gone to high school there since it was a school supported by the Presbyterian Church and his father was a Presbyterian Minister. The school during my time on the board was struggling to transition from a church owned to a privately supported school. I was happy to try to help in its transition, and very much enjoyed working with its Headmaster Joseph Loftin, and it's very dedicated board. After a few years, I was selected to be president of the board and was able to help secure the financing for the construction of a new Math-Science Building which triggered the future expansion of the school. For reasons unknown to me, Wynne was not happy in her job, and convinced Frank that it was best for them to move on.

They chose to move to Park City, a very attractive community with excellent schools for their children, Francis and Rachel. Wynne enjoyed her new role for a few months as a stay at home mom. Frank secured an information technology job at Deer Valley, a new upscale ski resort in Utah. There he developed a computer chip to imbed into skis to help families keep track of the whereabouts of their children on the hill. Unfortunately what appeared to be a very happy marriage to Wynne Smith ended in a divorce. Frank returned to Wasatch Academy in Mount Pleasant Utah where he is in the process of adapting the curriculum of his old alma mater to the modern age of digitized learning. He at this point in his career had morphed into a serious educator.

I recently (December-2012) spent a very exciting evening with him discussing the importance of focusing on the educational process of the learner rather than the experiences of the teacher. He has had a great deal of success in this approach with the slow or perceived non-learner. I have challenged him to find out why some (possibly many) inspired learners seem to lose their enthusiasm as they progress through their formal years of schooling. I should do the same for the medical students that I work with, since some in their senior years fail to appreciate the opportunities and excitement that derive from taking care of the sick.

Frank and I have had a lot of fun talking about some of our more interesting hikes on the trails along the Wasatch Front. For example, a hike up Lisa Falls in Little Cottonwood Canyon, which seemed rather benign became very risky when we turned around to go down. Our conversation had obscured the fact that the way up was seemingly easy, but the only way down was a sheer cliff. We finally, after several anxious moments, were able with cautious effort able to safely descend, much wiser for the experience. This brought to mind an additional, almost life ending experience (for me). We under estimated the difficulty of climbing Lone Peak (one of the highest mountains at the southern end of the Wasatch Front) from the Bell's Canyon trail. The final ascent found us climbing up a steep boulder field. I cautioned Frank W that we must be careful lest we disturb one of the large boulders that might hit the lower climber. I encouraged him to take the lead, and recognized my mistake as I looked up and saw a large boulder coming at me at a high speed. I took cover behind a large rock, just as the one that Frank W. had dislodged whizzed by me. Needless to say, profane words flowed from my mouth for several minutes. These are only a few of many harrowing events that we vividly remember and have lived to now talk about. I will relate below even a more risky situation which involved all of my children, as well as me.

Christine Vunder, Frank's partner is attending Snow College, pursuing her interest in sociology. She is a perfect match for

Frank, and they both enjoy their time with his two lovely daughters from his former marriage to Wynne Smith. The oldest, Frances is finishing up her studies in Journalism at the University of Utah. The youngest, Rachel, is a graduate of Wasatch Academy, and Snow College in Ephraim, Utah. She wants to be a horse trainer, and stays busy taking care of three horses, and managing the "coffee house" at Wasatch. She plans to complete her college education at the University of Utah while continuing to cultivate her skills in horsemanship.

My youngest daughter Jane also had no interest initially in medicine even though I had her working with me a few summers in the intake clinic of our bariatric surgical program at Utah. Her career path after graduating from Wasatch Academy took her to the University of San Diego and Cal Arts Institute where she pursued her interest in music before marrying her first husband Kevin Holt. Unfortunately their marriage lasted only five years, since along the way they had a lovely child named Donald who had Down's Syndrome. This led in some way to marital discord and a divorce.

But then as chance would have it, Jane met and married Bruce Karl Bjorklund, who became a wonderful surrogate father for Donald, having two young boys of his own. They established their home in Lancaster, California. Jane very rapidly moved up the home decorating ladder at Penny's Department Store in Los Angeles, and progressed to the position of Regional Sales Manager in the Custom Decorating Division. She then became Vice-President for Operations of a very successful company called For Windows Only. She also worked for Macy's Interior Design, and held contractors' licenses in the states of Arizona, California, and Nevada.

When Maja became ill, Jane, Bruce, and their children moved to Salt Lake City so that Jane could help in her mother's care. Jane initially established her own interior decorating business. Unfortunately a few years later she developed neurologic symptoms which ultimately led to an MRI Scan, and a diagnosis of Multiple Sclerosis. In the course of her illness and her treatment, she decided to work as a clinical coordinator at the University of Utah. In order to do so, and achieve her career goals, she had to become certified as a Clinical Research Coordinator with the FDA, which she did at the National Institutes of Health.

Then again, marital stress reared its ugly head, and she and Bruce have obtained what appears to me to be a friendly divorce. Jane and Donald live with each other in Park city Utah where Donald works for Home Depot. Donald is now 24, and is an accomplished drummer, and a well muscled weight lifter, and downhill skier. Jane is very happy with in her current role as Clinical Outreach and Education Manager for the Intermountain West Division of the Multiple Sclerosis Society. Words cannot express how much I appreciated her participating in and directing the prolonged terminal care of her paralyzed mother, Maja. She obviously is a very effective care giver as evidence by the successful development of her son Donald, and the many patients whose lives she touches in her work with the Multiple Sclerosis Society.

I obviously am very proud of the accomplishments of my children, and am pleased that each in their own way devoted at least a part of their life to service to others through medicine. I wish that Barbara Schmelzer Moody, their biologic mother was alive today. She did so much in the early years to get us all started on our career paths, and would be justifiably proud of her children's accomplishments, and those of her grandchildren Donald, Frances, Megan, and Rachel. Sadly, Barbara died on November 15th, 1975 from bleeding from a ruptured ovarian cyst at age 42. We thank her for the many contributions that she made during the formative years of our lives together as a family.

I would be remiss not to mention the wonderful times that we had together as a family during our stay in Salt Lake. Much of our time was spent in the mountains. The children were never too excited about hiking with me since they felt I was too demanding as to pace and the desire to reach the top of the peak that lie ahead. I do recall a harrowing experience during a hike on the Pfeiferhorn, a long but not especially steep climb, except at the top. We were climbing it together one spring before all the snow had left the peak The snow was soft, and we could easily make our way on steps that we made along the steep summit trail. Unfortunately the sun went down early behind the peaks to the west of us, and the stairs we had made turned to ice. We found a safer place to descend, but we could not see what was below us. I heard a shout from above "do not proceed you are heading for a cliff". We froze in our tracks. The caller was obviously a seasoned mountaineer. He had a rope and an ice axe which he tied the rope around. I, on firm ground, held the other end of the rope, as each of the children traversed to safer ground. He was correct. Our route of descent was heading right for a steep cliff. Obviously I lost all credibility as a mountain man.

I did better with the skiing, and could pretty well leave them quickly behind as they challenged me on the slopes. It was great fun to watch them perfect their technique on a rope tow hill at Alta, called Snow Pine. It did not take them long to become expert skiers, and to this day they can handle the Black Diamond trails with ease.

CHAPTER 17

ON THE ROAD AGAIN

I was very pleased with the progress that had been made with the program in surgery at Utah over an eleven year period. General surgery and all the divisions of surgery were expanding both clinically and academically. Orthopedic, pediatric, and neurosurgery were appropriately working towards being departments, as had been the case with the department of ophthalmology earlier. General surgery was strengthened by the recruitment of our former academic scholars, Cheung, Rikkers, Becker, Nelson, and McGreevy. I was very interested in helping these new faculty members get started on their surgical careers.

My major concern at Utah in 1982 was the imminent human trial of the placement of a totally implantable artificial heart. We had recruited Dr. William DeVries from Duke to head the division of cardiothoracic surgery. This was done with the enthusiastic support of Dr. Willem Kolff, the director of the division of artificial organs. Bill was recruited with the plan that he would have a joint appointment in the division of cardiothoracic surgery as its director, and as a surgeon in the division of artificial organs. Dr. DeVries was to implant the artificial heart when it was ready for human trial.

Dr. Kolff and I had discussed this issue in some detail, since the division of artificial organs was in fact a division of the department of surgery. I favored pursuing a bridge to transplant approach that had been recommended to us by Dr. Shumway at Stanford. Dr. Kolff was against this approach since he was concerned that there would never be enough human hearts to serve the need for heart replacement. He felt strongly that the only approach was to perfect the artificial heart to where it would provide long term survival for its recipients. Dr. Kolff and his group were obtaining long term survival in cows and sheep. His argument to move ahead with the program to replace a failing heart with the implantation of an artificial heart was persuasive, but not to the point where I was ready to give it my approval.

The progress that the Kolff group was making, however, was impressive. I was asked to serve on a committee for assessing whether the artificial heart was ready for implantation into a highly publicized patient Dr. Barney Clark, a dentist from Seattle. I was against implantation at this time, even though the recipient was aware that the current device would likely not provide long term survival. Elaborate arrangements had been made to publicize the event. In fact the University of Utah was enthusiastically behind the implant to the point where they were planning to build (with the help of a hospital chain) a 250 bed hospital for the artificial organ program. Rather than remaining, so to speak, a wet blanket on this very ambitious plan to catapult the University into prominence, I joined the others on the committee to give the implant unanimous support.

All of this took time to sort out, time that I used to look at other academic jobs. My visiting other universities when invited to consider moving to the chair of surgery elsewhere was not an unusual event for me since I looked at it as an opportunity to learn more about how to structure the program in surgery at Utah. I was invited to be a candidate over the years for the chair of surgery at UCLA, Stanford, University of Rochester, Harvard at the Brigham and Women's, and the University of Pennsylvania. I became a serious candidate at a few of these outstanding Universities, but never became interested enough to leave Utah. During this period of consideration of implanting an artificial heart at Utah, I was being actively recruited by the University of California in San Diego. I also was being approached by the University Of Texas Medical School in Houston to consider the Chair of Surgery there recently vacated under unpleasant circumstances by Stanley Dudrick. Stan was a close friend of mine, and the father of total parenteral nutrition (TPN). I told them that I was not interested.

I had to think long and hard each time I was approached to move to a new academic environment, not because of lack of academic opportunity at Utah, but because of what I would be leaving behind. Aside from the challenging administrative problem discussed above, I was quite happy with the surgical program at Utah. Our new University Hospital was esthetically appealing and very functional. I had been joined by extraordinary colleagues that had been schooled in the ways of surgery as well as science. I had the privilege of skiing two or three times a week in the winter. In the spring, I would hike on Saturday and ski on Sunday when the ski lifts and the slopes were abandoned by the church goers. I realized that I was addicted to the mountains. My home was nestled in the foothills, within walking distance of several trails that would take me up to over 11,000 feet from the 5000 feet elevation where we lived. I would do 30 or 40 hikes of varying lengths during the 6 month hiking season. During the winter, I would manage to ski all or part of 60 to 70 days.

My custom on the hiking days was to take off early in the morning with my dog, Honey, to climb the many peaks that surrounded my home. It would take us several hours or longer to climb the numerous peaks in the area (Olympus, Raymond, Superior, Red Pine, White Pine, Pfeifferhorn, Twin Peaks above Broads Fork, Deaf Smiths Canyon (no trail), Bell's Canyon, Lone Peak, or Timpanogos). It almost was a mandate to leave Utah if I wanted to continue to be academically active, rather than be a mountain hiker and a skier. I rationalized this passion by using my time on the mountain to review where we had been and where we were going as a department of surgery. These long hikes made me realize that there still was a lot to learn and to do to make surgical care more effective and safer for those who required it.

It was during this period of introspection that I received a call from **Dr. Ernst Knobil, PhD** (Ernie), the recently appointed Dean of the University of Texas Medical School in Houston. It was a lovely Sunday evening. Maja and I were setting in her studio, watching the moon coming up over the mountains. I imagine that we were sipping scotch and commenting on how lucky we were to be in such a beautiful place. Dean Knobil got right to the point, they wanted me to come down to Houston as the Chair of Surgery, and would not take no for an answer. Well, I said no, and thanked him for asking. He then requested that he be allowed to send up to Salt Lake a small search committee to present why I should join them. I said that that would be fine. He then asked me to at least come down and take a look at the job. I told him that I was too busy to travel at that time. He next made me an offer that I could not refuse. He said that they would come up and fly Maja and I down to Houston in a Lear Jet. I covered the phone and told Maja of the offer. Her answer was "I do not like to fly in small airplanes". With further coaxing, and her pleasant memories of the South during our days in Birmingham, she said let's go. I accepted his offer for a visit contingent on how our discussions went with the search committee on the following day.

I met the plane the next day at the Salt Lake City Airport, and greeted Dean Knobil, Dr. Rod Howell, the chairman of pediatrics and head of the search committee for the new chair of surgery, and Mr. William Smith, the chief executive officer of the Hermann Hospital, the major teaching hospital at UT Houston. Possibly there was a fourth person whose name I cannot recall. I tried to give them a travelogue as we skirted along the Wasatch Front, but they were only interested in the business of recruiting me to the chair. I often wondered why they were so interested in me. I was pushing 55, and thinking of spending more time in the mountains rather than the operating room. Maja served a super Swedish style lunch. We reviewed blue prints of space, and plans for the future of the hospital and the medical school. It was definitely something that was worth looking at. We arranged that the Lear would pick Maja and I up the next day for a two day visit to Houston.

As the Lear circled the next day with Maja and I on board to land at Hobby Airport close to the middle of Houston, Maja commented that the lush green foliage reminded her of Birmingham. She even welcomed the moist warm air as the pilot opened the door to the plane. I knew that I would not have to sell Maja on a move to Houston. We were met by Dean Knobil on the tarmac. Maja was taken to our hotel, and I was whisked away to the Medical Center by Dean Knobil. I was immediately impressed with the sheer size of the Texas Medical Center, and the relationship of the recently completed Medical School Building of the University of Texas to all of the marvelous medical facilities that it housed. Its physical attachment to the Hermann Hospital was of special importance to my interest in developing clinical scientists. Also important to our teaching and research activities was the proximity of the Baylor College of Medicine, the Methodist, St. Lukes, and Ben Taub Hospitals, and the MD Anderson Cancer Center. It was exciting to be considered for this important position in the largest medical center in the world which housed two giants in surgery, Drs DeBakey and Cooley. There was in addition a galaxy of other stars to include Dr. Stanley Crawford at the Methodist Hospital, Dr. George Jordan and Dr. Kenneth Mattox at the Ben Taub Hospital, and Dr. Lee Clarke and Robert Hickey at the MD Anderson Hospital, to name only a few of the outstanding surgical leaders at the TMC.

Dr. Knobil made it very clear that he wanted the School to be ranked within the top ten in the country within ten years. This was an extremely presumptuous ambition for a new school whose charter was to develop family physicians for South Texas. I was impressed with the space assigned to surgery for administration, faculty offices, teaching, and research. This was adjacent to several thousand feet of quality laboratory space. We immediately talked about resources. He told me that he would offer up front $200,000 for equipping the labs, and 3 million dollars each year of state money to run the department. I could not believe my eyes or my ears. I was only receiving $300,000 of state money to manage an academic program of similar size at Utah. I was pleased that my salary would be about $140,000 (in 1982 dollars), a bit less than I was earning at Utah. The difference was that this was guaranteed even if I never saw a patient, and to the extent that I engaged in caring for patients, I would be compensated for this by the formula of a well designed plan.

When I returned to the hotel to change clothes for a dinner party that was to be attended by Dr. Roger Bulger, the President of the University of Texas Health Science Center in Houston I told Maja of the offer and that I was going to accept it. She was in agreement. We were picked up at the hotel by Dean Knobil and his wife Julie, who also was a PhD scientist in the Department of Physiology. Maja entered the back seat next to Julie. As I entered the front seat next to Dean Knobil I said, "it seems like you really want me to be your chairman of surgery". He in return said "I do". I then shook his hand and said "I'll take the job". He was not only surprised but a bit angry. He explained to me that he wanted the President to make the offer and feel that he had recruited me. I told him not to worry, that I would play hard to get.

We had a lovely evening talking about all kinds of things. I got along well with President Bulger because I liked the idea of being part of a broadly based Health Science Center that included a Medical School, a Dental School, a School of Public Health, a Nursing School, and a School of Allied Health amongst other health facilities not known to me at the time. I did not realize until later that I was an odd man out on the issue of a broadly based Health Science Center. Most of the Medical School Faculty was not as enthusiastic as I for such an entity The Medical School was having trouble adjusting to the recent reorganization of the Health Science Campus. I correctly imagined then that the mixed feelings about an integrated comprehensive campus had something to do with money and power.

We returned to Salt Lake City (again on the Lear), and I immediately informed Dean Richard Lee that I was going to move to Houston on the 1st of January. This gave him a period of 6 months to find my replacement. I also needed a period of time to help the new faculty members that had joined the Department in Utah to settle in. Of equal importance, I wanted to have a smooth transition of our ongoing and funded research projects at Utah. A third complexity was how best to help Dr. Norbert Senninger, an International Research Fellow who had just arrived from Heidelberg initiate his research program during the move. We had already made preliminary plans to study the pathogenesis of acute necrotizing pancreatitis. The move of my laboratory to Houston provided for him the experience of setting up a research laboratory from scratch. It also provided for us time to plan how we might be able to challenge the Opie Theory that considered the reflux of bile as the cause of biliary pancreatitis. By initiating this research in Utah, we became familiar with the unique anatomy of the opossum, whereby the pancreatic duct joins the bile duct outside of the duodenal wall. We also learned how to measure the myoelectric complexes of the biliary sphincter, a technique that we planned to use in our initial experiments in Houston.

We were fortunate in being able to recruit Dr. Charlotte Zalewsky PhD to Houston to help us set up an electron microscopic suite, and one of our senior technicians to organize an analytical laboratory. They were a great help along with Norbert in moving the Utah lab to Texas, and helping to purchase whatever analytical equipment that we thought we would need for making the Surgical Laboratories functional upon our arrival in January 1,

1983. Fortunately the administrative and teaching space of the department was adjacent to that of the department of physiology chaired by Dr. Stanley Schultz a world class epithelial physiologist. The department of physiology already contained several basic scientists who had already collaborated in the past with Stan Dudrick and his group. This culture of interdisciplinary collaboration at UT-Houston was not just by chance. It was planned by the first Dean, Dr. Cheves Smythe, MD, in order to avoid all barriers to a free association between basic and clinical scientists. This was ideal for my purposes of training surgical leaders in the ways of science, and was the reason for my making up my mind to move to UT Houston without prolonged deliberation.

Dean Knobil was most generous and flexible in how I initially allocated my time between July 1st of 1982, and January 1st of 1983. I was to assume the administrative responsibility of the department of surgery in Houston on October 1st. Dean Lee in Utah was equally generous. He retained me as chairman of surgery until January 1st of 1983. Yes. I was being paid by each school for three months. Those were the good old days. My major concern was that the work load would interfere with my ski week-ends but that was not the case. Dr. James Parkin, the director of the division of otorhinolaryngology (ENT) became the acting chairman of surgery in Utah. Dr Joseph Corriere, director of the division of urology, and acting chairman in Houston continued to run things in Houston during my move.

Maja was just terrific at managing the move of the household. She sold the house in Salt Lake, bought a house in Houston, and moved the household with almost no help from me. I was in the air most of the time, not only flying back and forth between Salt Lake and Houston, but also participating in the governance of several national and international societies. Jane, our youngest daughter was a great help in this regard since she drove my car down from Salt Lake to Houston, keeping Maja company on the road and helping to transport our seven cats and my favorite hiking partner, Honey. I met them in Houston shortly after they and the moving van had arrived. It was one of the smoothest of the several previous moves we had made.

During this interim period, an artificial heart was implanted into Barney Clark. Initially the heart seemed to be working well. I was asked to see him in consultation about three weeks after the implant because he had a persistent ileus with marked distention of his abdomen. I was concerned that he might have ischemia (poor blood supply) to his intestine, and that was what was found at a later exploration of his abdomen. He subsequently died. This put a damper on the program that later moved to a not for profit hospital in Louisville, where after several additional failures, the total artificial heart program was abandoned, and has been replaced by a left ventricular device (LVAD) as a bridge to transplant. In fact, LVAD not only serves as a bridge to transplant, but also keeps people alive for a prolonged period of time. Former Vice President Cheney is a poster boy for the quality of life enjoyed while on the device prior to his own transplant a few years go.

CHAPTER 18

CHAIRMAN YEARS AT UT HOUSTON (1983-1994)

The Department of Surgery at the University of Texas Health Science Center in Houston (UTHSCH now UT Health) was first established as a division within the then new Medical School in 1970. Dr. Stanley Dudrick from the University of Pennsylvania was named its 1st director. Stan was already well known for his success in developing total parenteral nutrition (TPN). He was quite adventuresome to take an academic leadership position in a medical school that did not as yet have a building, and in addition had a tenuous relationship with a private hospital, the Hermann. Stan was and still is a visionary, and an inspirational leader. Within a few years he had recruited Dr. Edward (Ted) M. Copeland MD, Dr. James (Red) H. Duke MD, and Dr. Bruce V. MacFadyen MD (initially as a chief resident) as a core faculty for a Division of Surgery. The division was advanced to departmental status in 1972, and Stan Dudrick was designated its 1st chairman. All four of these individuals were interested in the biochemistry and physiology of surgical nutrition, and set about with great success in assessing the role of TPN in the management of patients with cancer (Copeland), trauma (Duke), gastrointestinal fistula (MacFadyen), and surgical patients in general (Dudrick). The accomplishments of this group put TPN and UT on the map.

I do not know the real story, but apparently Stan's success put him at odds with the administration. This led to the abrupt termination of his role as Chairman in 1980. Dr. Joseph Corriere, the Director of the Division of Urology became the acting Chairman of the Department. He strengthened the management systems by hiring David Miles MBA, ME, a graduate of the Naval Academy, the Tuck School of Business and the Thayer School of Engineering at Dartmouth. The latter schools were attended after graduating from the Naval Academy and serving several years in the Naval Submarine Corp. Dr. Joseph Corriere MD, and David Miles MBA, were an effective management team. By the time I arrived on the scene in the fall of 1982, they were well on the way to correct a sizeable Departmental financial shortfall.

The department of surgery at UT Houston was staffed with well trained clinical surgeons in all of the divisions. I assumed the role of director of the division of general surgery and the title of program director of its residency. Dr. Thomas Miller an excellent academic surgeon was assigned the role of co-director of the program and the day to day manager of the residency in general surgery. The other members of the division included Drs. Duke, Fischer, Copeland, Rowlands, and Flynn. The specialty divisions also had designated directors: oral-maxillofacial (Roche), neurosurgery (Miner), orthopedic surgery (Smith), pediatric surgery (Brooks), Plastic Surgery and Burns (Parks), thoracic and cardiovascular (Walker), transplantation and immunology (Kahan), and urology (Corriere). Dr, Copeland had assumed the Chairmanship of the Department of Surgery in Florida before my arrival.

Hermann was a 950 bed hospital when I first arrived, but many of the patients were no pay or low pay patients. The Hermann Foundation would defray some of the cost of caring for the trauma patients, but it was never enough. There was a gradual reduction in the availability and occupancy of surgical beds. Possibly this related to the increasing activity of the Doctor's Hospital that had been developed by the clinical staff at the Hermann Hospital. They apparently were not pleased with the arrival of the UT Medical School. An intense focus on billing and collection improved our profit margin from a 3 million deficit to a 3 million profit. This encouraged me to increase our pay line in order to retain those already on board, and to recruit an additional person to help Benjy Brooks in Pediatric Surgery. I also wanted to develop surgical endocrinology and peripheral vascular surgery within general surgery, and work towards establishing departmental status for the surgical specialties as was the trend elsewhere.

We were successful in recruiting Dr. Richard Andrassy from San Antonio to join Benjy Brooks in pediatric surgery, Dr. Ronald Merrell from Stanford to develop surgical endocrinology and a pancreatic islet transplant program, and Dr. Stuart Myers from Dallas to develop peripheral vascular surgery. Drs. Merrell and Myers had been trained at Washington University in St. Louis. Each had a strong interest in developing bench research as well as clinical programs in their areas.

Administration advised me not to recruit from other UT departments if it could be avoided. I, however, was very interested in recruiting Dr. Richard Andrassy to UT-Houston from UT- San Antonio where he was the director of pediatric surgery. I discussed this with my dear friend Dr. Brad Aust (now deceased), the chairman of the department of surgery at UT-San Antonio, and he agreed that Richard Andrassy was a pediatric surgeon who could compete against the world famous Texas Children's Hospital in Houston and he gave me permission to proceed with the recruitment. I knew Rich Andrassy from my days of visiting Wilford Hall as a consultant to the Air force Surgeon General. I also was aware of the fine training he had received at Wilford Hall in general surgery and pediatric surgery at the Los Angeles Children's Hospital. I was equally impressed with his unique surgical, academic, and administrative skills. Bringing him to Houston was one of my most important recruitments.

Dr. Andrassy's record at UT-Houston speaks for itself. He has developed a strong academic department in pediatric surgery in conjunction with Dr. Kevin Lally, also a well respected academic pediatric surgeon. Since being appointed chairman of the department of surgery when I retired 19 years ago, he has done a remarkable job in continuing to build strength in many areas. I am impressed that he returned to adult general surgery so that he could have an interaction with the residents in the areas of endocrine and hernia surgery, and continued to do pediatric surgery. He was instrumental in helping Dr. Lally develop the Hermann Memorial Children's Hospital and elevating the pediatric division to departmental status. The educational programs in surgery at both the medical student and residency level are the best that they have ever been. Dr. Andrassy has brought the Department way beyond where I thought it would be at this point in time. There still is a ways to go for the department to be considered to be one of the top tier departments of surgery in America, but it clearly is on a path to be so in the future.

I first met Dr. Ronald Merrill (Ron) in the mid sixties when he was a medical student at the University of Alabama, and I was impressed with his intellect, quick wit, and gift for innovation. I kept close track of his progress in the residency at Washington University because of the expertise in islet cell transplantation there. When Ron finished his residency at Washington University he joined the surgical faculty at Stanford. In addition to his surgical and investigative skills, he was a superior teacher. With the help of the start-up funds from Dean Knobil, I was able to recruit him to Houston. He emerged as one of our outstanding educators, and was very successful in developing a fine referral practice.

Generous funding from the UT Medical School allowed Ron and his Fellow Dr. Giacomo Basadonna, MD, to establish a strong program in human islet cell biology to include a storage bank for human islets. Unfortunately they were unable to get independent funding from the NIH for their islet research. When the Department's slush fund ran out, financing his lab became a contentious issue. When the Yale Chairmanship became available a few years later, Ron took it. Following a six year term there, he moved to the Chair at the Medical College of Virginia in Richmond. He retired last year (2012) to his home in Alabama. Jacimo returned to Italy after marrying my wonderful Administrative Assistant, Marilyn. They subsequently returned to the United States after starting their family, and Jacimo had established in Italy his reputation as a whole organ pancreatic transplant surgeon. He currently is director of organ transplantation at the University of Massachusetts.

Dr. Stewart Meyers, MD, came to my attention because of his interesting laboratory work on prostaglandins in the pathogenesis of acute cholecystitis. He was Chief of the Vascular Service at the Dallas VA, and was a product of the Vascular Training Program at UT-Southwestern. Stewart received his training in general surgery at the Barne's Hospital and the Washington University Medical School. I thought he would be ideal for developing vascular surgery in a town that was the mecca for this type of work. All Stewart would have to do was convert his interest in the biochemistry of epithelial cells to endothelial cells of the blood vessel wall in atherosclerosis. A condition of employment was that we provide him the resources to develop a state of the art clinical vascular assessment laboratory, which we did with our start up monies. After several productive years at UT, Stewart was recruited to the Chair of Surgery at Temple University in Philadelphia. For reasons not known to me, he subsequently joined Tom Miler at the Richmond Veterans Administration Hospital in Richmond. I saw Tom at the American Surgical Association Meeting in Indianapolis this year (2013). Tom was quite happy with his opportunities at the Medical College of Virginia but Stewart was not and has moved on to parts unknown.

In the course of writing these reflections, it became apparent to me that UT Houston has been a breeding ground for producing chairs of surgery from its faculty. These include Ted Copeland (Florida),

Rich Andrassy (UT-Houston), Ron Merrell (Yale and Medical College of Virginia), Stuart Meyers (Temple), Brian Rowlands (Belfast and Newcastle), Tom Miller (Saint Louis University), Dave Mercer (University of Nebraska), Bruce MacFadyen (Medical College of Georgia), and a former resident Dr. Wiley W. (Chip) Souba, MD MPH (the former Chairman of Surgery at Penn State, and Dean at Ohio State). He currently serves as Dean of the Geisel School of Medicine and Vice President for Health Affairs at Dartmouth. Chip was recruited to the surgical residency at UT Houston by Dr. Stanley Dudrick. Early in my tenure as Chair I took a long jog with him while he was a Graduate Student at the Harvard School of Public Health pursuing a Masters Degree in nutrition. It was clear that Chip was headed towards a strong position of leadership in surgery and medical education in general. Dr. John Daly MD was also one of the early graduates from the general surgical residency who has pursued a distinguished career as an academic surgeon having served as the Chairman of the Department of Surgery at the Cornell-New York Hospital Medical Center, and the Dean of the Temple University School of Medicine in Philadelphia.

I have already alluded to clinical advances made at Alabama by Hirschowitz (flexible endoscopy), and Utah (the Dixon endoscopic laser lab and the early mentoring of John Hunter) that brought us close to opening the doors to the era of minimal invasive surgery, but I missed it because of my myopic view of what a surgeon could and should be doing. My interest in developing knowledge to prevent disease prevented me from appreciating that minimal invasive surgical techniques were the next step in the refinement of our craft. Fortunately, Dr. Bruce MacFadyen, the first Dudrick Chief Resident in the program at UT-Houston, and subsequently a full time faculty member and a visionary saw the future very clearly. He approached me one day to see if he could have a customized sabbatical to go to Cleveland to pursue a fellowship in invasive endoscopy with Dr. Jeff Ponsky, a pioneer and recognized expert in the field. I greeted this proposal with enthusiasm. Bruce within a short period of time became an expert in both upper and lower flexible gastrointestinal invasive endoscopy. Unfortunately for UT-Houston he was recruited to the University of Georgia to introduce minimal invasive techniques to that community and serve as its Chairman for several years. I was delighted when he returned to his home base at UT-Houston (2013) to further pursue his very productive career.

This list above, which I am certain is incomplete, represents only a few of those who have worked with us and have achieved positions of leadership in American Surgery. Many others who pursued their residencies with us are successfully pursuing careers in academic surgery. These include Doctors Charles (Chuck) Cox (pediatric surgery at UT Houston), Ara Vaporciyan (non-cardiac thoracic at MD Anderson) Steve Yang (director of thoracic surgery at John's Hopkins, David Vega (cardiothoracic surgery at Emory University), Paula Termuhlen (endocrine surgery at the Medical College of Wisconsin), Catherine Musemeche, Lisa Florence (liver transplantation, University of Washington), Rafik Ghobriel (liver transplantation, Methodist Hospital Houston), Phillip Adams (acute care surgery—Houston), David Van Buren (organ transplantation), George Van Buren (organ transplantation, St. Lukes Hospital Houston), James Cross (director burn service UT Houston), Emily Robinson (breast and endocrine surgery UT Houston), Brijesh (Billy) Gill (trauma/acute care surgery UT Houston), Michelle McNutt (trauma/acute care surgery), John Hwang (liver transplantation University of California Los Angeles) and many others that I have not seen since they left our institution. This represents a respectable output of academic surgeons for a school that is only 40 years old.

The Surgical Specialties have also enjoyed a high level of success. Four have developed into autonomous Departments (Neurosurgery, Orthopedic, Pediatric and Cardiovascular/Thoracic Surgery). This has been a very important development from my point of view. Each had my full support as they put together their programs. Dr. Andrassy, my successor in the Chair was even more involved in nurturing their success.

CHAPTER 19

THE SURGICAL LABORATORIES AT UT HOUSTON

My major thrust during the early years at UT Houston was to develop a modern, well equipped and staffed research facility devoted to addressing surgical problems that involve the gastrointestinal tract, liver, bile ducts, and pancreas. These facilities were called as they were in Utah, the Surgical Laboratories. The intent was to have laboratories without walls where students, residents and faculty could pursue promising ideas. The key was to find scientists who would be willing to share their skills and knowledge freely to whomever sought their collaboration. Only a few of our own residents took advantage of this opportunity in the early years since most that joined our residency program were attracted to it because of our relationship with the MD Anderson Cancer Center and the Texas Heart Institute. We strongly encouraged these individuals to pursue their research with the excellent programs that existed at these institutions.

Dr. Miller had established a very strong and well funded laboratory program in gastric physiology that was contiguous to but separate from the Surgical Laboratories. He was from the beginning very supportive of my ideas, and helpful in bringing them to fruition.

Dr. James Cross who currently is director of the Hermann-UT Burn Center was one of his outstanding fellows during the early years. Dr. Jose Borreto, a PhD postgraduate student was also an early participant in Dr. Miller's very successful scientific enterprise.

I decided to put aside my interest in gastric physiology, and focus on the pathogenesis of gallstones and their complications. Dr. Charlotte Zalewski, PhD, continued to explore the cellular biology of the stomach at the ultra-microscopic level as an independent investigator. I and others collaborated with her when our work required ultra-structural analysis. Other independent investigators that joined us over the years included Dr. Dianne Haley-Russell, PhD, Jerry Schlegel, BA, Dr. Bruce Grossie PhD, Kathrine Husband, MA, and Yael Harari, MA.

Dr. Yong Fang Li, MD was one of the early recruits to the laboratory staff. He was an accomplished investigator who played a very important role in helping students, fellows, residents and faculty such as myself utilize the diverse resources of the Surgical Laboratory. Dr. Li was an excellent surgeon and scientist, having been a transplant surgeon with the 2cd Department of Surgery at Shanghai University in China. A surgeon of his skill was welcomed by the non-surgeons in the lab. Li stayed with us for many years before entering our Family Practice Residency and then subsequently establishing a successful practice in this important discipline.

A second early addition to the laboratory staff was Mr. Tri Phan. Tri, a former citizen of Vietnam, came to us by an arduous route through refugee camps in Southeast Asia at the end of the Vietnam War. He assumed the role of lab manager, and without any formal training in science, learned many of the analytical techniques that we employed in our experiments. He was especially gifted in histology and photography. The latter was important in documenting the lively activities of our laboratory and departmental parties.

The key to the success of the Surgical Laboratory in its early years was a constant flow of residents from abroad who we called International Fellows. These Fellows included Norbert Senninger from Heidelberg, Germany, Dr, Julio Coelho from Curitiba, Brazil, Dr. Dirk Gouma from Maastricht, Holland, Dr. Norbert Runkel from Heidelberg, Germany, Dr. Peter Kueppers from Heidelberg, Germany, Dr. Klaus Klemm from Heidelberg, Germany, Dr. Richard Calabuig from Barcelona, Spain, Dr. O.P. Cavouti from Santiago, Chile, and Dr. Rosario Vecchio from Sicily. These individuals were outstanding in their ability to work effectively with each other. They spent a year or two with us, sometimes together, but more often in successive years. They all worked very hard, spending many weekends in the lab in order to maximize their time with us. They overlapped in their participation, thereby being able to pass along in some cases, work in progress, to be finished by their replacement. They were critical in many instances to keeping the continuity of the research to its conclusion. They also played a very important role in our Summer Medical Student Research Program.

I was very careful in being sure that everyone who made a significant contribution to the work was listed in the publications referenced in the Appendix of this book. An especially attractive feature was that most of the International Fellows were sponsored by the residency program that they were training in. I was very active at the time in several of the International Societies that brought me together with their Chiefs. This provided an opportunity to receive inquiries as to whether we had room for one of their promising residents that wanted to be an academic surgeon. Most of the residency programs in Europe did not provide opportunities for a laboratory experience. The German Government attempted to remedy this deficiency by providing a one or two year scholarship to support International Scholars funded by the Deutsche Forschungsgemeinershaft (DMG) in Bonn. The Surgical Laboratory at UT-H was well suited for fulfilling this deficiency and much to its advantage since the sponsors also required the writing of a thesis of the work performed. **Dr Norbert Senninger MD** from Heidelberg was our first International Scholar sponsored by this program.

Dr Senninger was not only instrumental in moving the labs from Utah but also the key investigator on two important projects initiated in Utah and completed in Texas. One involved a study of the role of bile reflux in the pathogenesis of pancreatitis. Ligation of the bile duct below the junction of the bile and pancreatic ducts in the opossum leads to severe necrotizing pancreatitis. Simple ligation of the pancreatic duct alone leads to a low grade edematous pancreatitis and atrophy of the gland. The simultaneous obstruction of the bile and pancreatic duct also leads to severe pancreatitis whether the ligation is done below or above the junction of the ducts. Dr. Osmar Cavouti from Chile made an important contribution to this work by showing that prolamine (Ethibloc) injected into the pancreatic duct prior to low bile duct ligation attenuated the necrotizing pancreatitis associated with this model. External drainage of the bile in the Ethibloc instilled animals unfortunately confounded the results, since it relieved the biliary obstruction associated with low bile duct ligation in the test animals. These studies by Norbert and Osmar provided two pieces of scientific evidence that bile reflux as proposed by Opie in 1910 was not an essential feature in the provocation of acute necrotizing pancreatitis associated with the passage of a gallstone. Apparently the simultaneous obstruction of the bile and pancreatic ducts was the trigger for the development of necrotizing pancreatitis in this model.

Norbert made a second unique observation, with the help of Julio Coelho and David Van Buren, a surgical resident in our program. They clearly showed that placing a pancreatic segment into a Roux limb of jejunum of a dog protected the animal from the systemic effects of severe acute pancreatitis induced by the injection of a solution of bile salts into its main duct. This technique has been used clinically in the performance of human pancreas transplantation, but has not become a popular approach to pancreatic reconstruction after transplantation. Norbert's extensive work with us formed the substance of his Habilitation Thesis that led to his being awarded a Medical Degree in Surgery at the completion of his residency in Heidelberg. After several years on the surgical faculty at Heidelberg, Norbert was appointed to the Chair of Surgery at Muenster, Germany, where he has had a very distinguished career.

Dr Julio Coelho, MD, PhD, an International Fellow from Brazil, was very active in the Surgical Laboratories. He was the lead author on 16 refereed publications during his two year stay with us (see appendix). His major interest was in the myoelectric activity of the papilla of Vater and its effects upon pressures within the bile and pancreatic ducts. He did an extensive survey of the effects of a variety of hormonal and neural mediators on the function of the biliary sphincter of the opossum. One of his most interesting observations was that the instillation of alcohol into the stomach of an opossum led to an immediate increase in the electrical and mechanical activity of the biliary sphincter of this species. The experiment was performed in a way that the alcohol could not reach the papilla directly because of duodenal occlusion and a proximal gastroenterostomy. This is an interesting observation that deserves further study since it may lead to an explanation of how the "belting" (rapid ingestion of alcohol) can induce an episode of acute pancreatitis.

Dr. Coehlo, in collaboration with Jerry Schlegel made some of the early observations of the effects of gastrointestinal peptides and inflammatory mediators on the myolectric activity of the small bowel. An important observation was that cholecystokinin when administered exogenously was an agonist (increased the myoelectric potentials and contractions) of the biliary sphincter of the opossum. The significance of this finding only became clear to us several years later when Dr. Richard Calabuig, a Fellow from Barcelona working with Dr. William Weems in the Department of

Physiology established that the biliary sphincter of the opossum was a propulsive pump rather than a resistor as is the case in man. This made sense when viewed in terms of the feeding behavior of this animal that eats at night and hangs upside down by its tail during the day to digest its meal and avoid its predators. It has to pump the bile into the duodenum against the force of gravity. This observation may explain in part the findings of Geenen and his associates in Milwaukee that some patients with unexplained biliary type pain after cholecystectomy had a sphincter of Oddi that contracted rather than relaxed when they were administered cholecystokinin intravenously. We speculated that the simultaneous contraction of the gallbladder and the sphincter of Oddi i.e. biliary dyskinesia, was the cause of pain in this population of patients.

Dr. Julio Coehlo MD was a great help to all of us in the laboratory. Before returning to Brazil to assume the Chair of Surgery at Parana University, he spent some time with Norbert Senninger in Heidelberg. He then moved to Maastricht to receive a second PhD on the work he had done in part with us. He has emerged as one of the leading academic surgeons in Brazil, specializing in liver transplantation. It was a delight for Inger and I to meet Julio and his family at the meeting of the ISG in Hong Kong last November (2012), and he and his wife Karla at the Ghent meeting in August, 2013,

Dr. Dirk Gouma MD was referred to our program by his Chief at Maastricht University, the late J.M. (Coe) Greep MD. Dirk had a primary interest in the effects of external and internal drainage of bile on the outcome of patients undergoing surgery for obstructive jaundice. He studied this systematically in externally and internally drained bile ducts of rats. The studies revealed that prolonged external drainage of bile was bad for liver function because of the bile salt wasting incurred by this technique. He also showed that endotoxemia produced by bile duct ligation in the rat was increased by external drainage and decreased by internal drainage. After completing his residency at Maastricht, Dirk joined the faculty in Amsterdam where he serves as Chairman of the Department of Surgery, and is one of the top Academic Surgeons in Europe.

Dr, Richard Calabuig MD was referred to our International Fellowship Program by Dr. Puig LaCalle MD, one of the leading biliary surgeons in Spain. Richard helped us close out the opossum era while working in the laboratory of Dr. William Weems, PhD, a Professor within the Department of Physiology at UT-Houston, and an expert in the physics of fluid hydraulics. Bill had fashioned a unique way to determine the directional flow of fluid within a hollow tube such as the papilla of Vater, and to measure the forces that caused it to flow in one direction or another. As mentioned above, they convincingly showed that the biliary sphincter of the opossum was a pump rather than a resistor. He further described with Drs. Weems, Weisbrodt, and Mr. Seggerman (a graduate student in the Department of Physiology and Cell Biology) the effects of hemorrhagic shock on gallbladder contractility and intestinal motility of the opossum. Dr. Calabuig was a great help to me, along with Rosario Vecchio, and Norbert Runkel, in writing up some thoughts on the pathogenesis and treatment of stenosing papillitis. Richard was a delight to work with. He was very precise in his research and writings. To my knowledge, he practices as an academic surgeon in Barcelona. Why go anywhere else; it is such a beautiful town. Unfortunately my friend Puig LaCalle died unexpectedly over a decade ago and the presence of he and his lovely wife are greatly missed on the world stage.

Dr. Norbert Runkel, MD, a junior resident at Heidelberg was encouraged to join us by Norbert Senninger who was completing his residency at Heidelberg at the time. Norbert Runkel was interested in the infectious complications of biliary pancreatitis. He in collaboration with other workers in the laboratory established very early in his stay with us that the opossum harbored numerous strange parasites and bacteria, especially salmonella within their biliary tree. The latter studies were done in the bacteriology laboratory of the Trauma Research Center with the assistance of Lilliana Rodriquez (director of the bacteriology lab established within The Center), Terry Blaisdell (from Animal Care Center), and Dr. Mark LaRocco, PhD, a member of the Trauma Research Center, and Faculty within the Department of Pathology.

The availability of the Trauma Research Center and its activities will be discussed in detail later. Needless to say, it played a very important role in the ability of Dr. Runkel to pursue his interest in infection in the outcomes from acute pancreatitis. He pursued his early work under the mentorship of Dr. Thomas Miller, MD, with the assistance of Dr. Gregory Smith, PhD, Dr. Liliana Rodriquez, PhD, and Dr. Mark LaRocco, PhD. They clearly showed that the pancreatitis that follows low bile duct ligation in the rat leads to the translocation of gut bacteria into nodes adjacent to the gut wall and to organs further upstream. The low bile duct model of pancreatitis replaced the opossum model because of the similarity of the gut flora of the rat to that of humans. The development and detailed analysis of the effects of low bile duct ligation on pancreatic inflammation and gastrointestinal function set the stage for more than a decade of work in the Surgical Laboratory. It also provided a focus for our work in the Trauma Research Center.

Before returning to Heidelberg to complete his residency, Norbert Runkel made the important observation that slowing down intestinal transit by the exogenous administration of morphine led to bacterial overgrowth within the lumen of the gut. This was accompanied by bacterial translocation through the gut epithelium into lymph nodes adjacent to the wall of the intestine. This observation potentially had important implications to the clinical situation where sepsis from gut bacteria is the major cause of death in injured patients and those with severe pancreatitis. Furthermore, large doses of morphine were used (and still are) to keep patients comfortable when they are on the ventilator. Dr. Runkel returned to Heidelberg, wrote his thesis, and subsequently joined the surgical faculty at the Free University of Berlin. He later was appointed the Chief of a teaching Hospital in the South of Germany close to Lake Constance, a highly coveted position. We are very much in his debt for shifting our experimental model from the opossum to the rat. Unfortunately the rat does not have a gallbladder but it does have communications with the pancreatic duct along its length which allows the induction of pancreatitis by ligation of the bile duct as it enters the duodenum.

Dr. Peter Kueppers MD, also from Heidelberg, took up where Norbert Runkel had left off in his studies of the consequences of low bile duct ligation in the rat. He showed while working with Tom Miller, Greg Smith, Liliana Rodriquez, and Chung Chen that enteral deprivation (nothing by mouth) accompanied by total parenteral nutrition (TPN) caused translocation from the lumen of the gut in half of the rats so treated. The addition of morphine increased the translocation rate to 100%. This was a very important observation since at that time every severely injured or ill patient received TPN, and most were sedated with large doses of morphine. This was before the era of early institution of enteral nutrition to tolerance in patients with severe pancreatitis.

Peter, working with Dianne Russell made a second important and clinically relevant observation. He showed in a very clever model that recirculation of bile after establishing pancreatitis by bile duct occlusion in the rat could rapidly reverse the progression of the pancreatic inflammation. This is the clinical correlate of what happens clinically when a gallstone transits rapidly through the papilla of Vater. I was proud of his accomplishments in the laboratory but disappointed to learn that after returning to Heidelberg, Peter changed his specialty to radiology. I hope that his change in career choice was not due to my being too hard on him during his time with us. While his shift of professional interest was a loss for the world of surgery it was gain for radiology that possibly needed his unique talents.

I will defer my comments on Dr. Klauss Klemm's work with us as an International Scholar since he joined us several years later after we had established an NIH Sponsored Trauma Research Center. Klauss played an important role in the success of this Center in the 90s, and taught me how to ski Snowbird "kamikaze" style. As you probably have surmised, the International Fellows played a very important role in establishing the Surgical Laboratories at UT-Houston.

CHAPTER 20

TRAUMA RESEARCH CENTER AT UT HOUSTON (1988-2004)

The Hermann Hospital, with one of the largest and most active trauma services in the world, offered a unique opportunity to study the pathophysiology of traumatic injury. Having been successful in bringing an NIH sponsored Trauma Center to Utah where there was no trauma to speak of made me think that developing one at UT Houston would be a piece of cake. As Chairman of the Study Section for Bioengineering and Surgery for 2 years (1978-1980), the Study Section that reviewed the Trauma Center Grant applications, I learned that the National Institute for General Medical Sciences was looking for a way to bring basic and clinical scientists together to study the problems associated with major disease to include trauma. It suddenly dawned on me during one of our laboratory meetings in 1984 that that was precisely what we had to offer at UT-Houston.

The research laboratories and faculty offices of the Departments of Surgery and Physiology were perfectly aligned in terms of location and interest to study the effects of traumatic injury on the function of the gastrointestinal tract. It took a few years to re-establish a close working relationship with the basic scientists in Physiology as Stan Dudrick had previously done. Once that occurred, we as a group decided to study the pathogenesis of multiple organ failure (MOF). This was a timely topic in the early 1980's since it was just being described clinically by Arthur Baue at Yale, Ben Eiseman at Denver, and others. It is a disease characterized by the progressive of loss of vital organ function during optimum care in an intensive care environment. Our previous work led us to the hypothesis that MOF was the result of failure of gut propulsive activity leading to bacterial overgrowth, and a breakdown of the epithelial barrier to the inward migration of intestinal bacteria and its toxic products. We had established experimental evidence for this concept with the help of the International Fellows through the use of a rat low bile duct ligation pancreatitis model and studies of the bacteriology of the gut.

By 1988, we had put together a multidisciplinary team to examine the above hypothesis in rats and mice. The preliminary results from the previous work of the International Fellows and their mentors led to the NIH funding of a Trauma Research Center at UT-Houston. We were able to successfully renew the Center for 3 cycles (15 years) during my tenure as its Principal Investigator. Drs. Norman Weisbrodt PhD, Dr. Gilbert Castro PhD, and Dr. William Weems PhD, faculty in the Department of Physiology, were the key to the success of the Center. The fact that we had not translated our research findings into clinical applications was a frequent criticism of our work by site visit teams. Our rebuttal included the fact that our research group contained no clinically active trauma surgeons. They were too busy taking care of the injured.

This was corrected for the fourth renewal of the Center by the recruitment of Dr. Frederick Moore to UT-Houston by our Chairman, Dr. Richard Andrassy, with my enthusiastic concurrence. Fred initially served as Co-Program Director until he established his own research team, and subsequently became Program Director for years 15 to 20. Fred Moore came to Houston from the Trauma Program at the University of Colorado where the participants in the Trauma Research Center were surgeons who also had a strong interest in clinical research. It did not take long for Fred Moore to incorporate clinical protocols into our ongoing Center activities. Dr. Rosemary Kozar MD, PhD had joined us by that time, and had established a biochemical laboratory that supported a program in enteral nutrition. She instituted an active collaboration with Fred, and together they examined the role of amino acid supplements in enteral nutrition. Fred, in a relatively short period of time was able to secure an NIH sponsored Trauma Research Training Grant to complement the activities of the Trauma Center.

Below is a summary of the progress made during the initial 15 years of the grant. First I would like to identify and thank all of the individuals who participated in our studies during this period. I have already mentioned the International Scholars who actually contributed along with the other investigators in the Surgical Laboratories to provide the background for the successful receipt of the designation as a Trauma Research Center. We had strong institutional support for the Grant thanks to Dean Ernst Knobil, PhD, Dean John Ribble, MD, and Stanley Schultz, MD, Chairman of Physiology and Cell Biology for their enthusiastic administrative support of the Center. Most of the participants in the Trauma Research Center have already been mentioned in the work carried out in the Surgical Laboratories with the International Scholars. What I plan to do in this section is to discuss in some detail the progress that was made in understanding how the gut might contribute to the progression of multiple organ failure. Drs. Weisbrodt, Castro, Weems, Miller, LaRusso, Pressley, Lodato, Mercer. Mailman, Zembowicz, and Grossie played a critical role in the success of the Center over the years. A special thanks to the late Yael Harari, who helped us in so many ways as she underwent numerous attempts at curing her ovarian cancer.

My group for the most part employed an inflammatory model of low bile duct ligation which leads to a mild form of interstitial pancreatitis in the rat. We chose this approach since the mildness of the inflammatory response, and its reversibility provided the effects on gut motility and bacteriology that we wanted to study. We in essence wanted to learn how a delay in intestinal transit could lead to the infectious phase of multiple organ failure. There was a clinical rationale for this approach since patients with severe pancreatitis also initially develop intestinal stasis (ileus), and multiple organ failure. Sepsis from gut bacteria comes late in the course of their disease.

We therefore set out to test the hypothesis that factors which slow intestinal transit induce bacterial overgrowth which in turn disrupts the mucosal barrier to movement of gut bacteria and their toxins into the host. In this way, sepsis from gut bacteria in some unknown way leads to sequential organ failure and death. The rat was chosen for the majority of these experiments since the bacterial species in their gut are easily identified and are similar to that found in man. Hemorrhagic shock, a prominent risk factor for MOF in humans surprisingly did not cause an interruption in intestinal transit or bacterial overgrowth except when pancreatitis was also induced in the rats. Severe ischemia/reperfusion in the rat however was associated with a delay in intestinal transit, bacterial overgrowth and translocation. This was a model that was studied extensively by others in The Center, since it was felt to represent what happens to individuals after recovery from shock.

For many of these studies the bacteriology was performed by Liliana Rodriguez and Mark LaRocco (Pathology), and the morphology by Dianne Haley-Russell in the Department of Surgery. Many of the experiments were performed by Debra Muncy, MD, (a resident in the lab) and Mr. Tri Phan (the lab coordinator). Their technical skills were essential to the success of these experiments. Once we established the time course of the decrease in intestinal transit, bacterial overgrowth, and translocation, we turned our attention the etiology of the decrease in intestinal transit.

A group of elegant experiments performed by Norman Weisbrodt (with the help of Thomas Pressley, Yong Fang Li, Malcorzata

Zembowicz, Sandra Higham, Arthur Zembowicz, and Robert Lodato) showed rather convincingly that the intraperitoneal administration of endotoxin produced a decrease in ileal contractility while reducing the activity of an inducible form of nitric oxide. Dr. David Mailman, PhD, and Chairman of Physiology at the University of Houston was most helpful to the group through his participation in a weekly Trauma Center research conference where we discussed the potential role of various cytokines in the stasis-mucosal injury sequence. These were exciting findings that subsequently led us to examine the role of signal transduction in gut pathophysiology. This scientific interaction would probably have not occurred in the absence of the Trauma Research Center.

This is a good time to comment on the work of our fourth International Fellow from Heidelberg, **Dr. Klaus Klemm, MD**. Klauss joined our laboratory at the time that we became interested in how exogenously administered endotoxin derived from E coli produces a decrease in intestinal transit and translocation of intestinal bacteria through the mucosal lining of the gut wall. Using the distribution of fluorescein labeled- microspheres, Klauss demonstrated that the blood flow to the mucosa of the ileum was preferentially depressed during endotoxin induced shock. This outcome could be prevented by the simultaneous administration of the non-specific nitric oxide inhibitor, L-NAME. This turned out to be a very important observation since it brought to our attention that there was heterogeneity within the segments of the gut to endotoxin induced stress. The ileum clearly was more sensitive to this stressor than more proximal segments of the small bowel. This possibly had clinical relevance since the ileum by being adjacent to the colon had the highest levels of bacteria residing within its lumen compared to other segments of the small bowel. A decrease in its propulsive activity would therefore allow even higher levels of enteric bacteria and their toxins to accumulate.

Klauss returned to Heidelberg, and after completion of his residency in General Surgery, pursued further training in peripheral vascular surgery. I have had some contact with Klauss over the years since he married a girl from Houston. It is my understanding that he has an established practice in vascular surgery in a hospital not far from Heidelberg.

Klauss, along with the other investigators in the Trauma Research Center introduced into the Surgical Laboratories the powerful tools of molecular biology. We became very interested in the array of inflammatory markers that could be by now bought off the shelf. By this time in 1998, we were rearranging our thoughts and expanding our collaborations in order to utilize the new tools available to those doing sophisticated cell biology. Dr. Bruce Kone, MD, Professor of Medicine and Director of the Division of Nephrology, was most helpful in modernizing our laboratories to study the emerging field of signal transduction. He played a pivotal role in addressing areas of molecular biology that were relevant to the Centers activity in his role of Director of its Core Laboratory.

Dr. Frederick Moore had joined us in December of 1995, and was an active participant in our Friday Morning lab rounds. He brought to the table what was lacking in the Center, a unifying theme that would lead to a better understanding of multiple organ failure. He schematically showed us how our work to date fit in with his concepts of the role of inflammatory mediators in the pathogenesis of MOF.

The story goes something like this. Confronted with severe injury or illness (such as pancreatitis) the body responds by elaborating a large number of inflammatory mediators called cytokines. This clinical situation is referred to by the colloquial term Systemic Inflammatory Response Syndrome (SIRS). This cytokine storm during the first several days is lethal for some patients, but most survive, immunologically suppressed and physiologically compromised. Many additional mediators are produced to counteract the SIRS, thereby leading to healing in some, but a slowly progressive severe illness in others. Early after injury, the SIRS is accompanied by a loss of the propulsive function of the intestine (ileus) which leads to bacterial overgrowth within its lumen. Lack of enteral feeding (nothing by mouth), futile use of antibiotics, prolonged ventilator support, morphine sedation, suppression of acid secretion, bacterial overgrowth in the stomach, gastroesophageal reflux from the presence of a nasogastric tube, and poor ventilator hygiene leading to pneumonia are all factors that likely contribute to the breakdown of the enteric mucosal barrier within the gut, and progressive loss of organ function.

Dr. Moore thought that it was reasonable to consider as we had postulated that the gut was a primary factor in the ultimate septic death of many of these patients. His joining us from Denver was at the time that we were renewing the Center Grant for the third time. In other words we were already at the ten year mark, and badly in need of a clinical project. We decided to pursue five areas: I—The role of enteral nutrition in the management of injured patients (Moore and Kozar); II—The molecular pathways of signal transduction during the early phase of MOF (Kone); III—The mechanisms of gut smooth muscle contractility and propulsion following traumatic stress (Weisbrodt); IV—Gastric function during traumatic stress (Mercer); V—Bacterial mediation of gut function in post injury ileus (Moody). Drs. Miller and Myers, previous participants in the Center had moved elsewhere to assume Chairmanships. I had moved out of the Chairmanship at UT-H, and was looking forward to retirement and returning to Utah to renew my love affair with the Wasatch Mountains. I agreed however to remain in Houston as the Principle Investigator until Dr. Moore had time to get his own personal research well underway. The NIGMS staff felt comfortable with this arrangement, and in fact suggested that that is what we should do.

There are two individuals mentioned above in the third renewal, Dr. Rosemary Kozar, MD, PhD and Dr. David Mercer MD, who have made important contributions to the ongoing activities of the Trauma Research Center and the academic activities of the Department of Surgery in general. **Dr Rosemary Kozar MD, PhD** entered the general surgical residency at UT Houston after graduating from the Temple University School of Medicine in 1986. After a second year in our residency program, she joined Dr. Anthony Gotto's atherosclerosis laboratory when he was still the Chairman of Medicine at the Baylor College of Medicine. Under his mentorship during a four year formal bench research training experience, Rosemary received a PhD, and resumed her general surgical training at Temple University (1992-1995). Following three years on the surgical faculty at Hahnemann Medical Center in Philadelphia where she was primarily engaged in trauma and critical care, she joined our faculty in 1999, and became an integral part of the Trauma Division and Trauma Research Center. Her interest in enteral nutrition was a good fit to our ongoing research in gut integrity. Her critical care skills and knowledge of surgical nutrition was a great addition to the activities of the Center.

Dr David Mercer came to us as a fully trained investigator with an interest in the role of gastrointestinal peptides in intestinal function. He trained at Temple under Wally Ritchie, and consequently had developed a strong interest in the neuroendocrine control of acid secretion and its role in peptic ulcer disease. Dave was an outstanding surgical educator, researcher and clinician. His talents were recognized early in his surgical career as evidenced by the fact that he was elected to the Presidency of the Society of University of Surgeons. Because of his unique administrative skills, he was selected to be the Director of our Surgical Program at the LBJ Hospital. His talents were especially appreciated by the participants in the Surgical Laboratories since he was one of the few, possibly only surgeon in our group skilled in the techniques of modern biology. Because of his academic accomplishments he became a candidate for leadership roles elsewhere and was recruited to the Chair of Surgery at Nebraska just as we were facing our fourth renewal of the TRC. Fred Moore had moved to the Methodist Hospital and Dave was the interim PI of the Center at this critical point in its history. Fortunately we had several other research activities within the Surgical Laboratory to sustain its fiscal viability while we considered new directions for the Trauma Center.

CHAPTER 21

OTHER ACTIVITIES IN THE SURGICAL LABORATORIES

The Surgical Laboratories had several other research programs unrelated to the TRC. These included an NIH funded RO l Grant titled **Mechanisms of Biliary Stasis in Cholesterol Lithogenesis** (Moody, Li, and Weisbrodt). We in addition had received a P50 training grant entitled **Research Training in Digestive Disease and Nutrition** (Moody). This grant was designed to provide for surgical residents a three year PhD generating research experience that included course work and training in science with tutorials in three other disciplines. The intent was to educate highly motivated surgical residents to be the future leaders of surgical gastroenterology. We planned to have only two people a year enter the program. There was no problem in finding basic science mentors for such individuals, since funds were provided to pay the residents and support their research.

Dr. Norman Weisbrodt PhD was one of the more popular and successful mentors in the Digestive Surgery Training Grant. **Dr. Jose Ortega MD** was one of the first and most successful participants in the program. During his time in the laboratory (about three years) he perfected not only the surgical techniques involved in some elegant experiments to evaluate gut function, but also mastered the intricacies of the complex chemistry of cytokines and prostaglandins. In collaboration with Dr. Weisbrodt, he described the biochemical events that accompanied the contractile function of the biliary sphincter of the opossum. They, together with Dr. Pressley PhD, developed unique probes to detect the DNA of the pro-inflammatory cytokines IL-1 beta, and TNF-alpha in the smooth muscle and cellular infiltrate of the gallbladder wall during cholesterol feeding and the development of gallstones in prairie dogs. The course work required, and the laboratory time involved in testing these ideas left little time for Jose to write his thesis. In fact it was never written, since when he returned to the residency program, he had little time left at the end of the day to even sleep. This experience along with his concern about supporting his family dissuaded Jose from going into academic surgery full time. He did however join our clinical faculty when he completed his surgical training and is the chief of one of our affiliated hospital's surgical service, much smarter for his experience in the lab.

Several other candidates entered the program, but dropped out for various reasons. I learned from this experience that the best way to train surgeon clinician-scientists was to provide them with a shorter period in the laboratory after they have acquired basic surgical skills. This usually required two years in the clinic prior to spending two years in the laboratory. This improved the chances that when they returned to the clinical rotations they would still be familiar with the routines of surgical care and the technical aspects of operative surgery. The research years gave them time to establish or reestablish a family, and to pay off some bills with our monitored moonlighting program. I have always been amazed at how productive and successful residents have been who pursued this two year research experience during a seven year residency. The PhD model was obviously not well suited for our residents who even at that time had already incurred a considerable amount of debt. In addition they were more interested in obtaining advanced surgical training so that they could compete in the marketplace. The model that I personally pursued (seven clinical years followed by two years of basic research), worked out well for me, but as you possibly have surmised, it placed a huge burden on my family life.

The evolution of general surgical specialties (vascular, oncology, breast, endocrine, hepatobiliary-pancreas, trauma-critical care, minimally invasive surgery, and more recently acute care surgery) provides a large number of options for general surgeons when they complete their residencies. This has resulted in a decrease in the number of residents who desire to spend a few years in a basic science laboratory during their general surgical training. Furthermore, there is increasing concern about the lack of broadly trained general surgeons in the community, especially in rural areas. At the time of this writing (2013) there is an increasing need for general surgeons to work in small towns and rural communities.

The opportunity for surgeons to engage in clinical practice and bench research will only be available for those residents who have a strong passion to learn about something in depth, and the energy, patience, and will to master the tools of both clinical surgery and modern biology. While they will be rare birds, they will not become an extinct species since society will appreciate and reward them for the fruits of their extraordinary effort.

CHAPTER 22

TOWARDS RETIREMENT

I retired from the Chairmanship of the Department of Surgery at UT Houston in 1994 at the age of 66. My plan to return to Utah at that time was delayed by numerous responsibilities that required my presence in Houston. I was the only surgeon in the department primarily involved in the surgical management of obese patients, and was attempting to develop a comprehensive multidisciplinary obesity center. I still served as the Principal Investigator of the Trauma Research Center, and was still active in the laboratory pursuing how bacteria within the intestine obtain access to the general circulation. I also was co-editor of the Yearbook of Digestive Disease with Norton Greenberger, an outstanding gastroenterologist and at that time the chairman of medicine at the University of Kansas. In addition, I was in the middle of publishing an atlas of ambulatory surgery, and was considering how to produce a third edition of a multi-authored book titled "The Surgical Treatment of Digestive Disease" which had become outdated. All of these projects required my presence in Houston.

Dr. Andrassy was named interim chairman during the search for my replacement. He was most generous in providing for me an academic office and space for my staff, which included Flora Roeder, who was essential for my editorial responsibilities. Dr. Andrassy within the year became the Chairman of the Department, and allowed me to stay on as the Denton A. Cooley Professor of Surgery until it became the named Chair of Surgery in 2000 at Dr. Cooley's request, a decision that I strongly supported.

Dr. Andrassy since that time has supported and encouraged my work as a professor of surgery, including me in all the activities of the department. It has been a pleasure to work with he and his administrative staff over the ensuing 19 years. He has developed a superb department that I enjoy being part of. Recall that during my recruitment I told Ernst Knobil, the Dean in 1983 when I was appointed to the chair, that I would come down to Houston for a ten year period with the intent of curing my addiction to the mountains that surround Salt Lake City. Thirty years later (still addicted to the Wasatch Mountains), I am still here in Houston enjoying the city and the opportunity to participate in the educational programs at the Medical School. I spend the weekends at my home in Sandy Utah, and the week days at the UT Medical School in Houston. Initially, weekly visits to Salt Lake were essential in order to care for Maja's needs during the terminal phase of her long illness. Now I fly to Salt Lake about twice a month with my fiancée Inger in order to visit family and marvel at the mountains. I still travel to near and far away places, and interact with the faculty, residents and students at the medical school, and my colleagues at surgical meetings around the world.

Retirement from the Chair has offered me the freedom from day to day activities to spend more time with my work and my family. My plans for retirement changed rather dramatically almost 20 years ago when at 2:00 AM one morning after returning from a medical meeting in Milan, Maja (my former wife now deceased) awoke with a dislocated jaw. I gave her a pain pill and a half hour later popped her jaw into place and went back to bed. Suddenly it occurred to me that this was a strange event. I woke her up and she started to speak in a way that I recognized that she had had a stroke. I dialed 911, and within ten minutes the paramedics arrived, and transported her by ambulance to Hermann Hospital.

They admitted her to the intensive care unit. Fortunately, she was still breathing on her own since she had put in her will that she did not want any heroic measures if a life threatening event should occur.

Except for an initial febrile course, she made a rapid recovery, but was left with weakness of her upper and lower extremity on the left side. They suggested that she stay in the hospital for a few weeks for rehabilitation, but she had other ideas. She was found one day dangling over the side of her bed in her Posey Belt which was used in those days for restraint. A few days later she was found walking around in the basement with a new pair of tennis shoes that her daughter Jane had bought her, seeking a way out. We finally convinced the neurologist that we could manage her rehabilitation at home. We were allowed to take her home with the idea that we would supervise her use of the walker. This was a joke, because after one trip around Glenn Haven Drive where we lived, she threw away the walker, and did many laps each day under her own steam, and without our company. We knew from the many years of living with her that she was a "tough Swede".

Her recovery was rapid, and within a month she started to drive her car. What she and I did not know was that she had lost vision in the left side of each eye. In other words she could not see things on her left side. As a consequence, she got to where she wanted to go in her car by always turning right, including getting home from the store. This became almost a lethal issue a year later when we had a party at our week end retreat in New Ulm, a rural town about 90 miles west of Houston. We had purchased a lovely small home surrounded by giant pine trees and a white picket fence on the spur of the moment while driving one Sunday to view the blue bonnets. A large sign was displayed on the front of the house proudly stating "For Sale by Owner". We could not resist stopping and knocking on the door. We were greeted by a scantily clad, deeply tanned young man who wanted a quick sale since he wished to return to San Diego, and his surf board. After he had showed us around, I asked him how much he wanted for his house. He said about 70 thousand dollars. I said "sold", and within a few days, we had a lovely retreat in the country.

We moved an historical old school house to the property from Industry, a town about 10 miles north of New Ulm. We converted it into a gallery/studio for Maja's 200 oil paintings that she had produced in Salt Lake and Houston during the past decade. We used to go out a few Saturdays a month to tend to things, but we never stayed overnight since Maja was afraid of the coyotes that used to start whelping as darkness approached,

About a year after her stroke, we had a large barbecue party at the Ulm House for students, faculty and friends. It was catered by one of the local barbecue pits. As you can imagine, a good time was had by all, especially after the beer kegs were popped. As we prepared to return home, my car would not start, and it had to be towed to a garage on 290, the road to Austin. Fortunately we had come to New Ulm in separate cars, so we had transportation home. On picking up my car a week later, Maja was sideswiped by a pickup truck as she followed me across a two lane highway. She did not see the oncoming pickup truck because it was coming from her left side. I saw the accident out of my rear view mirror. The impact had spun her car around several times and had blown out the windows but it was still upright. I quickly ran to the site and found her clinging to the steering wheel. Her window was shattered. She calmly asked what had happened. I told her that she was in an accident and should not move.

An ambulance arrived within minutes, and she was taken to a local hospital. As I entered the hospital I met one of our general surgeons on the clinical staff at Hermann Hospital. I asked what he was doing there and he said he had been called off his ranch nearby to see an accident victim. I thanked him for coming, and told him it was my wife. I waited in the corridor and in about an hour or two I received the good news that he could find no evidence of injury, except for bruising on her chest. He reported that the vital signs, blood chemistries, EKG, and radiographs were normal and that I could take her home and observe her closely. She had an uneventful night except for pain at the site of her bruised ribs.

I examined her in the morning, and felt comfortable leaving for a flight to Chicago for a meeting which was interrupted by an urgent call from my associate Dr. David Thomson. He informed me that Maja had been admitted to the Hermann Hospital with a heart attack. I took the next plane back to Houston to find Maja setting up in bed in the Cardiac ICU, smiling and looking quite well. Work up revealed that she had advance coronary heart disease with a small area of left ventricular apical necrosis. It was judged that she did not need to have interventional therapy at the time. Within a few days, she was sent home on a medical regimen which included restrictions in her activity. It was obvious that this was the time to return to Salt Lake where we could be closer to family and friends.

The house that we had bought on Newcastle Drive in Sandy Utah, primarily for skiing shortly after leaving for Houston, was too small to accommodate all the things that we had accumulated over the years. We disposed of the New Ulm house with all of its furnishings by giving it to Wasatch Academy where my son Frank and daughter Jane had gone to school, and where I had served on the Board for ten years. This helped to defray the cost of a large pledge that we had made for the construction of a Math-Science Building when I was President of its Board. On completion, it was named after Dr. Keith Reemstma, a former student at Wasatch, and my predecessor in the chair of surgery at Utah. He and his wife Judy were generous benefactors to the school, Judy continues to participate in the activities of the Board after Keith's untimely death in 2000. Keith at the time was serving as the chairman of the department of surgery at the Columbia-Presbyterian Medical Center in New York City. I am sure that he would be most pleased to see the remarkable development of Wasatch Academy since his passing, a school that he so dearly loved. The school has almost tripled in the size of its student body, as well as in size of the physical facilities required to handle their educational activities.

It was obvious that we had to build a larger house in Salt Lake to accommodate the re-establishment of our family home in Utah. Fortunately a new sub-division was being developed that I had had my eyes on for several years. It abutted upon a piece of land that was owned by the city of Sandy, and was planned to be in the future an ecological park. We were most fortunate in obtaining a large corner lot that had an unobstructed view of the Wasatch Mountains, the Great Salt Lake, and a glimpse of the peaks of the Oquirrh Mountains across the valley. We proceeded to build a large retirement home appropriate for older folks with disabilities. The construction included wheel chair ramps, extra railings on the stairs, room for Maja's baby grand piano, wall space for her art work, and an abundance of windows that would bring her outside while still setting inside. In short, it was designed for the day that one or both of us would become incapacitated.

We enjoyed watching the construction crew prepare the site and build the home over a several month period during the summer and fall of 1996. Meanwhile, we fixed up and sold both the Houston and the Sandy homes, the former at a loss and the latter at a profit that balanced out each other and left us with enough money for the down payment on the new home. We moved to Sandy in the late fall of 1996. It did not take us long to settle in, but it did take very long to unpack the several hundred moving boxes that contained our treasures, much of which was Maja's art. Fortunately we had a lot of closets, wall space, and a large garage.

Delta Airlines offered very convenient and reasonably priced flights between Houston and Salt Lake City. Once we were settled in, we called it home, and I began what now is 19 years of commuting back and forth to work, home on Fridays, and back to work in Houston on Mondays. I am a 2 million plus mile Diamond Frequent Flier, and enjoying it. The airplane keeps me away from cell phones, and provides time to read the New England Journal of Medicine, Science, and the Economist each week.

CHAPTER 23

ADMINISTRATIVE CHALLENGES (1983-1994)

The retirement from the Chairmanship provided time to reflect on several unusual administrative challenges that kept me on my toes during my tenure as the chair at UT. The first challenge related to the unexpected relief of Ernst Knobil of the deanship three years after he had accepted the job. Ernie was a friend, a brilliant scientist, and an effective leader. His dismissal from the deanship was very upsetting to me since he was the reason why I had moved to UT-Houston. Apparently there was some sort of disagreement with the President of the Health Science Center, his boss. To this day, no one has revealed to me the issue. The most I can get is the statement that he was "fired".

I served on the search committee for a new dean, and in view of the urgency of filling the post, we decided to consider two worthy internal candidates, Dr. John Ribble, MD, the associate dean for student affairs, and Dr. Frank Weber, MD, the chair of family practice. They provided a distinct choice between an individual that obviously could take up where Ernie had left off, John Ribble, and Frank Weber, who might be considered an "outsider" that could bring us some new ideas in the expanding field of family practice and community medicine. Frank had excellent relationships with the practitioners throughout the State. Possibly it was for this reason that he received the appointment.

Frank died suddenly five months later from a myocardial infarction. His death was tragic and unexpected even though he was known to have diabetes. I had the privilege of writing a poem that became his obituary. It is etched in stone, and is prominently placed on the Frank Weber Plaza between the UT Medical School and the Texas Medical Center Library. I drop by to read the words from time to time to remind myself what an individual can accomplish in a short period of time through selfless effort and will. This poem and stone will far outlive any memory of my contributions to this Medical Center, but hopefully not Frank's. Fortunately John Ribble was still with us, and was appointed Dean, not in desperation, but because he was highly qualified and the obvious choice.

Just as things were settling down, John Ribble called the departmental chairs to his conference room one afternoon, and reached up to a library shelf and pulled down and distributed a copy of a proposed revision of the by-laws that governed the relationships between the Medical School and the Hermann Hospital. That seemed at the time to be innocent enough since it was probably time to tidy up the original document. As we scanned its contents, we realized that the School's sole right to appoint the chiefs of service at Hermann Hospital was placed in jeopardy. We all assumed that our position as chairman of a department at the Medical School automatically conferred the title of chief of service at the Hermann Hospital. The change whereby the Hermann Hospital would play a stronger role in the designation of the chief of service was apparently a request from the Board of Trustees of the Hermann Hospital. John Ribble made it clear to us that he concurred in this action, since he still had veto power over whoever was appointed. You could have heard a pin drop, but for only a few minutes, for then the chiefs said that this change in the by-laws was unacceptable. Dean Ribble thanked us for our attendance and the meeting but not the issue was over.

A few days later I had a visit in my office from three of the more senior chairmen of departments at the Medical School who wanted me to support a formal protest that implied if this change in by-laws were adopted, the signers would resign from being chief of service at the Hermann Hospital. I listened to their protestation and said that I would think about it. When they returned a few days later I said that I could not sign such an ultimatum since I worked for the University of Texas, and that whatever action was to be taken had to be initiated by the Dean, the President of the Health Science Center, or possibly even at the level of the Chancellor of the University of Texas, or the President of the Board of Regents. I again steadfastly refused to be part of what I now considered to be a cabal. I however was obviously concerned that if the sole authority for the chief's appointment was left to the Board of Trustees, our educational programs could be placed in serious jeopardy.

The ultimatum was delivered as planned the next morning and as could be predicted, by early afternoon all of the clinical chiefs that signed the ultimatum (11 out of 14) were relieved not only of their chief of service designation at the Hermann Hospital, but also of their chairmanships at the University of Texas Medical School in Houston. Robert Creasy, the chairman of the department of obstetrics and gynecology, arranged an urgent meeting of the faculty so they could be informed of what had happened. Dean Ribble was in attendance with his director of communications since he realized that the press would have a field day with this state of affairs. The faculty was enraged, because they felt that they were abandoned by their leadership. I was asked why I did not sign the ultimatum, and I explained my position as stated previously.

Shortly after the meeting I was off to of all places, Fiji. By the time I returned to Houston I learned that several chairs immediately repented, but several did not. The chairs of medicine, pediatrics, psychiatry, anesthesiology, and pathology officially resigned. I do not know where President Bulger stood on the issue, but did know that the Board of Regents did not like negative publicity displayed in the press. Not long after this incident, President Bulger resigned and John Ribble was named the interim President of the Health Science Center. This was appropriate since he was the only one who understood why this unfortunate chain of events occurred in the first place.

Life went on rather well during this period of healing, while filling the vacant chairs, and recruiting a new president. John Ribble did very well handling the administrative load of a president and a dean at the same time. He had a very seasoned administrative staff in the dean's office, and the remaining chairs and the faculty closed ranks to assure that the teaching mission was in no way compromised.

Within a year or so, everything returned to normal, at least for the department of surgery until one day I received a telephone call from a distinguished dean in Philadelphia who asked if I would call a very respected CEO of a well known medical center there who I also knew through our work together at the American Association of Medical Colleges. After a few calls, we finally connected, and the gentleman asked what I thought about Stan Dudrick, the former chair of the department of Surgery at the University of Texas in Houston. I told him that we were friends, and that I held him in very high regard. He then inquired about his administrative skills, and I replied that some of his faculty who were still in the department felt that he had an unusual style of management, and I left it at that. The conversation was rather innocuous. I had nothing specific to say. Fortunately my conversation was monitored by my administrative assistant, Karen Winkler, who affirmed that I had made no negative comments about Stan.

A few hours after we terminated our conversation, I received a call from dean Ribble asking me why I was saying negative things about Dudrick. I told him of my conversation with the administrator in Philadelphia. I was thoroughly confused since somehow I was led to believe that my phone call had been recorded, and that the call to Ribble had been from one of the Regents. The next day, the CEO of the Hermann Hospital, Harry Neer, stopped me in the hall of the Hospital and reassured me that everything would be alright. I asked what was wrong and he explained that Stan Dudrick was returning to Houston, and wanted to establish a clinical program at the Hermann Hospital to treat coronary artery disease by total parenteral nutrition. I was aware of his preliminary results of a clinical trial based on this notion which he had presented to the American Surgical Association. His presentation was not greeted with enthusiasm. I was less pessimistic. I thought that Stan and his group might be on to something since they also planned to develop a nutritious anti-atherosclerotic supplement called a "Moon Cookie" in recognition of the Houston Oiler's star quarterback at the time.

A few days later I was asked to visit with Ed Guinn, Dudrick's long time laboratory manager who was to set me straight as to what was going on. Harry Neer and I met with Ed Guinn in my office and he informed us that what they wanted to do was to have Stan be the chief of surgery at the Hermann Hospital, but in title only. Ed made it clear that they did not want Stan to run the day to day operations of the department of surgery in the Hospital or The Medical School. I was amazed, confused, concerned, and scared because I sensed something sinister in my visitor's remarks. I pointed out to him that my friend Stan Dudrick could identify himself as chief of surgery at the Hermann Hospital if the Hospital and the Medical School wanted it that way. I pointed out that my title was surgeon-in-chief. Stan Dudrick and I were close friends and remained so, and have never talked about these early days of his clinical trial. I helped his group carry out their study in whatever way I could. The idea came and went like the tropical storms we get in Houston every few years, and I have yet to taste a "Moon Cookie".

What I did not appreciate at the time was that the Hermann Hospital was close to declaring bankruptcy, and the contracts involved with the Dudrick research to cure coronary artery stenosis was worth millions of dollars. Recently, twenty-plus years later, I learned that the clinical trial of altering coronary arterial stenosis conducted over a two year period was terminated because of some undisclosed irregularities according to the Houston Chronicle. Rumor has it that Atheromine (the generic name of the concoction studied) did not show efficacy. Apparently enough money was transferred to the Hermann Hospital to avert bankruptcy.

Several lawsuits were filed, but the outcome was not revealed. Harry Neer was fired, but for another reason. He allegedly had made a large purchase of fajita meat that was still on the cows grazing in the field rather than cooling in the freezer. This instigated a whole new series of investigations called "fajita gate". Looking back at a series of administrative missteps makes me wonder now how we were able to make significant progress in developing a first rate medical center in spite of our administrative shortcomings. Harry Neer and his relatively small but effective administrative staff during a relatively short period of time in the early 1990s made important contributions towards this end, in spite of "fajita gate".

I have mentioned only a few of the many challenges that I faced as the chairperson of a department of surgery of a new medical school and surgeon-in-chief of its major teaching hospital. My previous administrative challenges at Utah had taught me not to panic, but to patiently try to find out what the real problem was that led to contentious issues amongst the leadership. It has not been uncommon for outstanding candidates for academic surgery to tell me that they were not interested in being a chair of surgery because of administrative burdens that I have described. My response is always the same. It is part of the job that if done effectively will enhance your own personal contributions to academic surgery. I have enjoyed helping to solve the long range and day to day problems that confront being a departmental chair in an evolving first rate medical community. It has been a privilege to stay on and observe how my ideas have directly and indirectly influenced the development of UT-Health in Houston, the current brand name for the enterprise.

CHAPTER 24

THE SURGICAL RESIDENCY AT UT HOUSTON

I always felt that one of the main responsibilities of a chairman of a department of surgery in a medical school was to preserve the integrity and improve the quality of the residency in general surgery. It therefore came as quite a shock when early in my tenure as chair at UT-Houston (1983) I received a letter from the Residency Review Committee informing me that they were putting our residency in general surgery on probation. I wrote them a strong letter requesting more time to get the program straightened out, and they acquiesced. They left us alone for 4 years during which we had made major improvements in the program. Unfortunately the surgical landscape was changing. The Hermann Hospital was admitting more and more trauma victims, but the general surgical faculty was seeing less paying surgical elective cases. State support was dwindling. Our efforts to develop a UT service at the MD Anderson Hospital were unsuccessful. Dr. Charles Balch, the chairman of the division of surgery there, and a close friend and former resident from Alabama wanted to help us establish such a service, but was restricted by the rule that a chief resident and a fellow could not be on the same service. Dr. Balch was most generous however in providing excellent rotations for residents in lower years. The Lyndon Baines Johnson Hospital (a county/city hospital similar to the Ben Taub that was staffed by the Baylor School of Medicine) was at the time just on the drawing board. We assumed that we would be responsible for its staffing. This would solve our problem of case numbers and case mix. We were approved for 6 chief residents in our program but only had enough clinical material for 4. This also was at a point in the maturation of the Residency Review Committees that they wanted more oversight and control of the content of the program. Furthermore, they rightly pointed out that our residents needed to have an in-depth experience in upper and lower endoscopy.

I had not kept up with the times in terms of accountability of operative cases. Unfortunately we were still a year away from the LBJ Hospital solution. A few chief residents had less than the required number of operations to take the Boards. In addition we were deficient in developing a training experience in upper and lower endoscopy. This latter deficiency in retrospect surprises me since I was at Alabama when Hirschowitz was perfecting his flexible endoscope for examining the foregut, and the Japanese had perfected the flexible colonoscope. In fact, I had visited Shinya in New York, a pioneer in flexible colonoscopy and a surgeon, to see how he had organized his colorectal clinic to accommodate this new advance. To my surprise, one morning he performed 10 colonoscopies before we had Tea at 10:00 AM.

I wrongly felt at the time that the flexible scopes were for the gastroenterologists to use, and that the surgeons should be spending their time in the operating room treating gastrointestinal diseases that required their attention by a formal laparotomy. Clearly I needed to have help with the strengthening of the surgical residency by increasing the clinical load and instituting endoscopic training for surgical residents.

It was quite by chance that I ran into Dr. John Sawyers, chairman of the department of surgery at Vanderbilt at a surgical meeting and informed him of our dilemma. He told me that my old friend John Potts who had spent time with me in the laboratory in Utah

(1977) might be interested in returning to full time academia, and that he would be an excellent man for the job. John Potts was employed at the time by the Cleveland Clinic in Fort Lauderdale. I thought that it would be difficult to recruit him away from the good life, but to my surprise he was attracted to the job of being a program director of a distressed program. He joined us within a few months, and had the program off probation in 6 months. The program has received unconditional approval ever since, and is stronger now than at any other time in its history.

As mentioned earlier, John was not only an outstanding educator but also a superb surgeon. He quickly developed a very active practice in hepatobiliary and pancreatic surgery, and was well liked by the residents in spite of the fact that he demanded a high level of performance not only in the operating room but also in their logging in their operations. His leadership skills led to his being appointed Chief of Surgery at the LBJ Hospital. His commitment to graduate education led to his being designated Associate Dean for Graduate Education at UT-Houston. Within a few years he was elected to the Presidency of the Program Directors in Surgery Association, and shortly thereafter appointed to be a Director of the American Board of Surgery. More recently, John has accepted the position of Vice President for Surgical Education of the Accrediting Council for Graduate Medical Education (ACGME) in Chicago. John is a stellar example of being the right man for the right job at the right place at the right time. Thanks go to the late Dr. Rainey Williams of Oklahoma, Dr. John Sawyers at Vanderbilt in Nashville, and the late Dr. Dean Warren at Emory in Atlanta for training him. A special thanks to John Potts for his dedication to excellence in whatever he does. We wish him well in his new leadership position.

My involvement with the day to day activities of the residents had by my intent not been as intimate in Houston as in Utah. The reasons for this were two fold; I was less active clinically, and I was involved in a wide variety of national and international affairs in surgery. Dr. Thomas Miller, an outstanding academic surgeon was the program director of the general surgical residency when I arrived at UT Houston in 1983. He was doing an excellent job in managing the residency, and because of his success as a basic scientist, he was an ideal role model for an academically inclined residency program. The problems with the residency that led to our brief period of probation were not due to his management of the program, but more to my negligence in not adhering to the rules of the Residency Review Committee. Tom did not appear to be concerned when I recruited John Potts to get us straightened out. In fact I think that he was pleased. It was not long after John's arrival that Tom became Chairman at St. Louis University. He currently is the Chief of Surgery at the Richmond Veterans Administration Hospital.

As mentioned above, my research efforts were directed towards developing an NIH sponsored Trauma Research Center and a Training Program in Gastrointestinal Surgery and Nutrition. My collaborative work with Drs. Li and Weisbrodt on gallstone pathogenesis was consuming most of my bench research time. To say that I was over extended would be an understatement, but I felt that I was contributing to the academic energy of the department with these diverse research activities.

Many of our residents went elsewhere for their research experience. Several of our former residents are currently on our faculty (Eduardo Souchon, Charles (Chuck) Cox, James Cross, Emily Robinson, Ara Vaporcyian, Rosemary Kozar. Several others are on academic faculties elsewhere (Daniel Bethencourt, James Harrell, Bruce Kraemer, Wiley Souba (now Dean and Vice President for Health Affairs at Dartmouth), David Van Buren, Larry Gentiello, Janet Hoagland, Paula Termuhlen, Lisa Florence, Richard Hostetter, Stephen Yang, and Rafik Ghobrial). I feel certain that this list is not complete, and that there are others working in academic environments. These only include those that I got to know quite well before I quit operating in 2005.

Enough cannot be said of the quality of the surgical faculty during this period of time. James (Red) Duke personifies the consummate surgical educator. He does it all well, and is an inspiration for all of us as regards dedication to quality of patient care. Bruce MacFadyen, Ronald Fischer, Brian Rowlands, and Thomas Miller were already on board when I arrived. This mature faculty helped to develop the Surgical Laboratories, the International Scholar Program, The Trauma Research Center, and an excellent Medical Student and Resident teaching program. I have already mentioned the contributions of some of the faculty that joined us after my assuming the Chair (Richard Andrassy, Ronald Merrill, Stewart Myers, and John Potts).

The recruitment of Dr. Lawrence Reed to the Trauma Division was also timely, because the volume of injured patients being brought to our emergency room by the air ambulance program (Life Flight) pioneered by Dr, Duke was growing exponentially. Larry brought a great deal of experience and enthusiasm to the trauma team. He set about studying the effects of cooling on the coagulation properties of the blood of patients who entered our emergency room in hemorrhagic shock. His work progressed very rapidly, as did his reputation in the trauma field, so it was not long before he also was recruited away to run his own service elsewhere.

Dr. Bruce Houtchens was added to the trauma team soon after his arrival in 1983. As mentioned earlier, Bruce came to Houston from Utah with me for the purposes of setting up a space medicine program with NASA. Bruce had excellent credentials in this area since he also was an aeronautical engineer, an astronaut, and a jet fighter pilot. He was quite experienced in air transport of the injured. Bruce also had a special interest in Tele-Medicine, and was instrumental in the development of an interactive therapeutic program in Russia after the Chernobyl nuclear explosion. He married Maria, a Russian medical student and returned to Salt Lake City so that she could go to the University of Utah Medical

School to obtain a United States Medical Degree. Bruce resumed his prior work with the Salt Lake Veteran's Administration Hospital.

Bruce and I had spent a lot of time hiking the mountains along the Wasatch Front. We had also climbed Mount Rainier together several years earlier without difficulty. He was the strongest climber on our rope of 8. His association with the Astronaut Core required that he stay fully conditioned. It therefore was with surprise and shock when I received a call from his wife Maria that Bruce had just died on a rather modest hike with her on Black Mountain. The climb is basically a gradual ascent along a ridge line, with a steeper trail to the summit. Maria decided to wait for Bruce under the shade of a tree. Bruce went up to the summit and returned without incident. He told Maria that he was tired and wanted to rest for a few minutes before starting the descent. He appeared to fall asleep. She became alarmed when he could not easily be aroused. When he did wake up, she recognized that he did not look well. She told him not to move, and started running down the trail, hoping to flag a biker, since this was a popular trail for mountain bikers.

Unfortunately there were no bikers on the trail that afternoon, and it took her about a half an hour to get to a phone and dial 911. By the time Life Flight reached Bruce he was dead. Autopsy revealed that he had total occlusion of a dominant right coronary artery. This was a surprising finding since Bruce had just undergone a very thorough physical evaluation in preparation for his testing a special thermal wet suit for the marines. An additional tragic paradox was that the tree that he died under was within sight of the helipad at the University of Utah that housed the helicopter and the first responders. A further poetic coincidence was that the Life Flight Program that retrieved him had been established by Bruce shortly after he had joined our Faculty at Utah in 1983.

Bruce had a formal military funeral, complete with a ten gun salute and a folding and the giving of the flag to Maria, now his widow with the responsibility of bringing up their son as a single mom. I was asked to give his eulogy, which I did with tears streaming from my eyes. He was not only a former student, colleague, and friend, but also very much a part of our family. I was very impressed with the testimony of many of his former patients. They all described the very personalized attention that he gave to their lives during their time of need, not only for their surgical problem, but for the difficulties that they were facing in life. I had the privilege several months later to carry his ashes up Black Mountain to deposit them within and around the tree where he died.

Maria completed her studies at the University of Utah Medical School with distinction even with the burden of grief, and responsibilities of caring for their son Stepan. Maria was fortunate in having had the help of her Grandmother, Meri, who had come to the United States a few years earlier to help with the management of the home while Maria attended Medical School. It was quite natural for Maria to choose to become a neurologist, since Meri, her grandmother, and her father and mother had also been neurologists in Russia. Following her residency in neurology at Harvard, she has stayed on to pursue an academic practice in Boston. Stepan, Bruce and Maria's son, is now a young adult attending college "back East", hoping to follow in the footsteps of his father by becoming an engineer.

The availability of the Trauma Research Center and the LBJ Hospital at UT-Houston provided the resources for recruiting to our program individuals who wanted to pursue a career in academic traumatology and critical care. When I interviewed Dr. Christine Coconour, MD for joining our faculty, we both recognized that Houston was the place for her to begin her academic career. She had just finished her residency at Case Western Reserve in Cleveland, and was seeking a position that would allow her to have protected time to pursue her interest in the pathobiology of traumatic injury. It was not long before she assumed the leadership role in the Shock/Trauma Critical Care Unit. Unfortunately for us, her talents became appreciated nationally and she was recruited to a similar role at the University of California in Davis several years ago. Chris is as successful as she was in Houston in her new job, and enjoys the California lifestyle. Inger and I plan to visit with her in her newly built home in the near future in order to check out her pizza oven and selection of fine California wines.

I was fortunate in the early years in Houston to recruit one of our own residents, Dr. David Thompson, to become the nucleus for an emerging liver and pancreatic surgical unit. He was a natural for this area because of his superior judgment and technical skills. After a few years he decided to become a colorectal surgeon, which he did. Following his completion of his fellowship in this discipline, he joined a prominent colorectal group in Houston directed by Randy Bailey, the group that had trained him. I was disappointed that I could not hold David's interest in the liver/pancreas area, but realize now that my motives may have been selfish. It is possible that I was looking for someone to baby sit the increasing number of patients with necrotizing pancreatitis that I was attracting to my practice. It was also my good fortune to have had the opportunity to also train his wife, Gretchen Zimmerman, who has been a very active general surgeon in the Houston area for many years. I am very proud that both of them in successive years have been elected to the coveted position of Presidents of the Houston Surgical Society in recognition of their important contributions to the care of patients in our area.

In closing out this portion of my professional life at UT-Houston, I must comment on the burst of growth in hepatic and pancreatic surgery that followed the recruitment of Dr. Craig Fischer, MD. Craig was the son of Dr. Ronald Fischer, a world class trauma surgeon, who recently died after a prolonged cardiovascular related illness. Craig was recruited by Dr. Andrassy after he completed his residency at the Massachusetts General Hospital in Boston and a formal hepato-pancreatic-biliary fellowship in Edinburgh, UK, under the tutelage of Professor James Garden.

These are two premier programs in this discipline. Craig came to us well prepared to go to work in a demanding specialty. I recognized during Craig's early years with us as a medical student at UT-Houston that he had the energy and drive to propel him into the upper ranks of surgery. I therefore took a special interest to see how he would manage to develop this emerging surgical specialty in the shadow of the large and established program at the MD Anderson Cancer Center. I was pleased to observe that his practice grew very rapidly, as did his reputation for being a very bold and aggressive liver-pancreatic surgeon. I use to enjoy watching him very safely and efficiently take a Chief Resident through a Whipple Procedure. I was disappointed when he told me one day that he was moving his practice to the Methodist Hospital but delighted for my long standing surgical colleague and dear friend Dr. Barbara Bass, who recognizes talent when she sees it.

CHAPTER 25

TIME TO "PACK IT UP"

The administrative turmoil at the Medical School for the first five years of my tenure in the Chair was in a word troublesome but not an impediment to program development. The laboratory was immune to administrative happenings, and the students were protected from the internal problems of the Health Science Center. Unfortunately, the same could not be said of the Hermann Hospital. Unfortunately the Hospital and the School were enmeshed in the web of a poor payer mix and collection rate. The Hermann Hospital was downsizing in order to try to balance their books, and the Medical School was increasing in size in order to meet their educational commitment.

The leadership of both the Medical School and the Hermann Hospital had changed at least three times during my first few years in Houston. Mr. David Miles, the departmental management officer and I were having difficulty each year in the second half of my time in the chair (1988-1994) balancing the departmental budget. We managed to sneak by each year with imaginative book keeping, and utilizing as best we could the money received from the state, endowments, grants and contracts, and most importantly an assessment fee (tax) from the transplant immunology laboratory. I was never successful in getting the Hermann to pay us up front or even for that matter after the fact for caring for the patients that they brought in through the emergency room or off the helicopter by Life Flight.

The constant change in the Faculty Compensation Plan (higher taxation) was a chronic problem that was hard to deal with. The faculty wanted to know why they only received about 20 cents for each dollar of service they rendered. The fact that this related to the inefficiency of the central billing system and the poor payer mix of their practice did not satisfy their concerns. I thought that the best way to handle this dilemma was to have a departmental review, which I requested. This was in about year 8 of my tenure.

The Dean appointed a review committee which initiated a process of interviewing each faculty member including myself. Dr. Walter Kirkendal a former chair of medicine at UT-Houston before my time was the chairman of the committee. I thought that he was joking when he requested that I provide for him in a few weeks an internal review of the department. A few days later Dr. Barry Kahan, the director of the division of transplantation and immunology approached me in the parking lot and asked me "what are they after you for". He stated that he had just had a very negative interview with the surgical chairman recruitment committee. I said that I did not know, but that I did observe that some of my strongest detractors were on the committee. About a month later, I received a call from my administrative assistant Karen Winkler who wanted to alert me that I had just received by registered mail from the Dean who was away in Florida a very negative review. I asked her to FAX me a copy, and I would try to get my response back to his office before he returned from Florida. As I recall, there were 44 negative comments, 43 of which I easily answered or rebutted. The 44th was more difficult to answer since it involved our general surgical residency being on probation. I did inform the Dean that I was in the process of taking care of this through the recruitment of John Potts.

Fortunately, someone had put in the review that I was getting old (64), and probably not up to the job of providing leadership for the department. I pointed this remark out to the Dean, and stated that I thought that it was inappropriate in view of the current legislation on age discrimination. Fortunately the two external reviewers, George Sheldon, Chairman of Surgery in North Carolina, and Samuel Wells, Chairman of Surgery from Washington University in St. Louis', both at the top of the leadership ladder in American Surgery serving as an external review committee thought that I was doing a good job under the circumstances.

The cash flow problem that I had each year at budget time was more difficult to solve. I used the federal government approach of deficit spending. The Dean did not like my approach, but I had few options because of the poor collections and high taxation. The Hermann wanted me to develop departments of orthopedics and neurosurgery in the near future. These both were divisions of the department surgery at the time, and both were striving for departmental status. I requested from the CEO of the Hermann Hospital at the time that he provide me, in writing, IOUs for a million dollars each for establishing these units. Much to my surprise he did, which I handed over to the Dean. Unfortunately, the Dean was never able to cash in on them since they were signed by Harry Neer, the victim of "Fajita Gate".

The third million that we owed I requested be paid by the Medical School Faculty Development Plan (MSRDP). I thought that the Plan owed us this since the surgical department had paid more than its fair share of the move of the clinical practices of the Medical School Research Development Plan (MSRDP) from the Hermann Professional Building to the Hilton Hotel Annex, which was a money loser. In fact after a few years of "red ink", the MSRDP moved back to their original location. Mr. Miles and I worked hard on a Recovery Plan, which I had to review with the Director of the Plan. He was not sympathetic to our solution and thought that we should tighten our belts by reducing expenses and the size of some of our highly academic educational components. I thought that it was unfair to put me at odds with my colleagues when other solutions were available at the institutional level.

Shortly thereafter, in the fall of 1994 I told Dean Ribble that I would like to turn over the chair to someone else. Fortunately, Dr. Richard Andrassy, the director of the division of pediatric surgery, and a very capable administrator and educator was appointed as the interim chair, and shortly thereafter the permanent chairman of the department. This solved the problem rather quickly. Apparently the Hermann paid off the IOUs, and the issue went away.

For my part, I was most pleased with the progress that we had made in establishing a base for further development of a first rate department of surgery. This was what I agreed to with the late Dean Knobil upon my recruitment from Salt Lake City to Houston in 1983. He unfortunately died of pancreatic cancer on April 13th, 2000. I owe Ernie a deep debt of gratitude for his bringing me to Houston, and providing me with the resources to develop an academic department of surgery. His commitment to the academic purpose was a stimulus for all of us to try harder, and a key figure in the success that the medical school now enjoys.

CHAPTER 26

LIFE AS A PROFESSOR OF SURGERY (1994 TO PRESENT)

As described earlier, I had already initiated plans to return to Utah in 1996 because of Maja's illness. I was mindful however of my continued involvement in several ongoing projects that could only or best be carried out in Houston. Dr. Andrassy solved the leadership of the Trauma Research Center problem by the recruitment of Dr. Frederick Moore from Denver, a seasoned, card carrying academic trauma surgeon. I was delighted with his recruitment since it offered me an opportunity to focus on my own project within the Center. I surmised that the completion of this project would take about five years. I was still active clinically in the surgical treatment of morbid obesity, and had the privilege of being identified as the Denton A. Cooley Professor of Surgery. Dr. Andrassy encouraged me to develop a multidisciplinary approach to the treatment of morbid obesity, and I was happy to do so. This gave me an opportunity to utilize the experience I had gained in directing the multidisciplinary activities of the Trauma Research Center.

Chance again went my way as regards my research interest in the mucosal barrier of the gut. Dr. Gilbert Castro PhD, one of the basic science investigators in the TRC, and an expert on gut immunology was attracted to a major administrative position elsewhere. This left his long time collaborator Yael Harari available for whoever in the Center had a need for her professional skill set. I and my team had worked with Yael before and we appreciated her intellect and knowledge of the mucosal immune system, an area that we were interested in pursuing. She was very gifted in experimental design and execution. Norm Weisbrodt, my long time collaborator was her mentor as well as mine.

We had clearly shown in the rat that a variety of traumatic stressors (low bile duct ligation pancreatitis, morphine administration, intestinal ischemia/reperfusion, and endotoxemia) would slow intestinal motility, and lead to overgrowth of bacteria in the gut of rodents. We knew from the work of others that the mucosal surface was relatively non responsive to endotoxin produced by E. coli, a bacteria that inhabits the lumen of the gut in large numbers. E. coli however is a prolific producer of another toxic molecule, formyl-methionyl, lysyl, phenylalanine (FMLP). It had been previously shown by others that FMLP was a potent stimulus for activation and release of inflammatory mediators from leukocytes.

We became keenly interested into whether FMLP through its effect on the mucosal immune system might be involved in the break in the mucosal barrier that we observed in models of intestinal stasis and bacterial overgrowth. We were specifically interested in the role of the mast cell in this process. Normal and pharmacologically induced mastocytotic (too many mast cells) rats, and mutant mastocytopenic (too few mast cells) mice were studied for this purpose. Isolated segments of ileum without a blood supply or lymphatic drainage were placed into Ussing Chambers, and their mucosal surfaces were exposed to various concentrations of FMLP. The rats with increased numbers of mast cells in their submucosa showed a time dependent marked increase in the movement of Dextran 4000 from the surface of the ileal mucosa compared to the normal controls, while the mast cell deficient mice were unresponsive to similar doses of FMLP compared to normal controls Mast cells thus appeared to play a very important role in the activation of the mucosal immune system. Unfortunately Yael was unable to go the next step to pursue the mediators involved in the mast cell/FMLP response because of a rapid progression of her recurrent ovarian cancer. These experiments ended with her passing. Norm and I both closed our labs at about the same time in 2004. I became busy developing our program in obesity, and Norm became the chair of the Department of Cell Biology and Integrative Physiology. We are most appreciative of the contributions that Yael had made during her many years with us at UT-Houston. We dearly miss her presence amongst us.

There are four additional projects of personal interest that I should mention that were conducted during the late 1980's and early 1990's. The first, and of greatest interest to me was the establishment of a digital computer based program to educate patients and their caregivers on how a surgical disease is diagnosed and treated. This was done in collaboration with Julie and Phillip Mitchell, both experts in how to build such a computer based platform. We called it The Texas Virtual Clinic. It can still be accessed most easily by employing the Google search engine. What we did was to discuss several surgical topics such as appendicitis, reflux esophagitis, peptic ulcer, gallstone disease, colon cancer, and surgery for morbid obesity. The presentation utilized coached volunteers to simulate the patient interaction, and included radiographic imaging studies and operative schematics and video clips. Our intent was to make the site interactive so that patients and their physicians could actually query us, but we ran out of time and money to continue the project.

A second area of interest was the development of weekly rounds in surgical ethics. This was conducted by Dr. Stanley Reiser MD, a world class Ethicist, who in fact was a full time member of the Department of Surgery. Dr. Ronald Merrell played an active role in assisting Stan and I in this endeavor. The Rounds were attended by medical and nursing students, residents, surgical faculty, nurses, clergy, and hospital administrators. The format was an in-depth discussion of case material on my surgical service. I can assure you that we had plenty of material to discuss which included such issues as informed consent, patient autonomy, care of the financially destitute, the impaired physician etc. The forum provided the students an opportunity to express their points of view on these varied and often contentious topics. We transcribed the discussions and collected enough material for a book to be titled "Surgery at the Scalpel's Edge". Unfortunately we were a decade or more ahead of the times, and could not find a publisher. Furthermore, the Dean informed me that the students had complained to him that the Rounds were a waste of their time. I recognized from this encounter that there was a lot of work to do if we wanted to produce a well informed and empathetic work force in medicine. Possibly now is the right time to try again, with the high interest in patient safety and health care reform.

A third area of interest, surgical innovation, was enhanced by my serving as a medical consultant to the Woodland's Venture Capital Company. My learning curve was very steep in this activity since I am by birth a poor boy who prefers playing in nature rather than in the stock market. I quickly learned that if you wanted to make money as a venture capitalist, you had to be smart, bold, and understand the intimate nature of the relationship of rate of burn to the ultimate success and payout of sponsored products. Bringing new ideas to the care of patients depends critically on the entrepreneurs who enjoy the thrill of success in this high risk game, since the development of a new therapy is very expensive.

A fourth unique area of experience was the production of a monthly television show for Medical World Television. The show was initially filmed in Hollywood in a large theater were Gun smoke, a popular television show was filmed. I also had the opportunity of filming interviews on separate occasions at our studios in Houston with two well known pioneers in Cardiovascular and Thoracic Surgery, Drs. Michael DeBakey and Denton Cooley. To some surgeons, these activities would appear not be part of the responsibilities of a chairman of surgery. While it is true that it did take me away from the operating room, patients and students, it did provide an opportunity to project our Department into the community. More importantly, it was fun for me and those that participated in the activity.

CHAPTER 27

A MULTIDISCIPLINARY PROGRAM IN OBESITY

As described earlier, we had already previously developed a multidisciplinary obesity study group at the University of Utah. The situation there was quite different than in Houston because we had accumulated a large number of morbidly obese patients that had been operated upon (about 500), and had the resources and the need for a large number of professionals to help both follow and study them. With pun intended, this was a huge undertaking. When I moved to Houston in 1983, I had decided to perform only one obesity operation each week, and devote my practice to hepatobiliary and pancreatic surgery. I had only performed 186 small pouch gastric by-passes by the standard open technique between January of 1987 (the date when I switched from horizontal stapling to the by-pass) to March of 2002 (the time when we decided to organize the UT Houston Obesity Surgical Center). There were no deaths, and only six serious complications. I had performed over 800 gastric procedures for weight control since 1975 without a death or a law suit. It occurred to me that this would be an appropriate time for me to stop operating on obese people and shift my interest to the pathogenesis of the disease.

In January of 200l, we initiated a monthly meeting which we called The UT-Houston Bariatric Surgical Study Group. The participants were a mixture of basic and clinical scientists who were interested in various aspects of obesity and its complications. It was truly multidisciplinary. What was missing was an adequate flow of patients to support the clinical studies that the group was proposing. This was solved when Dr. Andrassy hired three general surgeons with an interest in developing and broadening the field of minimally invasive surgery. The first to come on board was Steve Glorsky, a well trained general and critical care surgeon. He was a great help in increasing the volume of cases flowing into the Bariatric Surgical Center for open surgery. The laparoscopic gastric bypass was still in the discussion phase. Connie Pollard, a Nurse Practitioner with a strong interest in caring for patients with morbid obesity was indispensible to getting the program underway. Connie has been the lynchpin in developing the management systems for patient recruitment, data acquisition, and follow-up for the hundreds of patients that ultimately have been treated by our group in subsequent years.

Dr. Bruce MacFadyen, Dr. Steve Glorsky, and I started to ramp up the number of patients seen in the Obesity Clinic from 3 to about 6 per week, with the idea of increasing the numbers so that we could develop a data base and a sufficient population to enter into clinical trials. At about this time we were joined by two fully trained laparoscopic surgeons, Terry Scarborough and Erik Wilson. Both were very interested in doing laparoscopic gastric by-passes. They spent time with the UT Obesity Group in Dallas to learn the technique of laparoscopic gastric bypass. Bruce, Steve. and I had already established a flow of patients for open by-pass surgery who were quite obese. Many were out of the range recommended by the Dallas Group for gastric by-pass. Their mean body mass index (BMI) was about 50. With some encouragement and careful selection, Erik and Terry started to do a few cases a week and they learned that it was much easier to do these patients by the laparoscopic technique rather than open. The patients did much better as regards a rapid postoperative recovery. The length of stay decreased from 5 to about 2 days.

This helped in obtaining support from the insurance companies, and obviously was appealing to the patients Their results were excellent, and within a year or so, they were performing 4 to 6 cases a week, a volume sufficient for initiating clinical studies.

The days of open gastric by-pass were over, and just in time (2003) for me to give up operating. I was 75 years of age, and somewhat symptomatic from paroxysmal auricular fibrillation from a sick sinus syndrome. Maja, my wife, was incapacitated by multiple strokes from her cardiac disease, but was well cared for in our home in Utah. I felt that it was unethical for me to burden my patients with my own infirmities and personal responsibilities.

CHAPTER 28

THE VAGARIES OF AURICULAR FIBRILLATION

I had been lucky and enjoyed relatively good health into my early eighties, but I did have a few events that in retrospect could have been serious. The first was sort of scary. It occurred about thirty five years ago when I was skiing at a resort in Utah called Snowbird. I was skiing pretty fast, and when I arrived at the bottom of the slope, I could not recall the last half of a rather difficult part of the hill. I had descended 3000 feet from 11,300 to 8,300 feet in about 8 minutes. I sat down in the tram room where there were chairs at that time, and the tram driver asked me if I was going up with him. I said, no, and drove down the mountain with no further problems.

A few years later I had another event while spring skiing with John Hunter, a chief resident in surgery at Utah at the time, and currently the chairman of surgery at Oregon. While climbing Tri-Peaks at Snowbird with our skis on our shoulder at about 11, 500 feet I became weak. John took my skis, but not my pulse and within a few minutes my strength returned. I likely had an episode of auricular fibrillation (irregular heart rate). We skied down the backside of the mountain without further problems. I was living in Houston at the time, and we ascribed the event to me being a wimp from the flat lands.

The third event was definitive. A year or so later, while hiking the 10th Mountain Division Trail with Ben Eiseman of Denver and Hank Bahnson of Pittsburg, I woke up at 2 in the morning with the bed shaking while sleeping in the McNamara Hut. I went over to Hank, he took my pulse, and said that I was fibrillating. He gave me a pill, and rolled over and went back to sleep. My fibrillation ceased in about 15 minutes, and that was the beginning of many episodes of fibrillation above 10,000 feet. Possibly these episodes of fibrillation is the reason why a few years later I was found to have an up going right big toe (a positive Babinski sign) when my right sole was vigorously scratched by Dr Philip Johnson, my primary care physician. I have not had an imaging study of my head, but I suspect that my brain looks like Swiss cheese from throwing clots to my brain those many years ago before I was placed on chronic anticoagulation.

My episodes of fibrillation became more frequent and symptomatic over the next several years. I finally sought help from Dr. Ward Cassells, an outstanding cardiologist recently deceased. He tried to control my rhythm with anti-arrhythmic drugs, with immediate but not long lasting success. Finally it was decided to ablate the electrical circuits in my right heart since my predominant rhythm consisted of runs of auricular flutter. This reduced the symptoms but not the auricular fibrillation, so Dr. Anne Dougherty, my cardiologist, inserted a pacemaker and placed me on beta blockade and chronic anticoagulation. The two chamber pacemaker has worked fine for 8 years, and was replaced two years ago (2011) without event.

Maja was less fortunate with her chronic auricular fibrillation. She was managed primarily by beta blockade and the anti-coagulant Coumadin. As mentioned earlier, she had survived six strokes, a major automobile accident, a heart attack, and a bleed into her brain which almost killed her. Her life was saved by an heroic operation to drain a blood clot from the right side of her brain. The circumstances of this latter event requires an ethical comment.

Maja had made it very clear in her will that she did not want to have any futile medical or surgical interventions, especially those that required endotracheal intubation. When she became unconscious from her inter-cranial bleed, she was transported to the Alta View Hospital which was close to our home in Sandy. I was on an airplane travelling from Houston and was not available to help with the decision to have Maja intubated for assisted ventilation and transport by helicopter to the University of Utah Hospital for a higher level of care. This decision was made by my daughter Jane in spite of the negative advice of the staff at Alta View.

I learned of all this as my plane landed at the Salt Lake Airport where Jane's husband Bruce Bjorklund greeted me at the gate with the words "Mom is dead"! She was being transported as we spoke to University Hospital. We arrived at the Hospital just as the Life Flight helicopter was landing. She in fact looked very ill even on the respirator. Fortunately within a short period of time, she was seen by Dr. MacDonald, a highly respected and aggressive neurosurgeon. He told me that her only chance for survival was to immediately evacuate the clot from her brain. He was not very optimistic as to the outcome. I said go for it, and he did. She survived the operation, but did not wake up for five days. When she did, she rapidly recovered without obvious loss of her previous functional state which could at best be described as only fair.

Surprisingly, she recovered well enough to be cared for at home after a period of time in a rehabilitation center. Several months later she suffered another stroke that resulted in almost total paralysis. We again chose to take care of her at home. We were able to find three experienced care givers who rendered excellent around the clock nursing and personal care under the supervision of our daughter Jane. Maja was fed through a tube that had been placed in her stomach through the abdominal wall. Her urine was managed by in and out urethral catheterization. I assumed the role of her physician. My main concern was whether she was comfortable and free of pain. She could only say yes and no in Swedish. I often asked her whether she agreed with our treatment and she always answered in the affirmative, except once, to which I ascribed as to her having a bad day. She seemed to enjoy her days listening to opera, watching television, and following the family chatter. She especially enjoyed visiting with her grandson Donald who in some way seemed to be able to communicate with her better than I. I never felt that she wanted us to withdraw life sustaining care, but as her husband and her physician, that might have been wishful thinking.

On the morning after Christmas of 2004, as I was getting ready to go skiing, Rosa, her week-end caregiver, called me to come quick. Maja was slumped over in her wheelchair, without a pulse. We placed her on the floor and initiated gentle cardiopulmonary resuscitation. Rosa dialed 911. The response team was there in several minutes. She in essence had died gently in my arms of natural causes at the age of 89 in the presence of her family on December 26th, 2004. Maja's death had changed the equation of my own life. I now was classified as a widower, and experienced the loneliness that follows forty wonderful years of togetherness. For some reason it never occurred to me that I now was free to roam the mountains of the earth.

CHAPTER 29

RETIREMENT IN PLACE

I had planned to return to Salt Lake City within a few years after retiring from the chair of surgery at UT Houston. Shortly after retiring, I was invited to Salt Lake to interview for a job as chief of surgery at the Salt Lake VA. An attractive feature of this job was their intent to develop a private service for veterans who were currently seeking their care at other private hospitals. I did not realize that this was a contentious issue with the private surgeons and hospitals within the area. I to this day do not know for sure if that was the case. It did explain why one of the senior surgeons who I had trained took me aside and told me that the University Group did not want me to come back to Salt Lake and steal their cases. I was flattered to have them think at age 66 that I could in fact compete with them. I told the VA that I was not available at that time, and that was the end of it.

Each year since then, I have weighed the pros and cons of retiring to my home in Sandy Utah in order to spend more time with Maja when she was alive, and to hike and ski the Wasatch Mountains. I also wanted to continue to attend surgical meetings here and abroad as long as I could travel, but it seemed that my work in Houston was never quite done.

I had two additional informal job offers. The most attractive was from my long standing friend and colleague Larry Carey who at the time was chairman of the department of surgery at the University of South Florida in Tampa. I was quite tempted to take the job. It entailed being the chief of surgery at the St. Petersburg Veterans Administration Hospital which was ideally located on a beautiful sandy beach. The staff at the VA Hospital was very happy with their situation, and emphasized that if I would take the job, they would gladly do all of the surgery and patient care with a resident staff that was part of the training program based at the Tampa General Hospital. I was tempted to pursue the matter further but was not prepared to become a beach boy.

My dear friend Gil Diethelm, then chairman of surgery at the University of Alabama also offered me the opportunity to become the Director of the John Kirlin Ambulatory Center at the University of Alabama. I also was very tempted to take this unique opportunity but declined since I still had not completed several ongoing projects at UT-Houston

Soon after retirement from the chair I became involved with the curriculum of the 3rd year medical students. My involvement went up a notch when our educational coordinator married and moved elsewhere. My interest went beyond the didactic and practical aspects of the course, but related more towards trying to understand how we could solve two problems; the sheer expense of obtaining a medical education, and the problem of attracting students to primary care. As I began to work more intimately with the students at the 3rd and 4th year level, I realized that they were well informed, empathetic care givers, and enthusiastic learners. My disappointment was that they as a group did not know what they wanted to do when they graduated from medical school. I use to facetiously ask, hold up your hand if you want to be a doctor. Almost all hands would go up. I then would ask how many planned to be a family or general medical physician. Only a few hands would be raised. Pediatrics did a bit better. As time went on, I noticed that more and more students wanted to go into ophthalmology, radiology, obstetrics and gynecology, a surgical specialty, or emergency medicine. It was only in the 2cd decade of the 21st century that the light bulb went off. Times were changing. There was less commitment to working long hours with relatively low compensation. Their educational loans were pushing 150,000 dollars, and they wanted to have a life outside of medicine. The opportunity to work in a group practice, or do shift work was appealing to both their life style and their need to pay off their debt.

One advantage of having mountain hiking as a hobby is that you have several uninterrupted hours to both work up a sweat and think. On each of the 20 or 30 hikes I made each year in the Wasatch Mountains, I would spend some time thinking about how to make the interval of medical education shorter, and the practice of primary care medicine more attractive. I was quite aware of the fact that most of the countries abroad have a six year medical curriculum after what we would consider a high school education on steroids. I was quite familiar with this model, since we spent several weeks each year at our summer home in Sweden. I also had the privilege of working in several of their medical centers, and was impressed with the quality of the physicians that their system produces.

It became apparent to me that we could shorten the 11 years required for the training of general practitioners by three years in the following way. Preparation for medical school could be reduced to two years and medical school could be reorganized into two segments, each three years in length. The first three years would provide a basic science/transitional clinical experience, and the last three years could be spent learning and applying the principles of clinical practice. In this 2 (premedical), by 3 (basic medical), by 3 (clinical medical) modeI, the student would enter a highly integrated and streamlined program in which the first two years would be involved with liberal arts (humanities, arts, literature, philosophy, ethics, mathematics, and physics) to prepare them for medical school. They then would enter medical school and pursue

3 years of basic medical studies to include introductory courses in medical practice to be carried out with simulation technology. The final three years would consist of rotations on the various clinical services (medicine, family practice, surgery, pediatrics, psychiatry neurology, and obstetrics and gynecology). In order to make this cost neutral, we could develop a way to compensate the students for the services that they render to patients in the clinics and hospitals during their last three years of medical school. In this way, the MD Degree would mean that at graduation they would be a physician capable of practicing general medicine or family practice, possibly with no debt.

Those that chose to enter a specialty could do so after the end of the 6 year medical curriculum. This means that those desiring specialty training would have to become more personally responsible for financing further training. I discussed this idea many years ago with one of our Deans who dismissed it as not being practical. It however seems to me to be an idea whose time has come. I plan to continue to participate in a small group setting with 3rd year medical students in order to keep my finger to the wind, and ear to the ground. Maybe by the time I complete these musings, the problem of medical student indebtedness will be solved. It is a serious impediment to the attracting students into family practice and general medicine. I would estimate that funds derived from the state, the teaching hospitals, and the various communities where students would render care would make it possible for students to pursue such a medical curriculum in 8 years after high school, free of debt. This issue is clearly worth pursuing further both locally and nationally.

CHAPTER 30

RESEARCH AND AN INNOVATED APPROACH TO WEIGHT MANAGEMENT

The University of Texas Houston Bariatric Surgical Program has grown very rapidly since Terry Scarborough and Erik Wilson established their practice in minimally invasive surgery. Their development of a multi-hospital training program in this discipline (The Minimally Invasive Surgeons of Texas—MIST) has allowed the rapid diffusion of this technology in our geographic area. It did not take long for the community to recognize that these were the surgeons to refer their obese patients to for a relatively safe and successful operation. The MIST Group also recognized the need for a team approach and an extensive screening and educational program for the large number of referrals that were soon to come to them. The Hermann Hospital was very helpful in procuring large operating tables, beds, wheelchairs and other equipment for the care of very large patients. They also provided space and equipment for educational seminars, and ambulatory services. Of equal importance was the provision of nurses and a separate nursing unit for their care. They allowed me to continue to participate in the organizational phase of establishing a multidisciplinary Bariatric Surgical Center which included clerks, nurses, nutritionists, a statistician, a bariatrician(a non surgeon physician caregiver), and a nurse coordinator, Connie Pollard PA. This all took a few years, but it was worth it in terms of providing a well cared for cohort of patients for the studies to be described below.

At the time that the UT Houston Bariatric Surgery Study Group was considering what to study, two Requests for Applications were announced by the NIH, one from the National Heart and Lung Institute entitled Mechanisms of Obesity-Associated Cardiovascular Disease and the other from the National Institute of Digestive Disease. The latter was concerned with outcomes from the surgical treatment of obesity.

Dr. Taegtmeyer (a world class academic cardiologist) was successful in obtaining funding from the NIH National Heart and Lung Institute. The over arching hypothesis was that the excess glucose and lipids that circulate in the blood stream in obese subjects affects the contraction of cardiomyocytes and in turn the pumping action of the heart. The title of the Grant, **Glucolipotoxicity and Cardiac Dysfunction** was self explanatory. What they proposed to study was the effects of excessive nutrient molecules on the functional capacity of the heart in animals and humans. They proposed to study cafeteria fed and overfed normal and genetically modified diabetic rats. The metabolic adaptation and maladaptation of cardiac muscle was to be analyzed during conditions of metabolic stress.

Parallel studies were also to be carried out on obese subjects before and at intervals following gastric by-pass. Biopsies of the skeletal muscle of the anterior thigh were to serve as correlates of the cardiomyocytes studied in the animal preparations. Cardiac function in the normal and obese rats was to be determined by the well described Langendorf Chamber technique. Cardiac function was to be determined by echocardiography in obese patients prior to and at intervals following a small pouch gastric by-pass. Lipid deposition was found by histological examination in the cardiomyocytes of the fat rats, as well as in the skeletal muscle of the obese subjects. The obese subjects showed improvement in their cardiac function as they lost weight over time. Dr. Taegtmeyer was assisted in the human work by his Fellow, Dr. Joshua Leichman MD. The animal work was carried out by a postgraduate student Dr Martin Young PhD, and an MD/PhD student Chris Anderson. Two bariatric surgeons, Dr Terry Scarborough MD and Dr. Erik Wilson MD, performed the bariatric surgical procedures, the muscle biopsies, and the postoperative follow-up of the study subjects.

The second Request for Application was of more interest to me. It was a proposal to characterize the genetic profiles of morbidly obese subjects in an attempt to predict outcomes after bariatric surgery. Dr. Molly Bray PhD, a recognized expert in the field of molecular genetics was the Principle Investigator on the proposal. The Grant also included a proposal to specifically study circadian rhythms in obese humans, especially those with sleep apnea. Genetically modified diabetic obese rats were also to be studied in order to identify relevant genes that might contribute to sleep apnea. This grant was not sent for formal review by the NIH Study Section because of an insufficient number of study subjects, and a lack of a track record of the surgeons in pursuing studies of this type. The genetic aspects of obesity still remains a fertile field for investigation that remains poorly understood in the human. Unfortunately, mutations responsible for obesity in rodents is not easily translated to the disease of morbid obesity in man.

Dr. Martin Young PhD, and Richard Castriotta MD, the chairman of pulmonary medicine and director of the sleep center had already collaborated on a study of the effects of obesity on circadian rhythm in obese diabetic rats. Their component of the grant might best have been submitted as an ROI Grant since their proposal was directed at a specific life threatening complication of morbid obesity, sleep apnea. The unique features of this grant should be revisited and repackaged since a large number of patients now exist for such studies, and there are several surgeons now involved at UT-Houston in the treatment of morbid obesity who likely would be happy to collaborate with such excellent scientists. I have found over the years that basic scientists are very interested in collaborating with enthusiastic, technically proficient surgeons. They are usually not only interested in sharing their knowledge with clinicians, but they also enjoy seeing where their work fits into the pathogenesis and treatment of human disease.

The UT Surgical Obesity Center in Houston is currently thriving under the leadership of its Director, Professor Erik Wilson. In addition to participating in clinical trials to assess new technical advances in the field of robotics, its major thrust is to develop a better understanding of the relationship between obesity and glucose metabolism. There currently is a high level of interest in studying the role of the gut in the control of insulin release and utilization in obese subjects. The focus in our Center is on the role of the known incretin (insulin stimulating) gastrointestinal peptide, GLP-1, that is secreted by the L cells in the ileum. A human trial is currently underway with Dr. Bradley Snyder MD, a member of the UT component of MIST, as the Principle Investigator. He plans to assess the efficacy of an ileal transposition to the upper jejunum in the treatment of refractory diabetes in obese subjects who also will undergo a sleeve resection for their obesity. There is much work to be done, and hopefully those treating obesity will seize the moment since the obesity epidemic and its associated diabetes is still with us and increasing its penetration into our society.

I have also had the privilege of participating vicariously in assessing the role of vagal blockade on weight control in human subjects. My involvement is through my service on the Safety Monitoring Board of a Phase III trial being carried out by Enteromedics, a device company located in Minneapolis. The engineers in this company have developed a set of electrodes that can easily and safely be placed around the vagi at the esophageal gastric junction laparoscopically. These electrodes are connected to a subcutaneously positioned electrical pulse generator that can be programmed to deliver an electric current to intermittently block the flow of current down (or up) the vagus nerve. They have shown in animal work (pigs) in collaboration with KT Tweeden PhD, a veterinarian working at Enteromedics, that when the vagus nerves are electronically blocked, there is cessation of pancreatic secretion, and change in feeding behavior accompanied by slowing of weight gain (a surrogate for weight loss) in the young pig.

Enteromedics is carrying out a well designed randomized controlled trial involving about 300 subjects in order to establish the safety and efficacy of the vagal inhibitory approach to weight control. The study thus far has shown that the technique has few adverse side effects, and no mortality. While long term efficacy shows promise, it has not yet been conclusively achieved. With the encouragement of the FDA, the trial is being repeated with a much improved electrical system that does not require the wearing of an external electrode for current delivery. The control subjects in this study have placement of a pulse generator without implantation of electrodes so that no current is delivered in contrast to the study subjects. If efficacy is established, the safety profile of this approach may make it an acceptable form of surgical therapy for patients with an intermediate stage of obesity.

My interest in this approach relates to its safety, since the integrity of the gastrointestinal tract is not violated. Recently, in a separate cohort observational study carried out in Adelaide, Australia by Dr. James Tooley (an International Surgical Group colleague and long time friend) and his associates observed that glucose metabolism in diabetics also responds to intermittent vagal blockade. If the results hold up, and a controlled clinical trial is organized, I plan to ask our bariatric surgical group to participate.

The existing popular surgical approaches that include gastric by-pass, gastric sleeve, duodenal switch, and even the less intrusive gastric band have risks and complications that may negate their benefits over the span of a lifetime. What is needed is a safe, simple, almost risk free approach that can be used as an adjunct early in the weight gain phase of the obesity. Also required is a concerted effort to understand and correct the dysfunctional genes that lead to excessive fatness in the first place. Emphasis on diet modification (even at the commercial level) and daily exercise should of course also be encouraged.

At the time of this writing (2013) the obesity epidemic is far from reaching its asymptote. Possibly we should just accept the fact that being fat is the new normal. Clearly there are some obese individuals that lead a nearly disease free life, but not many. The problem of human obesity and its sequela is real, not only in terms of the burden of disease, but also human suffering. Our best hope is that improving our educational system will allow the young to avoid this burden, and lead the way to a cure. This clearly is a disease where "An Ounce of Prevention is Worth a Pound of Cure", the title of my AOA Lecture at the University of Virginia in 1980.

CHAPTER 31

PROFESSIONAL EXTRA-CURRICULAR ACTIVITIES

Academic Surgeons lead a very privileged life. Not only do they have the opportunity to generate knowledge and pass it on to their students, and apply it to their patients, but they also have a chance to exchange their ideas with their colleagues both at home and abroad. My first exposure to the professional and personal value of attending a surgical meeting was early in my residency at Cornell when my chief, Frank Glenn, invited me to a meeting of the Southern Surgical Association (1960). The meeting was at a lovely resort in South Florida called the Boca Raton. He allowed me to make closing remarks on a paper we had written together. Trying to answer several questions posed by some of the "giants" in surgery at the time was an exciting experience for me. The topic was how to manage the stones and sepsis that occurs in patients with intra-hepatic strictures and cystic dilation of their bile ducts. The cases reported were treated in the 1950s and even the old timers did not have much experience with this problem. Since I was always studying and writing up cases, and pursuing problems in the laboratory, I had an opportunity to attend the meetings of several societies during my early years in surgery. What I noticed was that the meetings were always held in very nice places. Furthermore, the social aspects of the meetings sometimes exceeded their scientific quality.

My move to the Cardiovascular Research Institute at the University of California in San Francisco to work with Dr. Richard Durbin, PhD in 1963, introduced me to the world of the basic scientist. I soon learned that their meetings were in places more conducive to a serious scientific discourse. I especially liked the spring Carmel Meetings of the Western Society of Clinical Investigation, and the annual meetings of the Biophysical Society and the American Physiological Society. I at first had trouble understanding what they were talking about, but in time, I learned the language of the scientist. It was fun to meet people who I knew and respected as only a name in the literature. The meetings were very much alive, made so by the large number of medical students and graduate students that would attend to present their work. My learning curve was very steep at the time.

I can vividly recall one evening at a meeting in Carmel when Jim Freston, the Chief of Gastroenterology at the time in Utah, suggested that we move the evening party up the road from Carmel to one of our favorite hang outs at North Beach in San Francisco. During the course of the evening we began to dance with the medical students that were with us. I was fortunate in winning one of the "stop-dances" with a very attractive female fourth year student working in the GI lab. After we sat down, the band leader came over to our table and congratulated us. He sat down and put his arm around me and related that he had been into the Emergency Room at the San Francisco General Hospital and was being treated for pubic lice ("crabs"). He wanted to know if he had received the right medication. I told him as I quickly backed away that that was not an area of my expertise. I was waiting the rest of the evening for the itching to start but fortunately it didn't. Apparently he was well treated. A few weeks later, at a student party with my wife, my dancing partner at the San Francisco party came up and recounted how much fun it was to dance with me a few weeks ago. I had forgotten to tell my wife about this extracurricular activity, and had some explaining to do. My wife was not concerned because she knew from years of experience that I was student friendly and harmless.

As I review my Curriculum Vitae, I see that I am truly a joiner, and an active participant in both clinical and scientific organizations that deal with a variety of topics. I served on the Board of Surgery, NIH Study Sections Medicine A and Surgery B (Surgeons and Engineers), VA Review Boards, Internal and External Departmental Reviews, Editorial Review Boards, Visiting Professorships, the Council of Academic Societies as Chairman, the Executive Committee of the American Association of Medical Colleges, the Liaison Committee on Graduate Medical Education, and the Association of Surgical Chairman as its Chairman. The details of my involvement in these organizations are contained in my Curriculum Vitae (cf Appendix). My purpose in these activities was to be involved in the breadth of medical education from the undergraduate preparation to the production of a first rate surgeon.

While I enjoyed the interaction with my colleagues in these activities it was at the cost of being away from the office, the lab, the operating room, the students, and the patients. It also meant that I was away from home a great deal of the time. I made a conscious effort to include my family in the progress of my work and travel related activities. They even today remember the names of many of my students and faculty colleagues, and tell me that they did not mind my missing some of the high points in their own lives. I prefer the culture of today, where the training programs and faculty work loads are much more conducive to a normal family life. This more leisurely approach to learning however is probably less effective in providing continuity of surgical care. I don't think that the 80 hour work week of today would have made much of a difference in my work habit since so much of my 120 hour work week was spent in the library, the lab, and the record room.

My involvement in specific health and science related organizations mirrors for the most part my interests at the time. For example, early in my career I most frequently attended the annual meetings of the American Physiological Association, the Biophysical Society, the American Gastroenterological Association, the Society of University of Surgeons, the Society of Surgery of the Alimentary Tract, and the American Pancreatic Association. As I progressed in my own career, I started to regularly attend the American College of Surgeons meetings, with an emphasis on the Surgical Biology Club III and the Surgical Forum. These meetings were very important to me, since it was where I met my colleagues and their residents and mine were able to mingle and exchange ideas. I also increased my participation in the American College of Surgeons, the Society of Clinical Surgery, the Western Surgical Association, and the Southern Surgical Association. I also placed a priority on participating in the Houston Surgical Society (monthly) and the Texas Surgical Society (bi-annually) for the past 30 years since they provided an opportunity to relate to my colleagues that practice in the area.

I had the opportunity to serve on the Medical Student Advisory Committee, and subsequently the Research Committee of the American College of Surgeons. My election to the American Surgical Association was a special treat since it provided for me an opportunity to later sponsor my trainees for membership, and to occasionally present our work to this distinguished group of surgeons. It was an unexpected privilege to serve one year as its Second Vice President. I am especially proud that Dr. F. Layton (Bing) Rikkers, one of my initial academic trainees at Utah, is President of the American Surgical Association this year (2013). He richly deserves this Honor in view of his contributions to academic surgery through his research, teaching, clinical care, and role as Editor of the Annals of Surgery for 17 years. He made an outstanding surgical journal even more prestigious.

Most of my organizational work has been spent with colleagues interested in the diseases of the gastrointestinal tract such as the American Gastroenterologic Association (Governing

Board-1985-1988), the American Pancreatic Association (President—1979), the Gastrointestinal Section of the American Physiologic Society, and the Society for Surgery of the Alimentary Tract (President—1981). These meetings provided an opportunity to keep up with my major fields of interest in the laboratory. I consider this experience to represent the equivalent of a chronic sabbatical. While my involvement in several different areas of gastrointestinal physiology was stimulating, it likely made my contributions to specific areas less effective. However, it did keep a lot of residents productive in the laboratory. In addition, it provided for my students and me a better understanding of the causes and treatment of obesity, peptic ulcer, liver, gallbladder, biliary tract, and pancreatic disease. This experience also offered a background for our publication of a major text, **The Surgical Treatment of Digestive Disease** (2 editions), a **Yearbook of Digestive Disease** that was about 50% surgical (15 Editions), and a surgical journal co-edited with Dr. Larry Carey entitled **Surgical Gastroenterology**. We proposed to the Society of Surgery of the Alimentary Tract that this be adopted as their Journal in 1994, but we were ahead of our time. They turned us down. Several years later when the time was right the Society developed a very successful journal entitled The Journal of Gastrointestinal Surgery co-edited by John Cameron and Keith Kelly. The time to recognize that surgical therapy of complex diseases of the digestive system required a well focused period of training in the area had finally arrived.

The organizational work that provided me the most satisfaction was working with international surgical groups. Early on, I was very much involved with the Collegium Internationale Chirurgie Digestivae (President US Section 1975-77) which has morphed into the International Society of Digestive Surgery, and the Societe Internationale De Chirurgie (President, US Section, 1992-1994, and Honorary Member—2005). I was delighted when the latter adopted the name International Surgical Society and moved its home office to Berne, Switzerland. Under the Direction of Dr.

Martin Allgower as its Secretary General, The ISS developed a biennial meeting schedule. Gradually other international surgical societies joined together to form what was ultimately called International Surgical Week. The participating societies (the ISS/SIC Integrated Societies) include the International Association of Endocrine Surgeons (IAES), the International Association for Trauma Surgery and Intensive Care (IATSIC), the International Association for Surgical Metabolism and Nutrition (IASMEN), Breast Surgery International (BSI), and the International Society for Digestive Surgery ((ISDS). The development of International Surgical Week would not have happened if it was not for the organizational skills of Martin Allgower and his team in Berne (gnomes as he called them). Victor Berchi was a key member of the organization, and is the person to go to to get things done. Felix Harder did a superb job as Secretary General following Martin's retirement. The meeting in Adelaide in 2011 was attended by over 1000 registrants and participants. The recent meeting (2013) in Helsinki held in conjunction with the Finnish Surgical Society attracted over 2000 participants. The scientific quality of the program was superb, only to be outdone by the social program. I am obviously very proud to be an Honorary Member of the host organization, the ISS.

I also was involved in the early phases of the development of the International Biliary Association and had the honor of being its President in 1985. Several years later, it morphed into the International Hepato-Pancreatico-Biliary Association. Dr. Henry Pitt has been a prime mover in getting this organization off the ground after the International Biliary Association succumbed to the challenge of the younger generation of liver and pancreatic surgeons who wanted a broader, less eliteist club. I remained silent during this debate, since I had my hands full dealing with problems at home, but I have been very pleased with the outcome.

My favorite organization over the years has been the International Surgical Group (ISG) which I had the privilege of joining in 1980.

It was organized shortly after World War II by surgeons from Northern Europe, Scandinavia, North America and Canada. I attended my first meeting in Heidelberg Germany where I met Fritz Lindner, one of the founding members. I also met his successor to the Chair in Heidelberg, Professor Christian Herfarth. Christian and I have become close friends over the years. He invited me to the German Surgical Society Meeting in Berlin when he was the President. It was the first year that they had allowed East Germans into Membership. I was impressed with the marked difference between the quality of the work and its presentation by members from the Institutions from the East and the West. I was even more impressed when the ISG visited the Technical University in Dresden (formerly in the Eastern Bloc) twenty years later, hosted by Dr. Hans-Detlev Saeger, the Chairman of the Department of Surgery there. The East had caught up with the West in the quality of their educational programs in surgery. The unification of East and West was a bold, challenging, and very successful experiment.

The ISG has remained small by intent, consisting of only 60 active members divided in thirds between Europe and Scandinavia, North America and Canada, and Others (Australia, China, Japan, and South America). It has many loyal Senior Members, most of whom have never missed a meeting. I have only missed two, and that was when Maja was very ill. My daughter Jane accompanied me on four meetings after Maja became bedridden. They included a visit to Oxford, Edinburgh, Stockholm, and the Fjords of Norway. Each meeting was associated with extremely informative sightseeing tours. Jane and I took a lot of pictures on these trips, much to the delight of Maja during the last years of her life.

Inger has accompanied me to several of the most recent meetings to include London, Boston, Louisville, Zurich, Adelaide, Hong Kong, and most recently Ghent and Bruge Belgium (August. 2013). As I view the membership list I note that several of my former associates, Bing Rikkers, John Hunter, Norbert Senninger, and

Julio Coelho are members. In fact there are several other surgical lineages represented in the organization which suggests that the Group might best be characterized as a surgical family. The warmth of the gathering suggests that is what it is.

Inger and I treated ourselves to a visit to Moscow and St. Petersburg on the way to Helsinki and then to Ghent. We both were impressed with the esthetic beauty, cleanliness, and cultural maturity of both cities. But what impressed us most was the friendly demeanor of the people. From the brochures we had read we anticipated that there would be a nefarious character behind every street lamp, but such was not the case. I purposely had left my Delta/American Express Card at home just in case my pocket was picked, which it wasn't. You can imagine how angry I was when I returned home to find that my card had been hit for over a thousand dollars by someone in Houston. We will be less cautious the next time we go to Russia, but not when we go again to Venice, where my pocket was picked by a 6 year old boy. How embarrassing!

CHAPTER 32

SOME INTERESTING FOREIGN VISITS

My interest in surgery in the United States and throughout many parts of the world has provided me with some unique experiences. One that immediately comes to mind occurred when I visited a hospital in Jinan, China. It was just a few months after the end of the Cultural Revolution (1976). As we approached the landing strip in Beijing in the middle of the night, Maja and I noted that there were no lights on the landing strip. The airport was almost completely dark. When the plane came to a stop, the stewardess advised us not to deplane until we were picked up by our hosts. Two individuals appeared who I recognized by their name tags as our hosts. They told us to follow them but not to talk. We took a short taxi ride to the railroad station, which was also without lighting. They instructed us to sit down and wait for them, but not to move or talk. We could hear many people sitting around us, whispering in Chinese. Our hosts returned and without speaking a word motioned for us to follow them, which we did. We boarded a train and entered a sleeping car. Our hosts now said, welcome, and you can now talk. Maja and I were not at all frightened by this experience, and in a way expected that things would be different in China after such a dark period in its history.

I was invited the next day to give a few lectures to a very large audience of physicians who had ridden their bicycles for miles to hear my presentation. There were almost no cars on the roads at that time, but thousands of bicycles. I was surprised how intent they were on listening to my lecture, since I do not believe most of them understood English. I then was taken on rounds to meet a middle aged lady who had gallstones. While bile duct stones were common in this area, multiple stones in the gallbladder were uncommon. She had had typical episodes of biliary colic for many years. I learned that she had been in the hospital for about a month, supposedly to wait for me to remove her gallbladder. I informed her through an interpreter what we planned to do the next day. She was most appreciative, and not at all concerned. The only imaging study was an oral cholecystogram which revealed multiple small stones. The hospital was well constructed, and had about 400 beds, and 10 operating rooms. It had been built by the Germans at the turn of the century.

The next day I was taken to an operating room that looked familiar except for one detail, it was hot, and the windows were open. One of the circulating nurses had been assigned the job of swatting the flies. The scrubbing of hands, gloving, gowning, prepping and draping of the patient was also very similar to what we do in the States. I had a tall, very attractive scrub nurse who understood English well enough to follow my requests. She passed me the scalpel very carefully, and when I asked for a clamp to control the few bleeders from the wound edge, she vigorously slapped the clamp into the palm of my outstretched hand like a pro. I quickly entered the abdomen through a right upper quadrant incision, explored the abdomen by gentle palpation, and then examined the under surface of the liver where the gallbladder was supposed to be, but the gallbladder was nowhere to be seen. There were a lot of ohs and ahs from the large audience that had gathered around the table. I began to sweat because of the heat and the absence of the gallbladder. Fortunately they had assigned a nurse to wipe my brow. As I examined the undersurface of segment

IV of the liver, I saw a cleft which I pried open and found a small shrunken gallbladder, which I teased out of its lair, eliciting again a lot of ohs and ahs from the gallery. I was able to safely dissect the gallbladder down to a small common bile duct, and remove the gallbladder without event. There was no capacity for an operative cholangiogram. I visited with her the next day, and she was without pain and enjoying an uncomplicated recovery.

We looked in on two major surgical procedures that I vividly remember. The first was a man who was lying on his stomach on the operating table with a long incision in his back. I inquired what was going on and the surgeon explained that the man had symptomatic disc disease, but they could not indentify an abnormality. They only had a plain film of the thoraco-lumbar spine. I did not make a comment, and we moved on to the next room. There I found a man lying on his right side with a long incision in his left chest. He was awake, his pain being controlled by acupuncture. I was told that he was having a Heller myotomy (division of the circular muscles at the lower end of the esophagus). There was a single anterior-posterior view of the barium filled esophagus hanging on the wall. They did not have the capacity for performing esophageal manometry. I again made no comment. It was obvious that the Cultural Revolution had slowed down their pace of adopting technology that was readily available in hospitals of comparable size in the United States. I was impressed with how quickly the Chinese have caught up with the rest of the world in the utilization of both diagnostic and therapeutic technology. On subsequent visits, I was also impressed with how successfully they have applied the principles of capitalism in their daily life. The thousands of bicycles have been replaced by an equal number of cars, many of them Mercedes.

We had two very interesting experiences on this trip. The first involved a visit from Beijing to the Great Wall. We were picked up by a car driven by a very tall Chinese woman who spoke little English. She took us directly to the Wall where we spent a few hours walking on the path on the top and then returned to Beijing. I noticed as we rode along a stream next to a residential district that we were driving through a military reservation that displayed a large number of tanks. Shortly thereafter, the taxi was waved down by a group of soldiers. I was impressed with how young they looked, as they waved their guns at us. They seemed to be interested in Maja's blond hair. We were asked for our passports, but we refused to give them to them and requested that we be taken to the American Consulate. Our taxi driver advised against this, and said for us to give her our passports, and that she would straighten things out. She was escorted to an old fashion crank telephone, and after two hours of talking, returned with our passports and we were allowed to proceed to Beijing. We never did get an explanation of why it took so long to get clearance. Probably we were lucky that we were not detained longer. I noticed that the soldiers were afraid of our large taxi driver as she talked sternly to them, raising her voice and her hands.

The most interesting part of the visit occurred when we visited the birthplace of Confucius. As we were walking through the gardens, our host said that we must rest. We really did not feel tired but followed our hosts' instruction to sit down in a small room within a guest house nearby. We then heard a rather loud discussion outside our window in Chinese, but we did not know what was being said in such a heated manner. In about an hour, our hosts returned, and one said not to worry, that the police chief was his brother- in- law. The issue was very serious; we had not obtained permission to visit the site. Fortunately the close relationship between the police chief and our host got us off the hook.

The remainder of our trip was relatively uneventful. We were treated like royalty on our last evening by attending a going away party at the Peking Duck Restaurant. Maja almost fainted when they brought out the duck fully prepared but not yet cooked and asked if she wanted the eyes when served, a Chinese delicacy.

We were presented with numerous gifts, one of which was a bottle of their very strong alcoholic drink. Fortunately for me it was packed in Maja's suitcase, since it broke at some point on our way to Sweden.

One of my more memorable trips to the East was when I was invited to be a guest of the Japanese Surgical Society. Professor Sato, chairman of the department of surgery at Tohoku University in Sendai was its president. When I stepped off the bullet train in Sendai, I spotted a very attractive young lady with a sign with my name on it. I walked up to her, gave her a hug, and said "I am Professor Moody". She backed away and said "I am married to an orthopedic surgeon". I responded, "that is okay, I am married to a Swedish artist". Her assignment was never to let me out of her sight. She taxied me around to the meeting place. I only had to give two lectures, and was not expected to stay for the other papers since they were in Japanese. We had a marvelous two days visiting traditional restaurants in the area, a spa for a swim and massage, and a shopping tour to buy a camera. Maja was quite envious when I showed her the pictures of my visit, and she insisted that she accompany me on future visits.

We visited Sendai several years later during which we attended a dinner at the largest geisha house in Sendai, said to be owned by Professor Maki, a very famous Japanese surgeon. Maja was the only female in attendance. At the end of the meal, our host told her how tired she looked, and that he had made arrangements for her to return to our hotel. Maja said that she felt fine, but sensed that she was obliged to leave, realizing that the party was just beginning. She was right. I had broken open the sake keg at the 1st party, and the meal, with a performance by the geisha girls (who also were the waitresses) represented the 2cd party. After Maja had left, I was ushered out of the hall and driven to a very elegant restaurant for the 3rd party where my associates were greeted by the girls that had just entertained and waited on us. As I walked into the restaurant I was greeted by a lovely Malaysian looking older lady who told me that she was the teacher for the geisha, and my host for the evening. She gave me a very detailed description of the training and the life of a geisha which had a lot to do with a classical education and little to do with sex. I excused myself from the 3rd party, and returned to my hotel wondering how to tell Maja that it was an innocent, beautiful evening.

There is an additional Japanese story that I must tell since it is so unique. On returning from a Visiting Professorship in Northern Honshu, Maja and I were extended the privilege of staying in Emperor Hirohito's summer home on Crater Lake. We were greeted by the staff of six, and treated as if we were the President of the United States and his wife. What I learned was that only one foreign couple a year had the privilege of staying there. I invited my host, a Professor of Surgery to join us for dinner but he refused, since it would be improper. He missed a fantastic seven course dinner. Maja and I strolled around the grounds after dinner. The views were spectacular. We then decided to take a bath, but changed our minds when we encountered the smallest bath tub we had ever seen.

We had one additional brush with Japanese Royalty, and that was when Prince Ahito and his wife awarded me a Distinguished Achievement Award from the International College of Surgeons at its meeting in Kyoto. It has been a great treat to have had the opportunity to visit Japan so many times since my first visit over sixty years ago. I had an opportunity to reciprocate their hospitality when we hosted the International Biliary Association Annual Meeting in Houston (1985). Many Japanese surgeons attended, and enjoyed riding an artificial bull at a rodeo we arranged for the occasion. They enjoyed the ride so much that they ended up with sore butts for several days. Inger and I had the opportunity to visit Yokohama a few years ago, and paid a visit to Sapporo where I first lived over 65 year ago at the pleasure of the United States Army. We were impressed with the remarkable sports facilities that they had developed for the 2002 Winter Olympics.

There are several other foreign visits that provided interesting experiences that I will describe briefly. During my Internship at the New York Hospital in 1956, I was asked to accompany a patient with end stage cancer who had a tracheostomy and needed medical care during his airline flight back to his home in Peru. This required a twenty-four hour flight on a propeller driven plane; jets had yet to be developed for civilian travel. I was not made aware of the fact that the patient was a political VIP. When we landed in Peru, several very large men boarded the plane and said that they would take care of my patient. They covered his tracheostomy against my protestations, and loaded the patient into an ambulance. I jumped in a taxi, and followed the ambulance to the hospital only to learn that the patient I had cared for was pronounced dead on arrival. I was told that I was no longer needed and to return to the United States as planned, which I did, without the two hundred dollars that I was suppose to receive on delivery of the patient. Living in New York City for a few years provided for me the insight to know that I was in a potentially dangerous political situation. Fortunately I had a round trip ticket which I used after a few days of wandering the streets of Lima. I was impressed with the fact that the poor people in Lima lived on the hills with beautiful views of the ocean and surrounding hills. Unfortunately they had to go up and down them for food and water.

I have subsequently had an opportunity to visit several other countries in South America. One of the most memorable was a visit to Buenos Aries, Argentina just after the conclusion of the Falkans War. Shortly after arriving at my hotel, I went for a jog to see the beautiful monuments that lined many of the broad boulevards. There was a large, very silent and somber crowd standing around one of the monuments. I asked a man who I could hear spoke English with a German accent what was going on. He was surprised that I did not know that people were disappearing in large numbers for reasons that at that time were not known. He also informed me that it was not a topic of conversation. I, with Inger, have recently visited Buenos Aries again, and found the answer. We were saddened to see under the buttress of a bridge that connects the extensive freeway system that surrounds this lovely city a large number of photographs and other momentos of those who had disappeared during what was called the "silent revolution". Apparently over a number of years an oppressive political group had been kidnapping and killing the opposition and burying them at sea. Our visits to Brazil were also taken with the admonition, be careful.

I had the opportunity to visit South Africa before and after the Mandela emancipation that did away with suppression of the black population under apartheid. My first visit was with the world renowned liver surgeon, Dr. Leslie Blumgart, MD. We visited the medical schools there, lecturing on topics of our choice, and having a good time in the evenings sampling wonderful wines and hospitality. I learned during the visit that Les was originally from South Africa and was a practicing dentist before going to medical school and becoming a liver surgeon. We both were impressed with the quality of the educational programs at these institutions. As I recall, there were 8 medical schools. One appeared to have only black students, and a mixture of black and white professors. I was impressed with the level of instruction and learning. The surgical faculty had a major interest in the treatment of thyroid disease. I had never before or since seen such a large number and variety of patients with thyroid disease. Making rounds was a great learning experience for me and I hope for the staff as I commented on how we would treat these diseases in the States. My prolonged and broad training in general surgery in the States under Frank Glenn, John Beal, Bjorn Thorbjarnarson, and Henry Mannix at the New York Hospital served me well in this situation.

I also enjoyed my visits to the transplant center in Johannesburg that had been established by Bertie Myberg, the hepatobiliary unit specializing in treatment of portal hypertension directed by John Terblanche at the Groote Schur Hospital in Cape town, and the comprehensive trauma program organized by Lynn Baker in Durban. On a subsequent visit to South Africa in 2005, I was impressed with the remarkable changes that occurred in the appearance of the countryside after the scrapping of apartheid. The shanty towns were disappearing at a rapid rate, being replaced by very attractive small homes. I was advised not to go downtown alone in Durban, and only by a specified route. This made me feel somewhat intimidated, and I wondered if possibly the transition from apartheid since my last visit there may have had some unanticipated negative consequences. It is my understanding that the health care system is underfunded, and that the academically inclined are moving elsewhere. I hope that this is not the case because it was my impression that the conversion to an open democratic society was progressing quite well. It appears at this point that South Africa will avoid the fate of Zimbabwe, at least as long as Mandela and his spirit remains alive.

CHAPTER 33

THE SWEDISH CONNECTION

It may appear that Sweden has played a very important role in my personal and professional life and it has. As mentioned in Chapter 8, it was quite by chance that I met Maria (Maja) Charlotta Stolpe in 1964 at a going away party for Gunnar Wallin, a Swedish colleague of mine at the Cardiovascular Research Institute at the University of California in San Francisco. This chance meeting initiated a long term relationship not only with Maja, but also Gunnar and his wife Kickan. We have had the privilege of seeing them frequently over these many years since they have a summer home very close to ours in Sweden. In fact, Inger and I have recently (June-2013) had an opportunity to meet with them at their summer home in Holmedal and discussed at length past and recent times with them.

My love affair with Sweden continues today through my marriage by common consent (formal engagement) to Inger Margareta Ardern (family name Ekstrand). Inger came into my life not by chance but by circumstance. I met her and her husband to be at her father's house in Örebro Sweden about 46 years ago when Maja, the children, and I were visiting Sweden for the first time as a family. Inger's father was a close friend of Maja's. He would deposit money into Maja's Swedish bank account each month that she would send to him from her work in her beauty salon in San Francisco. She planned to use this money to support herself when she returned to Sweden upon retirement.

Inger had known Maja from the age of five. They had kept very close contact over the years. I was not formally in the loop until the summer of 2005 when we held a memorial service for Maja at a small church that we have at our summer home in Klässbol, Sweden. Inger had been invited to the Service, but the invitation had been slow in getting to her and she did not have time to arrange to attend. She sent a card, and I made contact a few months later, which led to my visiting her home in Macclesfield, England (just south of Manchester) for the purpose of viewing several pictures of Maja I had not seen before. We had a wonderful week-end together. In fact, I flew back two weeks later in the fall of 2005 and I realized that I wanted to spend the rest of my life with her. She had a similar reaction—call it love at first sight—although by that time we had known about each other for over 45 years.

We now have been together for over 8 years, and became formerly engaged on my 80th birthday on May 3rd, 2008. On that date (which was easy to remember) we committed ourselves to each other for the rest of our lives with a handshake. Neither of us felt that a civil or religious ceremony was necessary. I had proposed marriage to Inger several years earlier on a chairlift at Snowbird. Her answer was "maybe, some day". But for now, we see no need for this formality. Inger had four years of formal art classes, two in Sweden and two in England, before she became a mother, and full time homemaker. During her early adult life she read Law, Psychology, Sociology, and French. While caring for the needs of her own children, she provided care for young patients with severe disabilities. At one point in her career she worked as a graphic artist for several years. She is surprisingly well informed about medicine as the result of helping to do the graphic layout for several books that described the clinical outcomes from the trials of the anti-cancer drug Tomoxifen. I consider her to be an intellectual. She always trumps me when we discuss literature, music, geography, history, cross word puzzles or movies. She can best be characterized as a human dynamo, with insatiable curiosity and energy. In addition, she is a marvelous cook, homemaker, and companion.

Even though Inger has spent most of her adult life in England, she remains very much a Swede. She has two young adult children, Krister and Kim, both Swedish citizens still living at home in Macclesfield, England. She has two older children, a son, Yestin, living in England and a daughter Catrine, who lives with her French husband (and excellent chef) Gilbert Cavallaro and two young children Lucio and Mateo in the Cayman Islands. Inger has five grand-children, Elly (14), Ellis (10), Mateo (9), Lucio (7), Ellie(3). She tries to spend as much time with them as she can. We visit the family in the Caymans each year around Thanksgiving. Inger is as a devoted grandmother as she has been a devoted mother. It is wonderful to see how she relates to the youngsters. Her motherly instincts really are impressive.

Inger and I enjoy our summer home (Tomta) in Klässbol, Sweden, in a county called Värmland where Inger spent many enjoyable summers with her grandmother as a child. Klässbol is famous for its old nineteenth century mill called Linneväveriet which makes the linens for the King and Queen of Sweden and the table cloths for the Nobel Award Dinner held at the Town Hall in Stockholm each year. Our home is ideally located in western Sweden not far from the Norwegian border. Arvika, a medium sized town is about 10 miles away. It lies at the upper end of a large, long lake called Glafsfjorden. At its southern end the lake connects with the largest lake in Sweden called Vänern which provides through locks a passageway to the Atlantic Ocean. This was a favorite retreat for the Vikings after their travels as attested to by the large number of huge burial mounds in the area.

I met the King of Sweden on two occasions. The first was at the 500th Anniversary of Uppsala University in 1978. He had just delivered a superb speech on the responsibilities of the 1st world countries to help the 3rd world countries feed its people. At a reception held in the Värmland Union (a faculty club so to speak of my district) I noticed that the King was standing apart from the rest of the group chatting with the organizer of the conference. I turned to my host Lars Thoren, the chair of surgery at Uppsala, and said that I was going to say hello to the King. Before Lars could catch my arm, I had bounded over and introduced myself to him. I congratulated him on his talk, and told him that my wife was Swedish and that we had a summer home in Klässbol, Sweden. We had a short, very pleasant chat. When I returned to my group, Lars was quite upset with me. He sternly said "we don't do that here". My somewhat impolite response was that if that was the President of the United States, the entire group would be surrounding him and exchanging greetings. Lars took the comment as well intentioned, and we remained very close friends.

The King of Sweden and I met again a few years later in Houston on the occasion of the Celebration of the 350th anniversity of the presence of Sweden in the United States (Delaware was ruled at the time for about 40 years by Sweden). I was asked to arrange the visit for the King and Queen of Sweden to Houston, and was honored to do so. We organized a day at the Texas Medical Center to include a morning tour of the Baylor School of Medicine hosted by Dr. Michael DeBakey, a conference in the afternoon titled Biotechnology of the Brain hosted by me, and an evening of music sponsored by the University of Texas. I was able to attract two Swedish Nobel Laureates and several other distinguished scientists to present at the afternoon conference sponsored by the Health Science Center. Dr. Roger Bulger, then President of the Health Science Center approved $50,000 to help sponsor two Swedish opera stars, Birgit Nilsson, and Elizabeth Södertröm to put on a program at the opera house downtown. Unfortunately this was at the time that President Bulger stepped down from the

Presidency, and John Ribble, Dean of the Medical School became the interim President of the Campus.

John called me into his office one day and said, "bad news Frank, we do not have the funds to support the opera". He directed me to Dr. John McGovern, a very successful and generous allergist in town. I discussed with Dr. McGovern the details of the impending visit from the King and Queen of Sweden, and the need for $50,000 to make it a success. He was most cordial and expressed an interest in sponsoring the operatic event, with one condition, that he be awarded a Swedish Medal (unspecified). I thanked him for his generosity, and flew off to Sweden to visit with the organizer of the New Sweden Program. It was easy to track him down in Stockholm, since he was Vice-President of Handelsbanken, and was intrigued by the publicity that would be generated surrounding the event. He made a few phone calls and said that all had been arranged. He would have a medal struck for Dr. McGovern at the request of and to be given by the King. I asked him what the Medal would be called and he said something to the effect of "The Order of the Northern Star".

This worked, and everything moved forward with only minor glitches. I met Dr. DeBakey and the King midway between the Baylor School of Medicine and the University Of Texas Medical School. I greeted the King by saying "so nice to see you again". He nodded with a quizzical look on his face. We proceeded to the front of a fully packed conference hall. I introduced the King to the Presenters and as he sat down, his seat slipped forward (by design for comfort) and the King slipped to the floor. Fortunately it was a slow slide. He smiled and slid back into his chair. This energized the security forces. The King was not injured, and the conference proceeded as planned.

The evening at the Opera, which included a reception, dinner, and performance by the opera stars also went well. The singing was superb. John was very pleased with his medal. Twenty photographers from various papers were lined up to take a picture of the Queen, with the King on her left side and John McGovern on her right. Probably a hundred or so pictures were taken. As the photographers were leaving, John came up to me and pointed out in rather excited terms that the left side of his tuxedo coat was turned back on itself. I told him before we restaged the photo op, let us see what the pictures look like. I could see by the look on the Kings face that he had enough pictures for one night. As luck would have it, John had stood so close to the Queen that his disheveled tuxedo jacket did not show up in any of the pictures. New Sweden had a happy ending.

Inger and I have spent several weeks each summer at Tomta, in Klässbol Sweden since we first visited there in 2006. It is an idyllic place, at the end of a dirt road with its own lake called Sojourn by the locals, and small heavily forested mountain called Klättern. A nature preserve at the top of Klättern provides a spectacular panoramic view of the surrounding lakes and rolling hills. The view is especially beautiful at around 11 PM on a clear mid-summer night as the sun just dips below its furthermost shore. We plan to spend an increasing amount of time there during the summer in the years ahead, watching the swans move slowly across the lake, and the deer and occasional elk feeding in the fields. When we get there early enough in the summer, we hear the call of the cuckoo bird echoing in the hills. It truly is a very special place. Cranes often come early in the morning to feed on the extensive fields of grass and even the lawn around our home.

Inger is a delight to live with. Not only is she a remarkable homemaker and companion, but also displays a sensitivity and appreciation for the planet earth and all that sustains it. She cares deeply for the life and the world around us. Conservation of the natural resources is a daily concern for her, and she is totally committed to recycling and eating organic foods. She is especially committed to the welfare of animals. For example, she is so sensitive to "road kill" that she cries whenever we see it, and wants me to stop to see if we can help the unfortunate victim. Of course this would be a foolhardy and even potentially lethal reaction on Texas highways. Her interest in the arts and general knowledge of the world makes her opinions worthy of thought and adulation. Her Swedish heritage and living for many years in England have molded her social conscience to where she could truly be labeled a socialist in the best sense of the word. Our only points of contention relate to my never turning out the lights, closing the closet doors, or turning off the water when I brush my teeth. My love of meat (especially sausage), and distaste for drinking water, and eating fruits and nuts in only small amounts is also of concern to her. I definitely would be labeled brown by her standards. Fortunately she makes me adhere to her standards when we are together, which is the majority of the time. As you can tell by the tenor of my remarks, I love her dearly.

CHAPTER 34

SUMMING UP A PRIVILEGED LIFE

I am often asked when I plan to retire, and my standard answer is probably never, since I have not worked in the usual sense where I could not wait to be free from my assigned or assumed tasks. Tending to the needs of sick patients, and teaching others how to do this successfully is an extraordinary privilege. To have been provided the resources to study why people develop their problems in the first place is an additional opportunity that I also appreciate and have utilized extensively throughout my career. My quest from the beginning of my surgical career has been to learn how to prevent the diseases that I treat. I have chosen to pursue this goal through research and the teaching of others. What I have described above primarily is my success in this regard through the work of my teachers, associates, students, patients, and the institutions that encouraged and supported my work.

I have included in my discussion aspects of my personal life that likely had an influence on my day to day work and the pace of its performance. My wives Barbara, Maja, and Inger, and my children Anne, Frank, and Jane have all been supportive of my work which for the most part has consumed my waking hours. I owe them a great debt of gratitude for their many kindnesses and sacrifices especially in the early years when opportunity was unlimited but money was scarce.

I owe a large measure of my success in medicine to my father who taught me humility and respect for those less fortunate than I. His obesity and its associated co-morbidities likely contributed to my interest in surgical approaches to its treatment. My mother's strong encouragement to go to Exeter and to strive to get the very best education that I could was in a way a reflection of her own ambition. Several years after my father had passed away, she went to work in the office of a very busy general practitioner who lived close by on Franklin Street, in Franklin, New Hampshire. She knew most of the patients who were cared for by this physician because she had worked with many of them. He recognized, as did she, that most of the patients were suffering from stress related disorders. He would end his conversation with such patient's by saying "See Elsie. She will fix you up". She allowed them to spend as a much time as they wanted talking about their problems, and then would give them a bag of pink pills with instructions to take three a day for two weeks. If they felt better, they would continue with the pink pills. If their symptoms persisted, she would shift them over to white pills. This was less expensive and probably as effective as "nerve pills".

My mother was very active in volunteer work that involved usually some elderly patient that could not care for themselves. In her later years, she moved down to Portsmouth, New Hampshire in order to be close to her daughter Alice. While in apparent good health at age 85, my mother developed acute ulcerative colitis and died a year later at age 86 from complications following total colectomy.

My sister Alice died at age 75 after a long struggle with chronic myelogenous leukemia. I went to visit her shortly before her death. She was in good spirits, and appeared quite healthy to me. I inquired from her doctor what was going on and she explained that there was nothing further to do for my sister. She required a withdrawal of fluid from her chest every few days, and that she was terminal. This explained the almost heavenly appearance of the hospital, and the soft organ music in the background. I was somewhat skeptical about the approach, but the Doctor convinced me that further interventions would be futile. My sister's only wish was that she be kept alive until Mother's Day a few weeks away. I regret now that I did not insist on at least one more drainage of the fluid in her chest, but I kept this thought to myself since the children were paying for her hospital stay.

It is hard to believe that it has been sixty years since I began to treat patients as a second year medical student at Dartmouth Medical School-Mary Hitchcock Clinic in Hanover, New Hampshire. My educational pace quickened when I transferred to Cornell Medical College in New York City in 1954 for my last two years of medical school. As mentioned in the beginning, my interest up to that time was to be a psychiatrist. It was quite by chance that my surgical rotation in the fourth year was a very positive experience. I enjoyed being part of the surgical team, actively participating in the care of the many complicated patients that we were treating on a daily basis. I found this all to be very exciting, and did not hesitate to sign up for the seven year program in general surgery after an experience in psychiatry that convinced me that the practice of psychiatry was not for me.

As I look back now during this current period of the restrictions imposed by the 80 hour work week, I wonder how under these conditions we could have taken care of the large number of patients that required our services each day during my residency. In fact, we only had time off when the work was done, and that usually was one night or so a week. I personally enjoyed the pace, and tried to use my time to the fullest. My wife Barbara rarely complained about my absence until the children came along several years later. In my senior residency years at the New York Hospital my work load continued to be heavy because of my interest in the laboratory, and studying problems on the ward. I was able however to spend time with the family a few hours on week-ends, since our apartment was across the street from the Hospital.

The surgical training provided by Dr. Frank Glenn, Dr. John Beal and their staff was invaluable to the development of my surgical skills and my commitment to personalized high quality patient care. My move to San Francisco to pursue basic science with Dr. Richard Durbin, PhD who had a primary interest in membrane transport from the point of view of its biophysical properties was the key to my success as a clinician-scientist. Dick Durbin was an excellent teacher. I was saddened by his untimely death from a heart attack some years later after he had moved to Puerto Rico.

My three years at UCSF were exciting for me since Bert Dunphy encouraged my efforts in the laboratory while fostering my career as a clinical surgeon. I learned a great deal from him about how to motivate students to pursue their areas of interest with passion. These formative years served me well as I moved up the academic ladder. During my Alabama years John Kirklin taught me how to organize a Department of Surgery, and how to pay attention to the details of a surgical intervention and its post-operative management.

My years at Utah (besides providing an opportunity to perfect my skiing technique) were an important period in my academic life. I learned how to stimulate others to consider a career in academic surgery. I also learned how to develop an outstanding medical enterprise with limited financial resources. I am especially indebted to John Reinertsen, the Chief Executive Officer of the University Hospital, who taught me how to keep my eye on the big picture, and to keep my ego in the background as I enthusiastically pursued my goals. John Dixon, the Dean and Vice President for Health Affairs at Utah, and a fellow surgeon, represented a role model of how to effortlessly provide leadership for your colleagues. He taught all of us how to "fast track" the building of a new University Hospital for which we had only enough money to build one floor at a time. He was great to work for, and a surgeon who during his six years as an administrator planned to lead our Department into the endoscopic minimally invasive age of surgery. Unfortunately his budding new career was interrupted by a myocardial infarction, but not until he had developed a gifted protégé, John Hunter, to continue his seminal work. John Dixon was the consummate mentor in that he would spend many hours in the laboratory, the endoscopic suite, or in the summer fishing on the streams of Utah with his pupil John Hunter.

The University of Texas Medical School in Houston has provided for me a unique opportunity to apply all that I had learned in my prior academic jobs. Ernst Knobil, during his short tenure as Dean (1982-1985), set the tone for the current success that UT HEALTH (current branding) in Houston is enjoying as it strives to enter the ranks of the upper tier of medical schools in the country. The Texas Medical Center is one of the largest in the world. Besides UT-Houston Medical School and its teaching hospital, the Memorial Herman and Children's Hospital, it includes the Baylor College of Medicine, the Methodist, St. Lukes, Texas Children's and Ben Taub Hospitals, and the MD Anderson Cancer Center. It also includes the UT Schools of Public Health, Nursing, Dentistry, Bioinformatics, and the Graduate School of Biomedical Sciences. The opportunity to make major advances in our understanding, treating, and ultimately preventing disease is infinite, and I am delighted to still be a small part of the action. I thank my Chairman, Richard Andrassy, and our President of the Health Science Center and Dean of the School of Medicine, Dr. Giuseppe N. Colasurdo, M.D. for this ongoing opportunity.

I have intentionally presented my life's experiences in an informal way in order to avoid being too pedantic in presenting the challenges of being an academic surgeon. What I have tried to convey is the tremendous satisfaction that can be derived by a total immersion in all aspects of an aggressive healing profession. This is not meant to be a highly referenced scholarly presentation. Most of the laboratory and clinical studies which it encompasses are contained within the articles and chapters listed in the appended Curriculum Vitae. I want to again thank all of those who have contributed to my journey, and apologize in advance for any erroneous commissions or inadvertent omissions. I invite comments from the readers as regards the latter oversights.

APPENDIX

I made a decision at the beginning of recalling my experiences as an academic surgeon to record them as I remembered them, and by intention planned not to produce a highly referenced manuscript. I have tried during my academic career to keep a complete record of my activities in a traditional Curriculum Vitae to include: personal information, education, professional experience, editorial experience, research awards, medical licensure, scholastic honors, professional honors, professional and scientific committees and organizations, professional community activities, university and hospital committees, named visiting lectureships, and bibliography. The latter includes published abstracts, surgical forum presentations, refereed original articles, invited articles, book chapters, and books. I cannot emphasize enough the importance of keeping a record of your work if you aspire to be an academic surgeon. I have told my students and colleagues over the years, "if you do not write it down, it did not happen". Your Curriculum Vitae defines who you are, where you have been, and where you are going. Reading my own reminds me what a wonderful privileged life I have had doing what I most enjoy doing, helping people through a variety of activities that includes direct patient care, research, and education.

CURRICULUM VITAE

NAME	**Frank G. Moody, M.D.**
PRESENT TITLE	Professor of Surgery
ADDRESS	7300 Brompton St., #5825 Houston, TX 77025 2913 Legacy Park Lane Sandy, UT 84093
Birth date:	May 3, 1928
Birthplace:	Franklin, New Hampshire
Citizenship:	U.S.A.

EDUCATION

Baccalaureate Degree:	Dartmouth College, 1948-1950, 1951-1953 BA
Advanced Degree:	Dartmouth Medical School, 1952-1954 Cornell University Medical College, 1954-1956, M.D.
Residency and Fellowship Training:	Internship, Assistant Resident, and Resident Surgeon, New York Hospital, Cornell University Medical Center, 1956-1963

Advanced Research Fellow, American Heart Association; Fellow, Cardiovascular Research Institute, University of California Medical Center, San Francisco, 1963-1965

Certification:

National Board of Medical Examiners—1957

American Board of Surgery—1964; Recertified—1980

Fellow, American College of Surgeons—1967

PROFESSIONAL EXPERIENCE

Clinical Instructor in Surgery, University of California Medical Center, San Francisco, 1963-1965

Assistant Professor of Surgery, University of California Medical Center, San Francisco, 1965-1966

Staff Surgeon, Veteran's Administration Hospital, (WOC) Birmingham, 1966-1971

Associate Professor and Chief, Division of Gastrointestinal Surgery, University of Alabama Medical Center, Birmingham, 1966-1969

Assistant Professor of Physiology and Biophysics University of Alabama Medical Center, Birmingham, 1966

Professor of Surgery and Director, Gastrointestinal Division, University of Alabama Medical Center, Birmingham, 1969-1971

Professor and Chairman, Department of Surgery, University of Utah School of Medicine; Chief of Surgery, University Hospital, University of Utah Health Sciences Center, Salt Lake City, 1971-1982

Staff Surgeon, Veteran's Administration Hospital (WOC), Salt Lake City, 1971-82

Denton A. Cooley Professor and Chairman, Department of Surgery, The University of Texas Medical School at Houston, Surgeon-in-Chief, Hermann Hospital, 1982-1994

Denton A. Cooley Professor, Department of Surgery, The University of Texas—Houston—Medical School, 1994 2000

Professor, Department of Surgery, The University of Texas Medical School at Houston, 1982-

Professor of Surgery, Graduate School of Biomedical Sciences, The University of Texas Health Science Center at Houston, 1988-

Editorial Experience:

Viewpoints on Digestive Disease, 1971-1973

Gastroenterology, Editorial Board, 1974-1978

Journal of Surgical Research, Editorial Board, 1975-1980

The Western Journal of Medicine, Editorial Board, 1976-

Surgery, Editorial Board, 1973-1981; 1984-1994

The American Journal of Surgery, Editorial Board, 1972-1998

Perspectives in Surgery, Editorial Board, 1978-1980

Digestive Diseases and Sciences, Editorial Board, 1980-1983

World Journal of Surgery, Consultant, 1980-1994

Butterworth's International Medical Reviews, Gastroenterology I, Foregut. J.H. Baron and **F.G. Moody** (Eds), Butterworth & Co., Ltd., 1981

Surgical Gastroenterology, Co-Editor, 1982-1984

Hepato-Biliary-Pancreatic Surgery, Advisory Board, l994

Current Concepts in Clinical Surgery, Advisory Panel, 1984

Digestive Surgery, Co-Editor, 1986 -1994; Editor Emeritus 1995

Lifetime Medical Television: Surgical Update, 1986-1989

Year Book of Digestive Disease 1984-1997

Research Awards

Clinical Investigation in Surgery for Postgraduate Training, 1968-1973, NIH, GM 01924, PI

Graduate Training Program in Surgery, 1971-1975 PHS training grant, GM 00839, PI

Mechanisms of Gastric Acid Secretion, 1967-1972 NIH, AM 16233, PI

Mechanisms of Gastric Acid Secretion, 1972-1975 NIH, AM 16233, PI

Mechanisms of Gastric Ulcerogenesis, 1975-1982, NIH, AM 16233, PI

	Quantitation of Physiological Reflux in Pancreatic Duct of Primates, 1975-1978, NIH-NCI CP 55709, PI
	Trauma and Burn Research Center, 1976-1985 NIH, GM 23095, PI
	Mechanisms of Gastrointestinal Adaptation, Core A, 1986-1991, NIH, AM 35588-01
	Mechanisms of Biliary Stasis in Cholesterol Lithogenesis, 1987-1990; 1992-95 NIH, RO1-DK-38888, PI
	NIGMS Trauma Research Center, Pathogenesis of Multiple Organ Failure, PI 1988-1993; 1993-1999; 1999-2003
	NIH, P50 GM38529, PI Research Training in Digestive Disease and Nutrition PI 1989-1994, NIH, DK 07565
	NIH, 3 P50 GM038529-14S2, Pathogenesis of Multiple Organ Failure, Budget Period: 8/1/2002-8/31/2004, Project Period: 5/1/1988-7/31/2004
	NHBI, 5RO1 HL073162, Glucotoxicity and Cardiac Dysfunction in Obesity, PI-Dr. HeinrichTaegtmeyer. Project Period: 2003-2008, with1 year extension to 2009. Moody Co-Investigator (10% time).
Medical Licensure	New York, 1957 (inactive)
	California, 1964 (inactive)
	Alabama, 1966 (inactive)
	Utah, 1971 (active)
	Texas, 1983 (active)
SCHOLASTIC HONORS	Phi Beta Kappa
	Alpha Omega Alpha (faculty)
PROFESSIONAL HONORS	Grand Gold Medaille, Milan, Italy, 1990

Olof Acrel Medal of the Swedish Surgical Society, 1992

Professor Honorario at the Hospital Universitario Doce de Octobre, Madrid, Spain, 1992.

Houston Surgical Society Distinguished Houston Surgeon, 1995.

Society of Surgery of the Alimentary Tract Founders' Medal, San Diego, 1995.

American Medical Association Scientific Achievement Award, Chicago, 1995.

International College of Surgeons Master Surgeon Medallion, Kyoto, Japan, 1996.

Honorary Member, International Surgical Society— Durban 2005.

Fellow, American Association for the Advancement of Science, Washington, D.C. February 2005.

Distinguished Service Award, International Hepato-Pancreato-Biliary Association. April 2005.

Dean's Teaching Excellence Award, University of Texas Health Science Center-Houston, 2006-2007.

Lifetime Achievement Award, Society of University Surgeons, 2008.

Medal of Honor, University of Texas Health Science Center at Houston, 2013.

PROFESSIONAL AND SCIENTIFIC COMMITTEES AND ORGANIZATIONS

Affiliated Medical Services, Board of Trustees, 1988-1994

Academy of Experimental Surgeons

Academic Surgery Training Committee, NIGMS, 1968-1971

American Association for Academic Surgery, 1991

American Association for the Advancement of Science

American Association for the Study of Liver Disease

American Association for Surgery Trauma, 1989-

American Board of Medical Specialties, 1975-1980

Executive Committee, 1977-1980

American Board of Surgery, Director, 1972-1978

American College of Surgeons, 1969-

Utah Chapter President, 1972-1982

Committee on Surgical Education in Medical

Schools, 1973-1978

Surgical Forum Committee, 1978-1982

Program Committee

Surgical Education and Research Committee, 1989-

American Federation of Clinical Research

American Gastroenterological Association,

Governing Board, 1985-1988

American Medical Association, 1968-

American Pancreatic Association, 1976-

President 1979

American Physiological Society, 1968-

American Surgical Association

Program Chairman, 1975-1978

Membership Committee, 1979-1983

International Relations, 1985

Committee on Honorary Fellowships, 1987-

Chairman, 1990

2nd Vice President, 1991-

American Trauma Society, 1993-

Association for Academic Surgery 1991-

Association of American Medical Colleges,

Committee on Financing Graduate Medical

Education, 1984-1986

Executive Council, 1985-1986

Executive Committee, 1986-1987

Distinguished Service Member, 1988-

Council of Academic Societies

Administrative Board, 1982

Chairman-Elect, 1985-1986

Chairman, 1986-1987

Biophysical Society

Collegium International Chirurgie Digestivae, United

States Section, President 1975-1977

National Delegate, 1978-1987

Conjoint Council on Surgical Research, Treasurer, 1985-89

German Society for Digestive and Metabolic Diseases,

Corresponding Member, 1988-

Houston Gastroenterological Society, 1986-

Houston Surgical Society, 1985-

Illinois Surgical Society,

International Biliary Association, President, 1985

International Society for Diseases of the Esophagus, 1983-

International Surgical Group, 1980-

John W. Kirklin Society, 1977-

La Society de Chirurgie de Quebec, 1984-

Liaison Committee on Graduate Medical Education, 1977-1980

National Association of Physician Hospital Organizations, 1993-

National Consultant in Surgery to the Surgeon General, U.S. Air Force, 1975-

H.C. Naffziger Society, 1976-

NIH Medicine Study Section A, 1972-1975

NIH Surgery and Bioengineering Study Section, 1976-1980, Chairman, 1978-1980

NIH Clinical Study Group, 1994-

New York Academy of Sciences

North Pacific Surgical Association

Pan Pacific Surgical Association

Pharmacology-Toxicology Clinical Management Study for the Dissolution of Gallstones, 1974-1982

Philippine College of Surgeons

Salt Lake County Medical Society

Salt Lake Surgical Society, President, 1975-1976

Societe Internationale de Chirurgie, 1977-

Council, 1985

U.S. Section, Secretary 1987-89, Vice President

1989-91, President 1992-1994

Society for Surgery of the Alimentary Tract, 1966-

Treasurer, 1973-1975, President, 1981, Board of Trustees, 1985

Society of Clinical Surgery, 1973-

Society of Medical Consultants to the Armed Forces, 1979-

Society of Surgical Chairmen, Secretary,

1977-79, Treasurer, 1979-1980, President, 1982-1984

Society of University Surgeons,

1966, Lifetime Achievement Award—2008

Southern Society for Clinical Investigation

Southern Surgical Association, 1982-

Southwestern Surgical Congress

Splanchnic Circulation Group

Surgical Biology Club III

Texas Surgical Society, 1985-

U.S. Dornier Bile Duct Stone Lithotripsy Trial

Director, 1987-1988

U.S. Northgate Gallstone Lithotripsy Trial, Director 1989-

Utah Society for Certified Surgeons, President, 1974-1976, 1979-1980

Utah State Medical Association

V.A. Merit Review Board (Gastroenterology), 1971-1975

Western Surgical Association 1974-

Membership Committee 1979-82

PROFESSIONAL COMMUNITY ACTIVITIES

Board Member, Salt Lake Area Chapter American Red Cross 1978-1979

Advisory Board, Houston Symphony 1987-1989

Board of Trustees, Wasatch Academy, Mt. Pleasant, Utah, 1991-

President Elect 1994; President 1995-1998

UNIVERSITY AND HOSPITAL

Administrative Council, The University of Texas Medical School, 1982-1994

Medical Board, Hermann Hospital, 1982-1994, Chairman, 1983-1985

Executive Committee, Board of Directors, 1983-1994

Medical Service Research and Development Plan, UTMSH

Clinical Chiefs Committee, Hermann Hospital, 1982-1994

Group on Services for Health, UTHSCH, 1986-1988

Operating Room Committee, Hermann Hospital, Chairman 1983-1987

The Woodlands Venture Capital Company, Scientific Advisory Committee, 1986-

Strategic Planning Committee, UTHSC, 1987

Clinical Policy and Planning Committee, UTMSH, 1988

Stroke Program Project Grant, Advisory Committee

Anesthesiology Search Committee, UTMSH Chairman, 1988

University Ventures, Inc., Board of Directors, 1989-1990

Affiliated Medical Services Board of Trustees, Harris County Hospital District, 1988-1994

Research Committee, UTMSH, 1991-

Research and Education Building Committee, LBJ Chairman, 1990

Board of Medical Advisors, Hermann Children's Hospital, 1990-1994

NAMED VISITING LECTURESHIPS

Annual William Beaumont Lecture University of Wisconsin, Milwaukee	September 1972
Annual Vera and Forrest Lumpkin Surgical Memorial Lecture The University of Texas Southwestern Medical School, Dallas	April 1976
Twenty-Seventh Annual Howard C. Naffziger Society Lecture University of California, San Francisco	April 1976
Edgar J. Poth Memorial Lecture, Twenty-eighth Annual Meeting Meeting of the Southwestern Surgical Congress, Houston, Texas	May 1976
Earl A. Connolly Memorial Lecture, Creighton University School of Medicine, Omaha, Nebraska	February 1977

W. Alton Jones Lectureship, University of Missouri, Columbia	April 1977
Theodore A. McGraw Lecture, Twenty-ninth Annual Banquet of Detroit Surgical Association, Detroit, Michigan	May 1977
Ralph R. Coffey Lecture, University of Missouri-Kansas City Truman Medical Center, Kansas City	May 1977
Alpha Omega Alpha Professorship and Lecture, University of Kansas Medical Center, Kansas City	March 1978
The Ninth Annual Kate and Dr. Harvey Cushing Lecture, New York, New York	November 1978
North Pacific Surgical Association Founders Lecture, Seattle, Washington	November 1978
Fourth Annual Leon Ginzburg Lecture, New York, New York	February 1979
J.C. Thoroughman Lecture, Emory University, Atlanta, Georgia	September 1979
James H. Fox Memorial Lecture, University of Colorado, Denver	November 1979
J.G. Probstein Lectureship, The Jewish Hospital of St. Louis, Missouri	February 1980
Fourth Annual Dragstedt Lecture in Medical Science University of Florida, Gainesville	March 1980
Distinguished Visiting AOA Professor, University of Virginia, Charlottesville	March 1980
W. Trevor Cook International Visiting Fellow, Ireland and England	July 1980
Dr. Frank H. Kidd, Jr., Visiting Professorship, Baylor University Medical Center, Dallas, Texas	February 1981
Sixth Annual Clarence E. Stafford Memorial Lecture, White Memorial Medical Center and Loma Linda School of Medicine, Loma Linda, California	May 1981

Eighth Annual Preston A. Wade Memorial Trauma Lecture, New York Hospital-Cornell Medical Center, New York City	May 1981
72nd Sommer Memorial Lecture, Portland, Oregon	October 1981
Annual Eisenberg Lecture, Brigham and Women's Hospital, Harvard Medical School, Boston, Massachusetts	May 1983
Annual Vezina Lecture, La Societe de Chirurgie de Quebec, Canada	April 1984
The Fourteenth Annual J. Murray Beardsley Surgeon-in-Chief Pro Tempore, Department of Surgery, Rhode Island Hospital, Brown University, Providence	June 1984
Leonard W. Edwards Lecturer, Vanderbilt University Medical Center, Nashville, Tennessee	October 1984
Charles Prothro Visiting Professor, Baylor University Medical Center, Dallas, Texas	October 1984
Distinguished AOA Professor, The University of Tennessee, Memphis	April 1985
Balfour Professor, The Mayo Clinic, Rochester, Minnesota	November 1988
Hodgen Lecturer, St. Louis Surgical Society, St. Louis, Missouri	March 1989
Thomas E. Jones Memorial Lecture, The Cleveland Clinic Foundation, Cleveland, Ohio	April 1989
Joel W. Baker Lecture in Surgery, Virginia Mason Medical Center, Seattle, Washington	May 1991
Richard P. Zimmerman, M.D., Memorial Lectureship, Johnstown, Pennsylvania	April 1992
Leon Sample Lecture, Yale University, New Haven, Connecticut	May 1992
Phillip Sandblom Lecture, Lund, Sweden	May 1992

Joseph Kuharich and William J. Moore, M.D., Memorial Lecture in Medical and Surgical Oncology, The Graduate Hospital, Philadelphia, Pennsylvania	January 1994
Val Williams Lecture, St. Louis University School of Medicine, St. Louis, Missouri	October 1996
Dorothy and Judson Rikkers Lectureship, University of Nebraska, Omaha, Nebraska	November 2002
Second Joaquim Aldrete Lectureship. University of Alabama, Birmingham, Alabama	September 2003
Reginald Smithwick Symposium and Lecture, Boston University Medical Center	November 2003
31st Warren H. Cole Surgical Lecture, Missouri Delta Medical Center,	August 2007

BIBLIOGRAPHY

ABSTRACTS

1. **Moody FG**, Durbin RP. Osmotic regulations of water flow in gastric secretion. Fed Proc 23:119, 1964.
2. **Moody FG**. Gastric blood flow and acid secretion during direct intra-arterial histamine administration. Gastroenterology 50:884-885, 1966.
3. **Moody FG**. Oxygen consumption during the thiocyanate inhibition of acid secretion. Clin Res XV:241, 1967.
4. **Moody FG**. Water movement through canine gastric mucosa during thiocyanate inhibition of acid secretion. Fed Proc 27:581, 1968.
5. Garrett JM, **Moody FG**, Godwin D. Disturbances in esophageal motility following lye ingestion. Clin Res XVII:25, 1969.
6. Cheung L, Stephensen LW, **Moody FG**, Torma MJ, Zalewsky C. Direct effects of endotoxin on canine gastric mucosal permeability and histological changes. Gastroenterology 66:A20/674, 1974.
7. **Moody FG**. Letter to the Editor: Ischemia and the gastric mucosal barrier. Gastroenterology 66:A-20/674, 1974.
8. Simons M, **Moody FG**: Carbenoxolone effects on gastric mucosal permeability and blood flow. Gastroenterology 68:A-100/957, 1975.
9. Zalewsky CA, **Moody FG**, Simons MA. The effects of p-choloromercuribenzene sulfonate (PCBMS) upon ultrastructure of canine gastric surface cells. Fed Proc 34:53, 1975.

10. Pipes EJ, **Moody FG**. Hepatic uptake of indocyanine green in phenobarbital treated versus non-treated rats. Clin Res XXIII:99A, 1975.
11. Reese R, Cheung LY, **Moody FG**. Effect of endotoxin on gastric mucosal microcirculation and electrical gradient. Clin Res XXIII:99A, 1975.
12. Cheung LY, Chang F, **Moody FG**. Canine gastric blood flow and its distribution during hemorrhagic shock. Clin Res XXIV:104A, 1976.
13. Simons MA, Bashioum RW, **Moody FG**. Inhibition of gastric acid secretion by epinephrine after alpha-blockage. Clin Res XXIV:135A, 1976.
14. Zalewsky CA, **Moody FG**. Correlation of parietal cell ultra-structure with acid secretion and inhibition. Gastroenterology 70:A-95/953, 1976.
15. Steur RR, **Moody FG**, McGreevy JM. Focal gastric blood flow measurements by photoelectric plethysmography-techniques and design. Proc Fed Am Soc Exp Biol 36:594, 1977.
16. **Moody FG**, Simons M, McGreevy JM. Effects of isoproterenol on cation exchange across the gastric mucosa. Proc of the International Union of Physiological Science, Paris, France, 13:523, 1977.
17. McGreevy JM, **Moody FG**. Capillary filtration does not prevent gastric erosions. Gastroenterology 74:1065, 1978.
18. Lazarus HM, **Moody FG**. Creation of a trauma and burn center. J Trauma 18:76, 1978.
19. Zalewsky CA, **Moody FG**. Mechanisms of mucus release from canine gastric epithelium. Gastroenterology 74:151, 1978.
20. **Moody FG**, McGreevy J, Zalewsky C, Cheung LY, Simons M. The cytoprotective effect of mucosal blood flow in experimental erosive gastritis. Upsula J Med Sci 82:264, 1978.

21. Becker JM, **Moody FG**. The effect of gastrointestinal hormones on the biliary sphincter of the opossum. Gastroenterology 76:1097, 1979.
22. Larsen KR, Davis EK, **Moody FG**. A proposed mechanism of acid-bile-shock ulcerogenesis. Fed Proc 39:326, 1980.
23. Zalewsky CA, **Moody FG**. Ultrastructural analysis of mucus secretion in human gastric mucosa. Fed Proc 39:768, 1980.
24. Larsen KR, Davis EK, **Moody FG**. Hydrogen ion back-diffusion, ischemia, and canine gastric lesions. Fed Proc 39:768, 1980.
25. Larsen KR, Jensen NF, Davis EK, **Moody FG**. The cytoprotective effects of (±)-15-deoxy-16-α, β-hydroxy-16-methyl PGE_1 methyl ester (SC-29333) versus aspirin-shock gastric ulcerogenesis in the dog. Conf. on Protective Action of Prostaglandins on Gastrointestinal Mucosa, Jan. 1981.
26. Jensen NF, Larsen KR, Davis EK, **Moody FG**. The dose response effects of two prostaglandin analogs (16-dimethyl PGE_2 and SC-29333) on the canine gastric mucosa, Clin Res 29:33A, 1981.
27. Larsen KR, Jensen NF, Davis EK, Jensen JC, **Moody FG**. Effects of SC-29333, A PGE_1 analog, and 16, 16-dimethyl PGE_2 on canine gastric total and mucosal blood flow. Gastroenterology 80:1205, 1981.
28. Larsen KR, **Moody FG**, Moran D, Russo J, Turner NC. Comparison of the acute effects of aspirin and paracetamol (acetaminophen USA) on canine gastric mucosa during shock. Proc of Fiftieth Anniversary Meeting of Brit Pharmacol Soc 259-260, 1981.
29. Rotering RH, Larsen KR, Davis EK, Dixon JA, **Moody FG**. The measurement of canine gastric mucosal blood flow with a laser doppler velocimeter. The Physiologist 24:15, 1981.
30. Moran DM, Larsen KR, Russo J, Davis EK, **Moody FG**. Naloxone does not prevent stress gastric lesions. Clin Res 30:37A, 1982.

31. Larsen KR, Ivarsson LE, **Moody FG**. Effects of pentagastrin on intramural distribution of 15μ microspheres in the gastrointestinal tract. Gastroenterology 82:1112, 1982.
32. Zalewsky CA, **Moody FG**, Davis EK. The effect of intraarterial acetylcholine on gastric epithelial permeability and water flow. Fed Proc 41:1124, 1982.
33. Zalewsky CA, **Moody FG**, Davis EK, Allen MA. Intra-arterial acetylcholine: a mucus secretory model. Gastroenterology 82:1217, 1982.
34. **Moody FG**. Methods and materials of the gastrointestinal tract suture. Jikeikai Medical Journal 29:424-425, 1982.
35. Tsoi CM, **Moody FG**. Weight loss and metabolic changes after gastric partitioning surgery of morbidly obese patients. Clin Res 31:66A, 1983.
36. Ridge BA, Zalewsky CA, **Moody FG**. Effect of cholesterol diet in prairie dogs on appearance of glucoseamine in gallbladder bile. Clin Res 31:34A, 1983.
37. **Moody FG**. Problems following cholecystectomy. Inpharzam Medical Forum 4:1-6, 1983.
38. Coelho JCU, **Moody FG**, Senninger N. Correlation between sphincter of Oddi and duodenum myoelectrical activities and pancreatic and biliary pressures. Dig Dis Sci 29:566, 1984.
39. Coelho JCU, **Moody FG**, Senninger N, Weisbrodt NW. Effect of alcohol on myoelectric activity of the sphincter of Oddi (SO) and duodenum (D) in conscious opossum. Gastroenterology 86:1050, 1984.
40. Senninger N, **Moody FG**, Van Buren DH, Coelho JCU. Pancreatic intestinalization in dogs: a new method to prevent lethal shock in acute pancreatitis. Gastroenterology 86:1244, 1984.
41. Senninger N, **Moody FG**, Van Buren DH, Coelho JCU. Biliary pancreatitis: the role of biliary reflux and obstruction in the onset of the disease. Eur Sur Res 16:24, 1984.

42. Coelho JCU, **Moody FG**, Gouma D, Senninger N. Myoelectric activity disturbance of the sphincter of Oddi and duodenum following alcohol administration. Dig Dis Sci 29:945, 1984.
43. Senninger N, **Moody FG**, Coelho JCU, Van Buren DH: A possible role for secretin in the etiology of necrotizing pancreatitis (NP) in opossums. Dig Surg 1:134, 1984.
44. Coelho JCU, Gouma DJ, **Moody FG**, Li YF, Weisbrodt NW. 5-hydroxytryptamine (5HT) increases the velocity of propagation and frequency of migrating myoelectric complexes (MMC). Gastroenterology 88:1351, 1985.
45. Li YF, Weisbrodt NW, **Moody FG**, Coelho JCU, Gouma DJ. Calcium-induced contraction and contractile protein content of prairie dog gallbladder following high cholesterol feeding. Gastroenterology 88:1475, 1985.
46. Coelho JCU, Gouma DJ, **Moody FG**, Senninger N, Li YF, Chey WY. Sphincter of Oddi and gastrointestinal disturbance following alcohol administration in the opossum. Digestion 32:173, 1985.
47. Rowlands BJ, Roughneen PT, Gouma DJ, Kilkarni AD, **Moody FG**. Impaired cell mediated immunity in extrahepatic biliary obstruction. Ital J Surg Sci 15:100, 1985.
48. **Moody FG**. Surgery for morbid obesity. Helv Chir Acta 52:408, 1985.
49. Coelho JCU, Gouma DJ, **Moody FG**, Chey WY. Phase III-like activity produced by instillation of alcohol into the duodenum is caused by motilin. Gastroenterology 88:1351, 1985.
50. Gouma DJ, Coelho JCU, Schlegel JF, Li YF, **Moody FG**. Mortality after infection in jaundiced rats and following internal and external drainage. Ital J Surg Sci 15:111, 1985.
51. Gouma DJ, Roughneen PT, **Moody FG**, Rowlands BJ. Changes in nutritional status associated with obstructive jaundice and biliary drainage in rats. Clin Nutr 4 suppl I:117, 1985.

52. Husband KJ, **Moody FG**, Dewey RB. Effect of cholelithiasis on gallbladder ion transport in the prairie dog. Fed Proc 44:1396, 1985.
53. Haley-Russell D, Husband KH, **Moody FG**. Effects of a lithogenic diet on the epithelium of the prairie dog gallbladder. Fed Proc 45:229, 1986.
54. Senninger N, Coelho JCU, Runkel N, **Moody FG**, Herfarth C. Autotransplantation intestinaliserter pankreasfragmente in hunden. Chirurgisches Forum pp 77-80, 1986.
55. Gouma DJ, Coelho, JCU, **Moody FG**. Endotoxemia of the biliary obstruction and following internal and external drainage in rats. Neth J Med 29:43, 1986.
56. Li YF, **Moody FG**, Weisbrodt NW. Impairment of myosin LC-20 phosphorylation in gallbladder smooth muscle from paririe dogs fed cholesterol. Gastroenterology 90:1521, 1986.
57. Coelho JCU, Gouma DJ, **Moody FG**, Li YF, Weisbrodt NW. Influence of autonomic drugs on the myoelectric activity of the sphincter of Oddi in the opossum. Gastroenterology 90:1375, 1986.
58. LI YF, Bowers RL, **Moody FG**, Weisbrodt NW. The use of strips of longitudinal muscle from the ileum of rats to study contraction and myosin phos-phorylation. Gastroenterology 91:1060, 1986.
59. Coelho JCU, Gouma DJ, Li YF, **Moody FG**, Schlegel JF. 16,16-dimethyl prostaglandin E_2 (PGE_2) increases the velocity of propagation of the migrating motor complex (MMC) in the gut of the opossum. Dig Dis Sci 31:117S, 1986.
60. Senninger N, Runkel N, Coelho JCU, **Moody FG**, Herfarth C. Intestinalization of pan-creatic fragments in dogs--a new method for pancreas preservation and study of acute pancreatitis. Z Vers Kund 28:208-209, 1986.
61. Bowers RL, Li YF, **Moody FG**, Weisbrodt NW. Maximal active stress (F_0) and muscle cell number/cross-sectional area in distal ileum from control and jejunoileal bypassed (JIB) rats. Fed Proc 46:684, 1987.

62. Li YF, **Moody FG**, Bowers RL, Weisbrodt NW. Contractility and myosin LC-20 phosphorylation in jejunal smooth muscle from prairie dogs and cholesterol. Gastroenterology 92:1506, 1987.
63. Senninger N, Runkel N, Schmidt-Gayk H, Belinger CH, Coelho JCU, **Moody FG**, Herfarth C. Biliary obstruction (BO) increases exocrine pancreatic secretion and circulating secretin levels in opossums. Dig Dis Sci 32:1192, 1987.
64. Li, YF, Weisbrodt NW, Foster JE, **Moody FG**,. Gallbladder bypass prevents the changes in contractility and phosphorylation due to high cholesterol feeding in prairie dogs. Gastroenterology 94:A261, 1988.
65. Li YF, Foster JE, Weisbrodt NW, **Moody FG**. Mild hemorrhagic shock impairs gallbladder contractility. Gastroenterology 94:A261, 1988.
66. Calabuig R, Ulrich-Baker MG, **Moody FG**, Weems WA. Propulsion in the opossum sphincter of Oddi. Gastroenterology 95:858, 1988.
67. Foster JE, Li YF, Weisbrodt NW, **Moody FG**. Gut smooth muscle derangements following hemorrhagic shock. Gastroenterology 95:865, 1988.
68. Runkel NS, Haley-Russell D, **Moody FG**. The cause of increased pancreatic duct permeability in biliary pancreatitis in opossums. Pancreas 4:639, 1989.
69. Calabuig R, **Moody FG**, Weems WA. Intrinsic propulsive behavior and associciated myoelectric activity of opossum jejunum. FASEB 3:A850, 1989.
70. Calabuig R, Weems WA, **Moody FG**. Sphincter of Oddi of the opossum as an in vivo pump. Gastroenterology 96:A69, 1989.
71. Li YF, Weisbrodt NW, **Moody FG**. Actin and myosin isoforms in GB smooth muscle following cholesterol feeding in prairie dogs. Gastroenterology 96:A300, 1989.
72. Runkel N, Russell D, **Moody FG**. Exclusion of the "pancreatic duct factor" by prolamin occlusion does not prevent experimental pancreatitis. Gastroenterology 96:A431, 1989.

73. Li YF, Russell DH, Myers SI, Weisbrodt, **Moody FG**. Effects of aspirin on gallbladder contractility in cholesterol fed prairie dogs. Gastroenterology 98:A254, 1990.
74. Calabuig R, Seggerman RE, Alizadeh H, **Moody FG**, Weems WA. Fluid propulsion and myoelectric activity after jejunoileal transposition in cats. Gastroenterology 98:A332, 1990.
75. Calabuig R, Li YF, Linzel MF, Weisbrodt NW, **Moody FG**. Gallbladder contractility in the prairie dog: Effects of dietary vs. non-dietary biliary cholesterol. Gastroenterology 98:A244, 1990.
76. Calabuig R, **Moody FG**. Gastrointestinal electrical activity in the prairie dog during fasting, feeding and after cholesterol diet. Gastroenterology 98:A332, 1990.
77. Harari Y, Calabuig R, **Moody FG**, Castro G. Immunological sensitization of gall bladder by naturally acquired gastric infection. Gastroenterology 98:A453, 1990.
78. Runkel NS, Smith GS, Rodriguez LF, LaRocco MT, **Moody FG**, Miller TA. Influence of shock on bacterial translocation during acute experimental pancreatitis. Gastroenterology 98:A233, 1990.
79. Calabuig R, Seggerman RE, **Moody FG**, Weems WA. Intestinal fluid propulsion and associated myoelectric activity in vitro. Gastroenterology 98:A333, 1990.
80. Calabuig R, Seggerman RE, Weems WA, **Moody FG**. Is the ileo-cecal junction a sphincter, a valve, or none of the above? Gastroenterology 98:A333, 1990.
81. Ortega JM, **Moody FG**, Weisbrodt NW. Mechanical and biochemical determinations in the opossum sphincter of Oddi. Gastroenterology 98:A257, 1990.
82. Ortega JM, Pressley TA, **Moody FG**, Weisbrodt NW. Detection of cytokine mRNA from prairie dog macrophages and gallbladders. Gastroenterology 100:A331, 1991.
83. Runkel NS, **Moody FG**, Smith GS, Rodriguez LF, Chen Y, Miller TA. Reduced bowel motility by morphine enhances bacterial translocation. Gastroenterology 100:A489, 1991.

84. Li YF, Weisbrodt NW, **Moody FG**. Effects of E. coli endotoxin on intestinal smooth muscle and epithelial function in rats. Gastroenterology 100:A463, 1991.
85. Kueppers PM, Russell DH, **Moody FG**. Signs of pancreatitis regress after reversal of pancreatico-biliary duct (PBD) obstruction in rats. Pancreas 6:706, 1991.
86. Kueppers PM, Weems WA, Sunderland GK, Russell DH, **Moody FG**. Intrinsic small intestinal pro-pulsive activity is decreased in opossums with sphincter of Oddi (SO) obstruction. Gastroenterology 102:A318, 1992.
87. Kueppers PM, Miller TA, Chen CY, Smith GS, Rodriguez LF, **Moody FG**. Bacterial translocation following total parenteral nutrition (TPN) is increased by morphine. Gastroenterology 102:A650, 1992.
88. Li YF, Newton TJ, Weisbrodt NW, **Moody FG**. Intestinal migrating myoelectric complexes in rats with acute pancreatitis and bile duct ligation. Gastroenterology 102:A474, 1992.
89. Li YF, Weisbrodt NW, **Moody FG**. Effects of interleukin-1β on muscle and epithelial functions of the ileum in rats. Gastroenterology 102:A475.
90. Muncy DM, Haley-Russell D, Stanislawska M, Vakil A, Rodriguez L, **Moody FG**. Bacterial trans-location following acute pancreatitis in rats. Gastroenterology 102:A490, 1992.
91. Ortega JM, Haley-Russell D, Li YF, **Moody FG**. Effects of interleukin-1 beta and interleukin receptor antagonist protein on gallbladder contraction. Gastroenterology 102:A326, 1992.
92. Haley-Russell D, Muncy DM, Stanislawska M, **Moody FG**. Measurement of inflammatory changes in rat pancreas following common bile duct ligation. Gastroenteorlogy 102:A268, 1992.
93. Haley-Russell D, Ortega JM, Li YF, Weisbrodt NW, **Moody FG**. Interleukin-1 beta (IL-1β) affects gallbladder contractility in vitro. Gastroenterology 102:A314, 1992.

94. Li YF, Weisbrodt NW, **Moody FG**. Nitric oxide is involved in muscle relaxation but not in changes in short circuit current to electrical field stimulation in rat ileum. Gastroenterology 103:1392, 1992.
95. Runkel NS, **Moody FG**, Mueller W, Senninger N, Herfarth Ch. Opie's biliary pancreatic reflux, common channel theory as a cause of acute pancreatitis tested in the opossum. Hellenic J Gastroenterol 5:302, 1992.
96. Senninger N, Runkel N, **Moody FG**, Herfarth Ch. The biliary factor in pancreatic atrophy. Gastroenterology 104:A335, 1993.
97. Li YF, Weisbrodt NW, **Moody FG**. Glucose enhances nitro-l-arginine transport in rat ileum. Gastroenterology 104:A542, 1993.
98. Li YF, Weisbrodt NW, **Moody FG**. Longitudinal muscle contraction and transmural potential difference in rat ileum. Gastroenterology 104:A542, 1993.
99. Kueppers PM, Chen CY, Rodriguez LF, Weisbrodt NW, Russell DH, **Moody FG**, Miller TA. Clonidine-induced bacterial translocation. Gastroenterology 104:A723, 1993.
100. Turnquest DG, Mobley SR, Smith GS, Miller TA, **Moody FG**. Rehydration and chemical sympathec-tomy restore intestinal transit in a bile duct ligation model of pancreatitis. Gastroenterology 104:A340, 1993.
101. Gray C, Li YF, Weisbrodt NW, Russell DH, **Moody FG**. Intestinal muscle contractility during acute pancreatitis. FASEB Journal 7:A26, 1993.
102. Li YF, Weisbrodt NW, **Moody FG**. Inhibition of no synthase and muscle relaxation by nitro-l-arginine is modified by sodium-glucose co-transport. J Gastrointestinal Motility 5:200, 1993.
103. **Moody FG**, Haley-Russell D, Muncy DM, Li YF, Weisbrodt, NW. Bacterial translocation in experimental acute pancreatitis. Intensive Care Med 20-S1:S16, 1994.
104. Lai ML, Harari Y, Ortega J, Castro GA, **Moody FG**, Weisbrodt NW. Molecular alterations in intestinal muscle occur

within 24 hours of a hypertrophic stimulus in the rat. Gastroenterology 106:A529, 1994.

105. Runkel N, **Moody FG**, Miller TA, Senninger N, Herfarth C. Promotion of bacterial translocation by altered biliary and pancreatic secretion. Gastroenterology 106:A763, 1994.
106. Runkel N, **Moody FG**, Senninger N, Herfarth C. The unidirectional valvular action of the opossum sphincter of Oddi prevents bile reflux. Gastroenterology 106:A356, 1994.
107. Higham SC, Li YF, Lodato RF, **Moody FG**, Pressley TA, Weisbrodt NW, Zembowicz A, Zembowicz MJ. Functional biochemical and molecular evidence for an inducible nitric oxide synthase-mediated decrease in ileal contractility. Gastroenterology 106:A510, 1994.
108. Armstrong JA, Russell DH, **Moody FG**. Decreased intestinal transit in a model of necrotizing pancreatitis. Gastroenterology 106:A284, 1994.
109. Li YF, Weisbrodt NW, **Moody FG**. Nitric oxide induces relaxation of ileal, but not gallbladder, muscle in prairie dogs. Gastroenterology 106:A345, 1994.
110. Li YF, Zembowicz MJ, Weisbrodt NW, **Moody FG**. Muscle responses to transmural electrical field stimulation (TMS) and nitric oxide synthase (NOS) activity in the ileum of endotoxic rat. Gastroenterology 107:1222, 1994.
111. Klemm K, Barreto JC, **Moody FG**. Nitric oxide is necessary for the maintenance of pancreatic blood flow in lipopolysaccharide induced shock in the rat. Gastroenterology 108:A366, 1995.
112. Klemm K, Barreto JC, **Moody FG**. Nitric oxide and differential regional mucosal blood flow distribution of the intestine in lipopolysaccharide induced shock in the rat. Gastroenterology 108:A296, 1995.
113. Li YF, Zembowicz MJ, Weisbrodt NW, **Moody FG**. Contractile activity and levels of cGMP and CAMP of prairie dog gallbladder and ileal muscle in response to S-nitroso-N-acetyllpenicillamine (SNAP). Gastroenterology 108:A423, 1995.

114. Hauschulz DW, Herbert JR, Li YF, Weisbrodt NW, **Moody FG**. Lipopolysaccharide (LPS), nitric oxide synthase II (iNOS), and intestinaltransit in the rat. Gastroenteorlogy 108:A611, 1995.

115. Zembowicz MJ, Higham SC, Fallow CH, Pressley TA, Weisbrodt NW, **Moody FG**. Immunohistochemical localization of inducible nitric oxide synthase (iNOS-II) in the ileum in a rat model of septic shock. Gastroenterology 108:A949, 1995.

116. Zembowicz MJ, Higham SC, Fallow CH, Zembowicz A, Weisbrodt NW, **Moody FG**, Presslley TA. Distribution of nitric oxide synthase-II in the intestine in a rat model of septic shock. FASEB Journal IX:A704, 1995.

117. Khan ARR, Lodato JA, Li YF, Chen ZQ, Weisbrodt NW, **Moody FG**, Lodato RF. Prevention of endotoxin-induced depression ofintestinal smooth muscle function bytumor necrosis factor-binding protein plus interleukin-1 receptor antagonist. FASEB Journal IX:A86, 1995.

119. Zembowicz MJ, Khan AR, Zembowicz A, Higham SC, Weisbrodt NW, **Moody FG**, Pressley TA, Lodato RF. Characterization of calcium-independent NO synthase expression in the ileum of healthy rats. Endothelium 3:S104, 1995.

120. LI YF, Zembowicz MJ, Weisbrodt NW, Lodato RF, **Moody FG**. NOS-II expression following ileo-jejunal transposition in rats. Gastroenterology 110:A343, 1996.

121. Klemm K, Mercer DW, Mailman D, **Moody FG**. Hypotension in septic shock is unrelated to endotoxin induced increase of systemic nitric oxide (NO) production. Gastroenterology 110:A1398, 1996.

122. Lazo G, Li YF, Weisbrodt NW, **Moody FG**, Lodato RF. Prevention of endotoxin-induced depression of intestinal transit by interleukin-1 receptor antagonist plus tumor necrosis factor-binding protein. Am J Resp Crit Care Med 153:A831, 1996.

123. Russell DH, Mercer D, **Moody FG**. Morphologic effects of lipopolysaccharide on the gastrointestinal (GI) tract. Shock S5:37-38, 1996.
124. Tran T, Li Y, Weisbrodt N, Russell D, **Moody F**. Inducible nitric oxide synthase (iNOS) and intestinal transit in response to lipopolysaccharide (LPS) administration in the mouse. FASEB Journal 11:A33, 1997.
125. Khalil S, Weisbrodt N, Russell D, **Moody F**. Time course of intestinal transit and inducible nitric oxide synthase (iNOS) after lipopolysaccharide (LPS) administration in the rat. FASEB Journal 11:A34, 1997.
126. Luviano D, Weisbrodt N, Russell D, **Moody F**. The effects of N^G-nitro-L-arginine-methyl ester (L-name) on intestinal transit in rats treated with lipopolysaccharide (LPS). FASEB Journal 11:A33, 1997.
127. Roberts MM, Russell DH, **Moody FG**. Laparotomy incision length affects intestinal transit in obstructive pancreatitis in rats. Gastroenterology 112:A814, 1997.
128. Runkel NS, Buhr HJ, **Moody FG**. Control of unidirectional flow across the sphincter of Oddi in opossums: Evidence against biliary-pancreatic reflux. Gastroenterology 112:A1470, 1997.
129. Elliott BJ, Mailman D, Weems WA, Weisbrodt NW, **Moody FG.** Nitric oxide synthase-II (iNOS) upregulation and intestinal propulsion in a guinea pig model of endotoxic shock. Gastroenterology ll4;A748, 1998.
130. Klemm K, Lodato RF, **Moody FG.** Interleukin I receptor antagonist (IL-1RA) prevents hypoperfusion of intestinal mucosa in septic shock. Gastroenterology 114:A387, 1998.
131. Grossie B., Weisbrodt N., **Moody F.G**. Enteral nutrition reverses the ischemia/reperfusion (I/R) induced reduction in transit in rats. FASEB J. 13, A219, 1999.
132. Harari Y, Phan T, **Moody F**. Effect of the bacterial product FMLP on intestinal permeability in controls and disease. Gastroenterology 116:A886, 1999.
133. Harari Y, **Moody F.** Ileal mucosal response to bacterial toxin (FMLP) challenge. Gastroenterology 118:A1345, 2000.

134. Harari Y**, Moody F**, Gordon J. Effect of morphine on Type I hypersensitivity. The FASEB Journal 15:A372, 2001.
135. Harari Y, **Moody F.** The role of morphine in the local immune response of the gut. Shock 15(6):A49, 2001.
136. Harari Y, **Moody F**. FMLP—Induced Intestinal Barrier Disruption In Transgenic and Knockout Mice. Gastroenterology 2003;124:A317.
137. Harari Y, **Moody F**. Effect of FMLP and Morphine on Ileal Epithelial Barrier Dysfunction in the Rat. Experimental Biology 2003:65;A165.22.
138. Tweden, KS, Sarr MG, Bierk MD, Camilleri M, Kendrick ML, Knudson MB, **Moody FG**, Wilson RR, Anvari M, Vagal Blocking for Obesity Control (VBLOC): Studies of Pancreatic and Gastric Function and Safety in a Porcine Model. Surgery for Obesity and Related Diseases 2006; 2:301 (presented at Annual meeting, American Society for Baratric Surgery, San Francisco, CA June 2006).
139. Toouli J, Kulseng B, Keller U, Kow L, Marvik R, Johnsen G, Frey D, Tweden KS, Wilson RR, Billington CJ, **Moody FG**. Vagal Blocking for Obesity Control: Ongoing Comparison of Weight Loss with Two Generations of an Active, Implantable Medical Device. Surgery for Obesity and Related Diseases 2008;4:305 (presented at Annual meeting, Amercian Society for Metabolic and Bariatric Surgery, Washington, DC, 15-20 June 2008).
140. Kow L, Toouli J, Freston JW, Tweden KS, Wilson RR, **Moody FG**. Comparison of Food Ingestion Disorders with Three Devices for Obesity Treatment. Obesity Surgery 2008;18:914 (presented at Annual Meeting, International Federation for the Surgery of Obesity, Buenos Aires, Argentina, 24-27 September 2008).
141. Kow L, Toouli J, Feston JW, Tweden KS, Wilson RR, **Moody FG**. Comparison of Food Ingestion Disorders with Three Devices for Obesity Treatment. Obesity 2008;15:S222 (presented at Annual Meeting, The Obesity Society, Phoenix, AZ, 3-7).

SURGICAL FORUM

1. Gilder H, **Moody FG**, Beal JM. Role of potassium in histamine stimulated gastric pouch juice. Surg Forum XII:287-289, 1961.
2. **Moody FG**, Gilder H, Beal JM. Perfusion secretory studies of the isolated canine stomach. Surg Forum XII:282-284, 1962.
3. **Moody FG**, Durbin RP. Mechanism of water flow in gastric acid secretion. Surg Forum XV:309-310, 1964.
4. **Moody FG**, Durbin RP. Effect of histamine on water permeability of dog stomach. Surg Forum XVI:325-326, 1965.
5. Bridges CL, Abendroth JF, **Moody FG**. Hepatic uptake of the organic anion indocyanine green during bile salt and secretion choleresis. Surg Forum XXI:406-408, 1970.
6. Archibald LH, **Moody FG**, Simons M. Effect of isoproterenol on canine gastric acid secretion and blood flow. Surg Forum XXV:409-411, 1974.
7. Olsen CO, **Moody FG**. Mechanism of histamine-resistant gastric acid secretion in rats. Surg Forum XXVII:388-390, 1976.
8. McGreevy JM, **Moody FG**. Protection of gastric mucosa against aspirin-induced erosions by enhanced blood flow. Surg Forum XXVIII:357-359, 1977.
9. McGreevy JM, **Moody FG**, Zalewsky C. Effects of topical 16,16-dimethyl prostaglandin E2 on aspirin ulcerogenesis. Surg Forum XXIX:413-415, 1978.
10. Becker JM, **Moody FG**. Effects of gastrointestinal hormones on the opossum biliary sphincter. Surg Forum XXIX:400-401, 1978.
11. Shaw BW Jr, Becker JM, **Moody FG**. Histaminergic responses of biliary sphincter in opossum. Surg Forum XXX:400-404, 1979.
12. Potts JR, **Moody FG**. Inhibition of spontaneous biliary sphincter activity by an H_1 agonist. Surg Forum XXXI:200-202, 1980.

13. Jensen NF, Larsen KR, Davis EK, Jensen EJ, **Moody FG**. Two prostaglandin analogs (16,16 dimethyl prostaglandin E_2 and SC-29333) and the gastric mucosal barrier: A dose-response study. Surg Forum XXXII:124-125, 1981.
14. Ridge BA, Zalewsky CA, **Moody FG**. Histologic change in prairie dog gallbladder epithelium after cholesterol diet. Surg Forum XXXIII:212-213, 1982.
15. McGreevy, JM, Zalewsky CA, **Moody FG**. Gastric mucosal potential difference does not correlate with membrane viability. Surg Forum XXXIII:155-156, 1982.
16. Senninger N, **Moody FG**, Van Buren D, Coelho JCU, Li YG. Effect of biliary obstruction on pancreatic exocrine secretion in conscious opossums. Surg Forum XXXV:226-228, 1984.
17. Li YF, **Moody FG**, Weisbrodt NW, Zalewsky C, Coelho JCU, Senninger N. Decrease of contractility of prairie dog gallbladder muscle strips following cholesterol feeding. Surg Forum XXXV:219-221, 1984.
18. Coelho JCU, **Moody FG**, Senninger N, Li YF. Sphincter of Oddi and duodenum electro-myography and common duct and pancreatic duct pressures in the conscious opossum. Surg Forum XXXV:219-221, 1984.
19. Foster JE II, **Moody FG**. Effect of hemorrhagic shock on intestinal motility in the opossum. Surg Forum XXXVIII:165-166, 1987.
20. Myers SI, Li YF, Weisbrodt NW, Russell DH, **Moody FG**. Endogenous gallbladder prostaglandin biosynthesis is not related to gallstone formation in the prairie dog fed a high-cholesterol diet. Surg Forum XL:157-158, 1989.
21. Runkel NS, Smith GS, Rodriguez LF, Chen Y, Miller TA, **Moody FG**. Biliary and pancreatic obstruction reduces bowel motility, disrupts intestinal microflora, and promotes bacterial translocation. Surg Forum XLII:122-123, 1991.
22. Turnquest DG, Smith GS, Russell DH, Miller TA, **Moody FG**. Evidence supporting a role for the hydroxyl radical as a mediator of acute pancreatitis in the rat. Surg Forum XLIII:190-192, 1992.

REFEREED ORIGINAL ARTICLES

1. Okinaka A, **Moody FG**, Dineen J, Beal JM, Martin KA. Experimental production of peptic ulcers without increased secretion of acid. Surgery 46:70-75, 1959.
2. Cornell GM, Gilder H, **Moody FG**, McSherry CR, Beal JMR. The use of jejunal inter-position with total gastrectomy. Ann Surg 152:430-444, 1960.
3. Gilder H, **Moody FG**. Components of body weight loss in surgical patients. Metabolism 10:134-148, 1961.
4. Glenn F, **Moody FG**. Intrahepatic calculi. Ann Surg 153:711-724, 1961.
5. Glenn F, **Moody FG**. Acute obstructive suppurative cholangitis. Surg Gynecol Obstet 113:265-273, 1961.
6. **Moody FG**, McSherry CR, Beal JM. Mucosal replacement of gastric explants by free autogenous graft. Surgery 50:540-543, 1961.
7. Cornell GN, Gilder H, **Moody FG**, Frey C, Beal JM. The pattern of absorption following surgical shortening of the bowel. Bull NY Acad Med 37:676-688, 1961.
8. Gilder H, **Moody FG**, Beal JM. Water distribution in surgical patients. J Surg Res 111:59-66, 1962.
9. **Moody FG**, Cornell GN, Beal JM. Pyloric obstruction complicating peptic ulcer disease. Arch Surg 84:462-466, 1962.
10. **Moody FG**, Asch T, Glenn F. Intrahepatic cholangiography. Arch Surg 87:475-482, 1963.
11. Gilder H, **Moody FG**. Relationship of K+ to H+ in histamine-stimulated canine gastric juice. Proc Soc Exper Biol Med 114:190-192, 1963.
12. **Moody FG**, Beal JM. Carcinoma of cecum associated with intussusception. Arch Surg 87:836-839, 1963.
13. Beal JM, **Moody FG**. Postoperative complications of duodenal surgery. Surg Clin N Am 44:379-386, 1964.
14. **Moody FG**, Thorbjarnarson B. Carcinoma of the ampulla of Vater. Am J Surg 107:572-579, 1964.

15. **Moody FG**, Durbin RP. Effects of glycine and other instillates on concentration of gastric acid. Am J Physiol 209:122-126, 1965.
16. Gilder H, **Moody FG**. Aldosterone effect on canine gastric juice. Proc Soc Exper Biol Med 121:913-918, 1966.
17. **Moody FG**. Gastric blood flow and acid secretion during direct intra-arterial histamine administration. Gastroenterology 52:216-224, 1967.
18. **Moody FG**. Oxygen consumption during thiocyanate inhibition of gastric acid secretion in dogs. Am J Physiol 215:127-130, 1968.
19. **Moody FG**, Durbin RP. Water flow induced by osmotic and hydrostatic pressure in the stomach. Am J Physiol 217:255-261, 1969.
20. **Moody FG**, Garrett JM. Esophageal achalasia following lye ingestion. Ann Surg 170:755-784, 1969.
21. **Moody FG**, Davis WL. Hydrogen and sodium permeation of canine gastric mucosa during histamine and sodium thiocyanate administration. Gastroenterology 39:350-357, 1970.
22. **Moody FG**. Water movement through canine stomach during thiocyanate inhibition of gastric acid secretion. Am J Physiol 220:467-471, 1971.
23. **Moody FG**, Aldrete JS. Hydrogen permeability of canine gastric secretory epithelium during formation of acute superficial erosions. Surgery 70:154-160, 1971.
24. **Moody FG**, Aldrete JS. Current status of surgically created portasystemic shunts in the management of portal hypertension. Am Surg 37:605-612, 1971.
25. Halpern NB, Hirschowitz BL, **Moody FG**. Failure to achieve success with remedial gastric surgery. Am J Surg 125:108-115, 1973.
26. Berenson M, Garde AR, **Moody FG**. Twenty-five-year survival after surgery for complete extrahepatic biliary atresia. Gastroenterology 66:260-263, 1974.

27. Rikkers LF, **Moody FG**. Estimation of functional reserve of normal and regenerating dog livers. Surgery 75:421-429, 1974.
28. Cheung LY, Englert E Jr, **Moody FG**. Dissolution of gallstones with bile salts, lecithin, and heparin. Surgery 76:500-503, 1974.
29. Rikkers LF, **Moody FG**. Estimation of functional hepatic mass in resected and regenerating rat liver. Gastroenterology 76:691-699, 1974.
30. **Moody FG**, Rikkers LF, Aldrete JS. Estimation of the functional reserve of human liver. Ann Surg 180:592-598, 1974.
31. **Moody FG**, Simons M, Jackson T. Effect of-cholormercuribenzene sulfonate on gastric parietal and surface cell function in the dog. Gastroenterology 68:279-284, 1975.
32. Cheung LY, Stephenson LW, **Moody FG**, Torma MJ, Zalewsky C. Direct effects of endotoxin on canine gastric mucosal permeability and morphology. J Surg Res 18:417-425, 1975.
33. Cheung LY, **Moody FG**, Reese RS. Effect of aspirin, bile salt, and ethanol on canine gastric mucosal blood flow. **Surgery** 77:786-792, 1975.
34. Archibald LH, **Moody FG**, Simons H. Measurement of gastric blood flow with radioactive microspheres. J Appl Physiol 38:1051-1056, 1975.
35. Zalewsky CA, **Moody FG**, Simons MA. Effects of p-chlormercuribenzene sulfonate upon ultrastructure of canine gastric surface cells. Gastroenterology 69:427-438, 1975.
36. Archibald LH, **Moody FG**, Simons MA. Comparison of gastric mucosal blood flow as determined by aminopyrine clearance and gamma-labeled microspheres. Gastroenterology 69:630-635, 1975.
37. **Moody FG**, Cheung LY. Gastrointestinal biliary conditions. Surg Gynecol Obstet 142:197-201, 1976.

38. Cheung LY, Reese RS, **Moody FG**. Direct effect of endotoxin on the gastric mucosal microcirculation and electrical gradient. Surgery 79:564-568, 1976.
39. **Moody FG**, Cheung LY, Simons MA, Zalewsky C. Stress and the acute gastric mucosal lesions. Am J Dig Dis 21:148-154, 1976.
40. Keller RW, Berenson MM, **Moody FG**, Freston JE. The effect of the detergent treatment of the gastric mucosa on drug transport (39295). Proc Soc Exp Biol Med 151:730-735, 1976.
41. Albo D Jr, Taylor CW, Page B, Chang FC, **Moody FG**. Multifactor evaluations of surgical trainees and teaching services. Surgery 80:115-121, 1976.
42. Simons MA, **Moody FG**, Torma MJ. Effects of carbenoxolene on gastric mucosal permeability and blood flow in the dog. Gastroenterology 71:603-607, 1976.
42a. Brantigan JW, Owens ML, **Moody FG**. Femoral neuropathy complicating anticoagulant therapy. Am J Surg 132:108-109, 1976.
43. **Moody FG**, Cheung LY. Stress ulcers: their pathogenesis, diagnosis and treatment. Surg Clin N Am 56:1469-1478, 1976.
44. Zalewsky CA, **Moody FG**. Stereological analysis of the parietal cell during acid secretion and inhibition. Gastroenterology 73:66-74, 1977.
45. **Moody FG**, Berenson MM, McCloskey D. Transampullary septectomy for post-cholecystectomy pain. Ann Surg 186:415-423, 1977.
46. Cheung LY, **Moody FG**, Larsen K, Lowry SF. Oxygen consumption during cimetidine and prostaglandin E_2 inhibition of acid secretion. Am J Physiol 234:E445-E450, 1978.
47. Nelson EW, Berenson MM, **Moody FG**. Accuracy and consistency of pancreatography. Am J Surg 136:740-743, 1978.
48. **Moody FG**, McGreevy J, Zalewsky C, Cheung LY, Simons M. The cytoprotective effect of mucosal blood flow in

experimental erosive gastritis. Acta Physiol Scand Special Suppl, p 35-43, 1978.
49. Becker JM, Ti TK, **Moody FG**. A model of biliary pancreatic reflux. Surgery 85:147-152, 1979.
50. Zalewsky CA, **Moody FG**. Mechanisms of mucus release in exposed canine gastric mucosa. Gastroenterology 77:719-729, 1979.
51. Holman JM, Rikkers LF, **Moody FG**. Sepsis in the management of complicated biliary disorders. Am J Surg 138:809-813, 1979.
52. Madsen AC, Rikkers LF, **Moody FG**, Wu JT. alpha-fetoprotein as a marker for hepatic regeneration in the dog. J Surg Res 28:71-76, 1980.
53. Moysaenko V, **Moody FG**. Effects of regional hypercalcemia on gastric acid secretion. J Surg Res 28:206-208, 1980.
54. Becker JM, **Moody FG**. The dose response effects of gastrointestinal hormones on the opossum biliary sphincter. Curr Surg 37:60-63, 1980.
55. McGreevy JM, **Moody FG**. A mechanism for prostaglandin cytoprotection. Br J Surg 67:873-876, 1980.
56. Larsen KR, **Moody FG**, Cheung LY. Controlled intragastric pH and cimetidine inhibition of histamine-stimulated gastric acid secretion in the dog. Surgery 89:196-201, 1981.
57. McGreevy JM, **Moody FG**. Focal microcirculatory changes during the production of aspirin-induced gastric mucosal erosions. Surgery 89:337-34l, 1981.
58. Becker JM, Duff WM, **Moody FG**. Myoelectric control of gastrointestinal and biliary motility: A review. Surgery 89:337-341, 1981.
59. **Moody FG**, Zalewsky CA, Larsen KR. Cytoprotection of the gastric epithelium. World J Surg 5:153-163, 1981.
60. Larsen KR, Jensen NF, Davis EK, Jensen JC, **Moody FG**. The cytoprotective effect of (±)-15-deoxy-16αβ-Hydroxy-16-methyl PGE_1,methyl ester (SC-29333) versus aspirin-shock gastric ulcerogenesis in the dog. Prostaglandins Suppl 21:119-124, 1981.

61. **Moody FG**. Surgical application of sphincteroplasty and choledochoduodenostomy. Surg Clin N Am 61:909-921, 1981.
62. Potts JR, **Moody FG**. Surgical therapy for chronic pancreatitis: selecting the appropriate approach. Am J Surg 142:654-669, 1981.
63. **Moody FG**. Postcholecystectomy syndromes. Prac Gastroenterol V:8-10, 1981.
64. Becker JM, **Moody FG**, Zinsmeister AR. Effect of gastrointestinal hormones on the biliary sphincter of the opossum. Gastroenterology 82:1300-1307, 1982.
65. Simons MA, **Moody FG**. Effects of beta-adrenergic agents on canine gastric acid secretion. Surg Gastroenterol 1:35-44, 1982.
66. Russo J Jr, Thompson MIB, Russo ME, Saxon BA, Matsen JM, **Moody FG**, Rikkers LF. Piperacillin distribution into bile, gallbladder wall, abdominal skeletal muscle, and adipose tissue in surgical patients. Antimicrob Agents Chemother 22:488-491, 1982.
67. Zalewsky CA, **Moody FG**. Mucus secretion in human gastric epithelium: an ultrastructural study. Surg Gastroenterol 1:39-53, 1982.
68. **Moody FG**, Becker JM, Potts JR. Transduodenal sphincteroplasty and transampullary septectomy for postcholecystectomy pain. Ann Surg 197:627-636, 1983.
69. Zalewsky CA, **Moody FG**. Stimulation of canine gastric mucus secretion with intra-arterial acetycholine chloride. Gastroenterology 85:1067-1075, 1983.
70. Ash KO, Smith JB, Kremp JW, Lynch MB, **Moody FG**, Raymond JL, McKnight MR, Williams RR. The effect of diet on ouabain binding to erythrocytes from obese subjects. Clin Physiol Biochem 1:293-299, 1983.
71. Tsoi CM, Westenskow DR, **Moody FG**. Weight loss and metabolic changes of morbidly obese patients after gastric partitioning operation. Surgery 96:545-549, 1984.

72. Senninger N, **Moody FG**, Van Buren DH. Effect of intestinalization of pancreas fragments with acute pancreatitis in dogs. Langenbeck's Arch Chir Suppl 183-187, 1984.
73. Moran DM, Larsen KR, Russo J, Davis EK, **Moody FG**. An evaluation of naloxone as a gastric cytoprotective agent during hemorrhagic shock. J Trauma 24:728-730, 1984.
74. Gouma D, **Moody FG**. Preoperative percutaneous transhepatic drainage: use or abuse. Surg Gastroenterol 3:74-80, 1984.
75. Coelho JCU, Solhaug JH, **Moody FG**, Li YF. Experimental evaluation of gastric banding for treatment of morbid obesity in pigs. Am J Surg 149:228-231, 1985.
76. Coelho JCU, **Moody FG**, Senninger N. A new method for correlating pancreatic and biliary duct pressures and sphincter of Oddi electromyography. Surgery 97:342-348, 1985.
77. Coelho JCU, **Moody FG**, Senninger N, Weisbrodt NW. Effect of alcohol upon myoelectric activity of the gastrointestinal tract and pancreatic and biliary duct pressures. Surg Gynecol Obstet 160:528-533, 1985.
78. Coelho JCU, Gouma DJ, **Moody FG**, Li YF. Gastrointestinal myoelectric activity following abdominal operations in the opossum. World J Surg 9:612-618, 1985.
79. Coelho JCU, **Moody FG**, Senninger N, Li YF. Effects of gastrointestinal hormones on Oddi's sphincter and duodenal myoelectric activity and pancreaticobiliary pressure. Arch Surg 120:1060-1064, 1985.
80. **Moody FG**. Pathogenesis and treatment of inflammatory lesions of the papilla of Vater. Jpn J Surg 15:341-347, 1985.
81. Gouma DJ, Coelho JCU, Greep JM, **Moody FG**. Drenagem biliar pre-operatoria. Revista Brasileira de Cirurgia 75:391-394, 1985.
82. Raymond JL, Schipke CA, Becker JM, Lloyd RD, **Moody FG**. Changes in body composition and dietary intake after

gastric partitioning for morbid obesity. Surgery 99:15-18, 1986.

83. Coelho JCU, Gouma DJ, **Moody FG**, Schlegel JF. Effect of feeding on myoelectric activity of the sphincter of Oddi and the gastrointestinal tract in the opossum. Dig Dis Sci 31:202-207, 1986.
84. Gouma DJ, Coelho JCU, Fisher JD, Schlegel JF, Li YF, **Moody FG**. Endotoxemia after relief of biliary obstruction by internal and external drainage in rats. Am J Surg 151:476-479, 1986.
85. Senninger N, **Moody FG**, Van Buren DH, Coelho JCU. Intestinalization of pancreatic fragments in dogs. Surg Gynecol Obstet 162:355-360, 1986.
86. Gouma DJ, Coelho JCU, Schlegel J, Fisher JD, Li YF, **Moody FG**. Estimation of hepatic blood flow by hydrogen gas clearance. Surgery 99:439-445, 1986.
87. Senninger N, **Moody FG**, Coelho JCU, Van Buren DH. The role of biliary obstruction in the pathogenesis of acute pancreatitis in the opossum. Surgery 99:688-693, 1986.
88. Coelho JCU, Gouma DJ, Li YF, **Moody FG**, Schlegel JF. Effect of 16,16-dimethyl prostaglandin E_2 on the myoelectric activity of the gastrointestinal tract of the opossum. J Physiol 377:421-427, 1986.
89. Coelho JCU, Gouma DJ, **Moody FG**, Li YF, Weisbrodt NW. Serotonin increases the velocity of propagation and frequency of the migrating myoelectric complexes. Eur J Clin Invest 16:252-256, 1986.
90. Coelho JCU, Gouma DJ, **Moody FG**, Li YF, Weisbrodt NW. The influence of autonomic drugs on the motility of the sphincter of Oddi in the opossum. Surg Gynecol Obstet 163:209-214, 1986.
91. Gouma DJ, Roughneen PT, Kumar S, **Moody FG**, Rowlands BJ. Changes in nutritional status associated with obstructive jaundice and biliary drainage in rats. Am J Clin Nutr 44:362-369, 1986.

92. Coelho JCU, Gouma DJ, **Moody FG**, Li YF, Senninger N. Gastrointestinal motility following small bowel obstruction in the opossum. J Surg Res 41:274-278, 1986.
93. Coelho JCU, Gouma DJ, Li YF, Senninger N, **Moody FG**. Efeito de estimulos fisiologicos sobre a motricidade do esfincter de oddi. Arq Gastroenterol, Sao Paulo 23:9-14, 1986.
94. Coelho JCU, Gouma DJ, **Moody FG**. Alteracoes da motricidade do esfincter de Oddi secundarias a administracao de algumas drogas. A Folha Medica 93:11-14, 1986.
95. Li YF, **Moody FG**, Weisbrodt NW, Zalewsky CA, Coelho JCU, Senninger N, Gouma D. Gallbladder contractility and mucus secretion after cholesterol feeding in the prairie dog. Surgery 100:900-904, 1986.
96. Coelho JCU, Gouma DJ, **Moody FG**, Senninger N, Li YF, Chey WY. Sphincter of Oddi and gastrointestinal motility disturbance following alcohol administration in the opossum. World J Surg 10:990-995, 1986.
97. Coelho JCU, **Moody FG**. Certain aspects of normal and abnormal motility of sphincter of Oddi. Dig Dis Sci 32:86-94, 1987.
98. Coelho JCU, Gouma DJ, Li YF, **Moody FG**. Correlation between biliopan-creatic pressure and electromyography of the sphincter of Oddi after various stimuli. ABCD Arq Bras Cir Dig, Sao Paulo 1:68-70, 1986.
99. Li YF, Weisbrodt NW, **Moody FG**, Coelho JC, Gouma DJ. Calcium-induced contraction and contractile protein content of gallbladder smooth muscle after high-cholesterol feeding of prairie dogs. Gastroenterology 92:746-750, 1987.
100. Gouma DJ, Coelho JCU, Schlegel JF, Li YF, Fisher JD, **Moody FG**. The effect of preoperative internal and external biliary drainage on mortality of jaundiced rats. Arch Surg 122:731-734, 1987.
101. Coelho JCU, Li YF, Gouma DJ, Senninger N, **Moody FG**. Dynamic study of Oddi's sphincter. Nat Med J China 67:206-208, 1987.

102. Senninger N, **Moody FG**, Coelho JCU, Van Buren DH. Intestinalization of pancreatic fragments in dogs--improvement in survival rate after acute segmental pancreatitis. Am J Surg 153:364-368, 1987.
103. Cavuoti OP, **Moody FG**, Martinez G. Role of pancreatic duct occlusion with Prolamine (Ethibloc) in necrotizing pancreatitis. Surgery 103:361-366, 1988.
104. Zalewsky CA, **Moody FG**, Allen MA, Davis EK. A morphological and radio-isotopic evaluation of water flow through the canine gastric wall after intraarterial acetylcholine chloride. J Penn Acad Sci 62:71-77, 1988.
105. Bland KI, Jones RS, Maher JW, Cotton PB, Pennell TC, Amerson R, Munson JL, Berci G, Fuchs GJ, Way LW, Graham JB, Lindenau BU, **Moody FG**. Extracorporeal shock-wave lithotripsy of bile duct calculi. Ann Surg 209:743-755, 1988.
106. **Moody FG,** Amerson JR, Berci G, Bland KL, Cotton PB, Graham JB, Jones RS, Maher JW, Munson JL, Pennell TC, Way LW. Lithotripsy for bile duct stones. Am J Surg 158:241-247, 1989.
107. **Moody FG**, Haley-Russell D, Li YF, Husband KJ, Weisbrodt NW, Dewey RB. The effects of lithogenic bile on gallbladder epithelium. Ann Surg 210:406-416, 1989.
108. Haley-Russell D, Husband KJ, **Moody FG**. Morphology and bile composition of the prairie dog gallbladder: normal characteristics and changes during early lithogenesis. Am J Anat 186:1-11, 1989.
109. Calabuig R, Ulrich-Baker MG, **Moody FG**, Weems WA. The propulsive behavior of the opossum sphincter of Oddi. Am J Physiol 258:G138-G142, 1990.
110. Calabuig R, Seggerman RE, Weems WA, Weisbrodt NW, **Moody FG**. Gallbladder and gastrointestinal motility after hemorrhagic shock. Surgery 107:568-573, 1990.
111. Li YF, Bowers RL, Haley-Russell D, **Moody FG**, Weisbrodt NW. Actin and myosin isoforms in gallbladder smooth muscle following cholesterol feeding in prairie dogs. Gastroenterology 99:1460-1466, 1990.

112. Calabuig R, Weems WA, **Moody FG**. Choledochoduodenal flow: Effect of the sphincter of Oddi in opossums and cats. Gastroenterology 99:1641-1646, 1990.
113. Runkel NS, Rodriguez LF, LaRocco MT, **Moody FG**. Mechanisms of pancreatic infection in acute pancreatitis in opossums. Curr Surg 47:460-462, 1990.
114. **Moody FG**, Calabuig R, Li YF, Harari Y, Rodriguez LF, Weisbrodt NW. Biliary and gut function following shock. J Trauma 30:S179-S184, 1990.
115. **Moody FG**, Calabuig R, Vecchio R, Runkel N. Stenosis of the sphincter of Oddi. In Pitt HA (ed) Surg Clin North Am 70:1341-1354, 1990.
116. **Moody FG**, Vecchio R, Calabuig, R, Runkel N. Transduodenal sphincteroplasty with transampullary septectomy for stenosing papillitis. Am J Surg 161:213-218, 1991.
117. Miller TA, Tornwall MS, **Moody FG**. Stress erosive gastritis. Curr Prob Surg XXVIII:459-509, 1991.
118. Runkel NS, Rodriguez LF, **Moody FG**, LaRocco MT, Blasdel T. Salmonella infection of the biliary and intestinal tract of wild opossums. Lab Animal Sci 41:54-56, 1991.
119. Li YF, Weisbrodt NW, Harari Y, **Moody FG**. Use of modified Ussing chamber to monitor intestinal epithelial and smooth muscle functions. Am J Physiol 260:G166-G170, 1991.
120. Li YF, Weisbrodt NW, **Moody FG**. Effect of bile diversion and sphincterotomy on gallbladder muscle contractility and gallstone formation. Am J Surg 162:31-35, 1991.
121. Runkel NSF, **Moody FG**, Smith GS, Rodriguez LF, LaRocco MT, Miller TA. The role of the gut in the development of sepsis in acute pancreatitis. J Surg Res 51:18-23, 1991.
122. Harari Y, Calabuig R, **Moody F**, Castro G. Immunological sensitization of opossum gallbladder by naturally acquired stomach roundworm infection. Comp Biochem Physiol 99C:531-535, 1991.
123. Calabuig R, **Moody FG**. Gastrointestinal electrical activity in the prairie dog during fasting, feeding, and after high-cholesterol diet. J Gastrointestinal Motility 3:117-122, 1991.

124. Calabuig R, **Moody FG**. Odditis estenosante. Una vieja controversia. Cirugia Espanola 51:135-140, 1992.
125. Rodriguez L, Calabuig R, LaRocco M, **Moody FG**, Miller TA. Bacterial flora of the gastrointestinal tract of opossums. Vet Med 30:289-295, 1992.
126. Haley-Russell D, Calabuig R, **Moody FG**. Anatomy of the bilioduodenal junction of the opossum. Anat Rec 232:579-586, 1992.
127. Runkel NS, Smith GS, Rodriguez LF, LaRocco MT, **Moody FG**, Miller TA. Influence of shock on development of infection during acute pancreatitis in the rat. Dig Dis Sci 37:1418-1425, 1992.
128. **Moody FG**, Senninger N, Runkel N. (Editorial) Another challenge to the Opie myth. Gastroenterology 104:927-931, 1993.
129. Kueppers PM, Miller TA, Chen C-Y, Smith GS, Rodriguez LF, **Moody FG**. Effect of total parenteral nutrition plus morphine on bacterial translocation in rats. Ann Surg 217:286-292, 1993.
130. **Moody FG**. Lithotripsy in the treatment of biliary stones. Am J Surg 165:479-482, 1993.
131. Runkel NSF, **Moody FG**, Smith GS, Rodriguez LF, Chen Y, LaRocco MT, Miller TA. Alterations in rat intestinal transit by morphine promote bacterial translocation. Dig Dis Sci 38:1530-1536, 1993.
132. Kueppers PM, Russell DH, **Moody FG**. Reversibility of pancreatitis after temporary pancreaticobiliary duct obstruction in rats. Pancreas 8:632-637, 1993.
133. Li YF, Newton TJ, Weisbrodt NW, **Moody FG**. Intestinal migrating myoelectric complexes in rats with acute pancreatitis and bile duct ligation. J Surg Res 55:182-187, 1993.
134. Gray CR, Li YF, Weisbrodt NW, Russell DH, **Moody FG**. Intestinal muscle contractility during acute pancreatitis. Neurogastroenterol Mot 6:37-42, 1994.

135. Li YF, Weisbrodt NW, Lodato RF, **Moody FG**. Nitric oxide is involved in muscle relaxation but not in changes in short-circuit current in rat ileum. Am J Physiol 266:G554-G559, 1994.
136. Li YF, Russell DH, Myers SI, Weisbrodt NW, **Moody FG**. Gallbladder contractility in aspirin- and cholesterol-fed prairie dogs. Gastroenterology 106:1662-1667, 1994.
137. Runkel NSF, Rodriguez LF, **Moody FG**. Mechanisms of Sepsis in Acute Pancreatitis. Am J Surg 169:227-232, 1995.
138. Mankarious R, Zaafran S, McDonald G, **Moody FG**. Jaundice and massive abdominal lymphadenopathy. Hospital Medicine, June 15, 1995, 31-32.
139. **Moody FG**, Haley-Russell D, Muncy D. Intestinal transit and bacterial translocation in obstructive pancreatitis. Dig Dis Sci 40:1798-1804, 1995.
140. Fuchshuber PR, Vecchio R, Turnquest D, **Moody FG**. Aberrant biliopancreatic duct. Arch Surg 130:1139-1141, 1995.
141. Zembowicz MJ, Zembowicz A, Khan AR, Higham C, Weisbrodt NW, **Moody FG**, Pressley TA, Lodado RF. Charazterization of calcium-independent NO synthase expressed in the ileum of healthy rats. The Biology of Nitric Oxide, part 5, Portland Press Proc, p. 296, 1996.
142. Clifton GL, Donovan WH, Dimitrijevic MM, Allen SJ, Ku A, Potts JR III, **Moody FG**, Coake C, Sherwood AM, Edwards JV. Omental transposition in chronic spinal cord injury. Spinal Cord 34:193-203, 1996.
143. Weisbrodt NW, Pressley TA, Li Y-F, Zembowicz MJ, HighamSC, Zembowicz A, Lodato RF, **Moody FG**. Decreased ileal muscle contractility and increased NOS II expression induced by lipopolysaccharide. Am J Physiol 271:G454-G460, 1996.
144. Calabuig R, Weems WA, **Moody FG**. Union ileo-cecal: valvula o esfinter. Un estudio experimental en la zarigueya. Rev Esp Enf Digest, 88:834-839, 1996.
145. Klemm K, Mercer DW, MailmanD, **Moody FG**. Hypotension during septic shock does not correlate with plasma levels of

nitric oxide metabolites in the conscious rat. J Gastrointest Surg I:347-356, 1997.

146. Klemm K, **Moody FG**. Regional intestinal blood flow and nitric oxide synthase inhibition during sepsis in the rat. Ann Surg 227:126-133, 1998.

147. Lodato RF, Rizwan Khan A, Zembowicz MJ, Weisbrodt NW, Pressley TA, Li YF, Lodato JA, Zembowicz A, and **Moody FG**. Roles of IL-! And TNF in the decreased muscle contractility induced by lipopolysaccharide. Am J Physiol 276 (Gastrointest. Liver Physiol. 39):G1356-G1362, 1999.

148. Ayra R, Grosssie B Jr, Weisbrodt NW, Lai M, Mailman D, **Moody F**. Temporal Expression of Tumor Necrosis Factor-alpha and Nitric Oxide Synthase 2 in Rat Small Intestine after Endotoxin. Dig Dis and Sci 45:744-49, 2000.

149. Harari Y, Wiesbrodt NW, **Moody FG.** Ileal Mucosal Response to Bacterial Toxin Challenge. J Trauma 2000;49:306-313.

150. Hassoun HH, Mercer DW, **Moody FG**, Weisbrodt NW, Moore FA: Postinjury multiple organ failure: The role of the gut. Shock 15:1-10, 2001.

151. Hassoun HT, Weisbrodt NW, Mercer DW, Kozar RA**, Moody FG**, Moore FA: Inducible nitric oxide synthase mediates gut ischemia/reperfusion induced ileus only after severe insults. J Surg Res 97:150-154, 2001.

152. Grossie, V.B., Jr, Weisbrodt, N.W., Moore, F.A., and Moody, F.: Ischemia/reperfusion-induced disruption of rat small intestine transit is reversed by total enteral nutrition. Nutrition 17:939-943, 2001.

153. Harari Y., Weisbrodt N., **Moody F.A**. The effect of morphine on mast cell-mediated mucosal permeabilty. Surgery, Volume 139 (1) 54-60, 2006.

154. Camilleri M, Toouli J, Herrera MF, Kulseng B, Kow L, Pantoja JP, Marvik R, Johnsen G, Billington CJ, **Moody FG**, Knudson MG, Tweden KS, Vollmer MC, Wilson RR, Anvari M. Intra-abdominal Vagal Blocking (VBLOC Therapy): Clinical Results with a New Implantable Medical Device. Surgery: Journal of the Society of University Surgeons 2008;143:732-731.

155. Camilleri M, Toouli J, Herrera MF, Kow L, Pantoja JP, Billington CJ, Tweden KS, Wilson RR, **Moody FG**. Selection of Electrical Algorithms to Treat Obesity with ntermittent Vagal Block Using An Implantable Medical Device (accepted with electronic prepublication, Surgery for Obesity and Related Diseases. September 2008).
156. Leichman JG, Wilson EB, Scarborough T, Aguilar D, Miller CC, Yu S, Algahim MF, Reyes M, **Moody FG**, Taegtmeyer H. Dramatic Reversal of Derangements in Muscle Metabolism and Left Ventricular Function After Bariatric Surgery. The American Journal of Medicine Volume 121 (11) 966-973.
157. **Moody FG**. Disease Prevention from a Surgical Perspective. The American Journal of Medicine 2011;201: 138-139.

INVITED ARTICLES

1. **Moody FG**. The surgical management of gastrointestinal cancer. South Med Bull 57:107-110, 1969.
2. **Moody FG**. The latest concepts in surgical management of peptic ulcer disease. J Alabama Med Assoc 39:464-468, 1969.
3. **Moody FG**. Choice of operation in surgical treatment of ulcer. Curr Med Dialogue 38:421-432, 1971.
4. **Moody FG**, Tessier C, Gross L. Preparing patients to live with an ileostomy. Medical-Surgical Review August-September 1971.
5. **Moody FG**. Town-gown relations and affiliated hospital residency programs. Surgery 74:474-478, 1973.
6. **Moody FG**. Rectal bleeding. N Engl J Med 290:839-841, 1974.
7. **Moody FG**. Surgical manpower: quality, quantity, and distribution. Am J Surg 132:688-690, 1976.
8. **Moody FG**. Answers to questions on stress ulcer. Hosp Med 13:8-25, 1977.
9. **Moody FG**. Cimetidine and prostaglandin: evidence for different modes of action on gastric mucosa. Gastroenterology 74:1333-1334, 1978.

9a. **Moody FG**. Sphincteroplasty with transampullary septectomy. Perspectives in Surgery 1:1-11, 1978.

10. **Moody FG**. Peptic ulcer surgery. Am J Surg 135:731, 1978.
11. **Moody FG**. Sclerosing cholangitis. Gastroenterology: A Weekly Update 1:154-159, 1979.
12. **Moody FG**. LCGME: A critical link to the future. Bull Am Coll Surg, March 1979.
13. **Moody FG**. Zalewsky CA, Larsen KR. Invited Commentary: Effect of bile on canine gastric mucosa. World J Surg 4:475-476, 1980.
14. **Moody FG**. An ounce of surgery for a pound of cure. The Pharos Alpha Omega Alpha 43:19-21, 1980.

15. Larsen KR, **Moody FG**. Editorial: Clinical significance of gastric blood flow autoregulation during stimulation. Dig Dis Sci 27:673-674, 1982.
16. **Moody FG**. Editorial: Diagnosis and treatment of obstructive biliary tract disease. West J Med 136:530-532, 1982.
17. Larsen KR, **Moody FG**. Editorial: 16,16-Dimethyl PGE_2 and HCO_3- efflux. Dig Dis Sci 28:649-650, 1982.
18. **Moody FG**, Carey LC. Editorial on Frank Glenn. Surg Gastroenterol 1:267, 1982.
19. Larsen KR, **Moody FG**. Editorial: Functional difference between ridges and valleys in gastric mucosal rugae. Surgery 91:243-244, 1982.
20. Potts JR III, **Moody FG**. Surgical approaches to chronic pancreatitis. Surgical Capsule and Comment p 2, November 1982.
21. **Moody FG**. Surgical gastroenterology: Problems and Solutions. Am J Surg 145:2-4, 1983.
22. **Moody FG**, Miller TA. Answers to questions on stress ulcer. Hospital Medicine 19:33-56, 1983.
23. **Moody FG**. Foreword: Transplantation Proceedings XV, Suppl 1:2207, 1983.
24. Herrington JL, Skinner DB, **Moody FG**, Cohn I Jr, Vazio VW. Symposium: General surgery problems. Contemp Surg 26:85-135, 1985.
25. **Moody FG**. Funding of graduate medical education: Perspective of a surgical educator. Curr Surg 43:271-274, 1986.
26. **Moody FG**. Invited Commentary: A healthy, disease-free society. West J Med 145:184-185, 1986.
27. **Moody FG**. Commentary: Biliary strictures as a cause of primary intrahepatic bile duct stones. World J Surg 10:874-875, 1986.
28. **Moody FG**. Book Review: Colorectal Cancer: Concepts in Diagnosis and Treatment. New Engl J Med 315:1360-1361, 1986.

29. **Moody FG**. Editorial: Clinical research in the era of cost containment. Am J Surg 153:337-340, 1987.
30. **Moody FG**. Book Review: Surgical Management of Morbid Obesity. N Engl J Med 318:387, 1988.
31. **Moody FG**. Moderator and Summation: The public's perception of medicine. The Medical Profession: Enduring Values and New Challenges. Conf Proc of AMA Section on Medical Schools, Feb 25-27, 1987, pp 139-194, 1988.
32. **Moody FG**. Pancreatitis as a medical emergency. Gastroenterol Clin North Am 17:433-443, 1988.
33. **Moody FG**. Editorial: Acute acalculous cholecystitis. Mayo Clin Proc 64:255, 1989.
34. **Moody FG**, Kuzin MI, Morino F. Morbid obesity. General Surgery: Current Status and Future Trends, pp 263-268, XXVI World Congress of the International College of Surgeons, Milan, Italy, July 3-9, 1988, Raven Press, 1989.
35. **Moody FG**. Laparoscopic cholecystectomy. In: Greenberger NJ (ed) Decision Making in GI Disease. 10 pp, Glaxo Pharmaceuticals, HP Publishing Co., 10 Astor Place, New York, NY 10003.
36. Toouli J, Lam SK, Stevenson G, Choi TK, Berci G, Mack E, **Moody FG**. Symptomatic gallstones: Management options for the 1990s. HPB Surg 4:255-260, 1991.
37. **Moody FG**. (Book Review) Gastrointestinal Emergencies. Surg Gynecol Obstet 175:577, 1992.
38. **Moody FG**, Potts JR III. Management of biliary tract injuries secondary to laparoscopic cholecystectomy. Surgical Rounds 16:651-659, 1993.
39. Weisbrodt NW, **Moody FG**. (Letter) Gallbladder contractility. Gastroenterology 102:741-742, 1992.
40. McGill, DB, **Moody FG**. (Commentary) Invasive endoscopy and the medical/surgical divide. Gastroenterology 107:306-308, 1994.
41. **Moody FG**. Two women with severe abdominal pain--indications for laparoscopic cholecystectomy. Gastrointestinal Diseases Today 3:1-18, 1994.

42. **Moody FG**. Definition of acute obstructive suppurative cholangitis. J Hep Bil Pancr Surg 3:1-3, 1996.
43. **Moody FG.** Bile Duct Injury During Laparoscopic Cholecystectomy. Surg Endosc 2000;14:605-607.

BOOK CHAPTERS

1. Durbin RP, **Moody FG**. Water movement through a transporting epithelial membrane: the gastric mucosa. In: The Statement and Movement of Water in Living Organisms, pp 299-306, Sixth Symposium of the Society for Experimental Biology, Cambridge University Press, 1964.
2. Kurihara M, **Moody FG**. The complications of general surgery. In: Concepts and Practices of Intensive Care for Nurse Specialists, pp 280-311, The Charles Press Publishers, Inc., 1969.
3. **Moody FG**. Water flow through gastric secretory mucosa. In: Gastric Secretion, pp 431-452, Academic Press, Inc., New York and London, 1972.
4. **Moody FG**. Role of mucosal blood flow in the pathogenesis of gastric ulcers. In: Holdon P (ed) International Encyclopedia of Pharmacology and Therapeutics, pp 339-360, Permagon Press, Oxford and New York, 1973.
5. Torma MJ, **Moody FG**, Cheung LY, Zalewsky C. Surface and microcirculatory effects of carbenoxolone on aspirin-induced erosive gastritis in dogs. In: Jones Sir FA, Parke DV (eds) Fourth Symposium on Carbenoxolone, pp 41-54, Butterworth Publishers, London, 1975.
6. **Moody FG**. Surgical implications of cholangitis. In: Najarian JS, Delaney JP (eds) Surgery of the Liver, Pancreas and Biliary Tract, pp 131-141, Symposia Specialists, Miami, 1975.
7. **Moody FG**. Portacaval and splenorenal shunts. In: Najarian JS, Delaney JP (eds) Surgery of the Liver, Pancreas and Biliary Tract, pp 601-609, Symposia Specialists, Miami, 1975.
8. **Moody FG**. Achalasia of the esophagus. In: Hardy JD (ed) Rhoads Textbook of Surgery, Principles and Practice ed 5, pp 756-762, J.B Lippincott Co., Philadelphia and Toronto, 1977.
9. **Moody FG**. Ulcerative colitis. In: Sabiston DC Jr (ed) Davis-Christopher Textbook of Surgery ed 11, pp 1115-1124, W.B. Saunders Co., Philadelphia, London & Toronto, 1977.

10. Zalewsky CA, Bauer RF, **Moody FG**, Brooks FP. Effect of vagal stimulation upon parietal cell ultrastructure. In: Brooks FP, Evers PW (eds) Nerves and the Gut, pp 41-50, Slack, Thorofare, NJ, 1977.
11. **Moody FG**. Surgical therapy for gallstones and their complications. In: Schoenfeld LJ (ed) Diseases of the Gallbladder and Biliary System, pp 235-279, John Wiley & Sons, New York, London, Sydney and Toronto, 1977.
12. **Moody FG**. Acute stress erosions and ulceration. In: Sleisenger MH, Fordtran JS (eds) Gastrointestinal Disease Pathophysiology, Diagnosis Management ed 2, Vol 1, pp 826-838, W.B. Saunders Co., Philadelphia, London, and Toronto, 1978.
13. **Moody FG**, McGreevy JM, Zalewsky CA. Role of gastric blood flow in the pathogenesis of erosion and ulcers. In: Peptic Ulcer Disease: An Update, pp 135-150, Biomedical Information Corporation Publications, New York, 1979.
14. Cheung LY, **Moody FG**. The use of microspheres to measure gastric mucosal blood flow. In: Fielding LP (ed) Gastro-Intestinal Mucosal Blood Flow, pp 27-34, Churchill Livingstone, Edinburgh, London and New York, 1980.
15. **Moody FG.** The basis of the methods to estimate mucosal blood flow. In: Fielding LP (ed) Gastro-Intestinal Mucosal Blood Flow, pp 83-86, Churchill Livingstone, Edinburgh, London and New York, 1980.
16. Cheung LY, **Moody FG**. Gastric blood flow: comparison of venous outflow, gamma labelled microspheres ands aminopyrine clearance methods. In: Fielding LP (ed) Gastro-intestinal Mucosal Blood Flow, pp 138-146, Churchill Livingstone, Edinburgh, London and New York, 1980.
17. **Moody FG**. Gastric operations. In: Schwartz SI (ed) Modern Technics in Surgery. Abdominal Surgery, Installment I, pp I-1-I-58, Futura, New York, 1980.
18. Rikkers LF, **Moody FG**. Abdomen. In: Wolcott MW (ed) Ambulatory Surgery and the Basics of Emergency Surgical

Care, pp 315-327, JP Lippincott Co., Philadelphia and Toronto, 1981.

19. Larsen KR, **Moody FG**. Selection of appropriate methodology for the measurement of blood flow in the gut. In: Granger DN, Bulkley DB (eds) Measurement of Blood Flow. Applications to the Splanchnic Circulation, pp 511-528, Williams & Wilkins, Baltimore, 1981.
20. **Moody FG**. Ulcerative colitis. In: Sabiston DB Jr (ed) Davis-Christopher Textbook of Surgery ed 12, pp 1099-1108, W.B. Saunders Co., Philadelphia, London, and Toronto, 1981.
21. **Moody FG**, Potts JR. The pancreas. In: Kyle J, Hardy JD (eds) Scientific Foundations of Surgery ed 3, pp 479-506, William Heinemann Medical Books Ltd, London, 1981.
22. **Moody FG**, Zalewsky CA. The gastric surface epithelial cell. In: Harmon JW (ed) Basic Mechanisms of Gastrointestinal Mucosal Cell Injury and Protection, pp 373-389, Williams & Wilkins, Baltimore, 1981.
23. **Moody FG**, DeVries WC. The esophagus and diaphragmatic hernias. In: Hardy JD (ed) Hardy's Textbook of Surgery, pp 469-496, J.B. Lippincott Company, Philadelphia, 1983.
24 **Moody FG**. Biliary, pancreas and papilla of Vater interrelationships. In: Blumgart LH (ed) Clinical Surgery V: The Biliary Tract, pp 197-208, Churchill-Livingstone, New York, 1982.
25. **Moody FG**, McGreevy JM. Stomach. In: Schwartz SI, Shires GT, Spencer FC, Storer EH (eds) Principles of Surgery ed 4, pp 1113-1145, McGraw-Hill Co., New York, 1983.
26. **Moody FG**, McGreevy JM. Complications of gastric surgery. In Greenfield LJ (ed) Complications in Surgery and Trauma, pp 425-446, J.B. Lippincott Co., Philadelphia, 1983.
27. **Moody FG**. Postcholecystectomy syndromes. In: **Moody FG** (ed) Advances in Diagnosis and Treatment of Biliary Tract Disease, pp 49-56, Masson Publishing USA, Inc., New York, 1983.
28. **Moody FG**. Papillary function and physiology. In Salmon PR (ed) Gastrointestinal Endoscopy: Advances in Diagnosis

and Therapy, Vol. 1, pp 163-180, Chapman and Hall Medical, London, 1984.

29. **Moody FG**. Postcholecystectomy syndrome. In: Cameron J (ed) Current Surgical Therapy 1984-1985, pp 211-215, B.C. Decker, Philadelphia, 1984.
30. Larsen KR, **Moody FG**. Anatomy of blood circulation. In: Abramson DI, Dobrin PB (eds) Blood Vessels and Lymphatics, pp 410-415, Academic Press, New York, 1984.
31. McGreevy JM, **Moody FG**. Pathophysiology, pathogenesis, and pathology of blood circulation. In: Abramson DI, Dobrin PB (eds) Blood Vessels and Lymphatics, pp 423-427, Academic Press, New York, 1984.
32. **Moody FG**. Surgery for benign disease of the papilla of Vater. In: Najarian JS, Delaney JP (eds) Advances in Hepatic, Biliary and Pancreatic Surgery ed 2, pp 261-269, Year Book Medical Publishers, Chicago, 1985.
33. **Moody FG**. Biliary stones. In: Najarian JS, Delaney JP (eds) Advances in Hepatic, Biliary and Pancreatic Surgery ed 2, pp 199-207, Year Book Medical Publishers, Chicago, 1985.
34. Becker JM, **Moody FG**. Sphincter of Oddi and biliary motility. In: Condon RE, DeCosse J (eds) Surgical Care II, pp 40-55, Lea & Febiger, Philadelphia, 1985.
35. **Moody FG**, Larsen KR. Acute erosions and stress ulcer. In: Berk JE, Haubrich WS, Kalser MH, Roth JLA, Schaffner F (eds) Bockus Gastroenterology ed 4, pp 1004-1012, W.B. Saunders Co., Philadelphia, 1985.
36. **Moody FG**. Consultant on Chapter 6, Biliary tract, liver and pancreas. In: Hickey RC (ed) Year Book of Cancer, pp 81-93, Year Book Medical Publishers, Chicago, 1985.
37. **Moody FG**. Stomach and duodenum. In: Beahrs OH, Beart RW Jr (eds) General Surgery--Therapy Update Service, pp 7-1-7-21, Harwal Publishing Co., Media, PA, 1985.
38. **Moody FG**. Surgical consultation in digestive disease. In **Moody FG** (ed) Surgical Treatment of Digestive Disease, pp 3-8, Year Book Medical Publishers, Chicago, 1986.

39. **Moody FG**. The postcholecystectomy syndrome. In **Moody FG** (ed) Surgical Treatment of Digestive Disease, pp 296-305, Year Book Medical Publishers, Chicago, 1986.
40. Becker JM, **Moody FG**. Ulcerative colitis. In: Sabiston DB (ed) Textbook of Surgery, pp 1011-1023, WB Saunders Co., Philadelphia, 1986.
41. **Moody FG**. Consultant on Chapter 6, Biliary tract, liver and pancreas. In: Hickey RC (ed) Year Book of Cancer, pp 95-107, Year Book Medical Publishers, Chicago, 1986.
42. **Moody FG**. Therapy in intractable gallbladder disease. In: Griffin WO Jr, Mandelstam P (eds) Selected Gastrointestinal Disorders: Intractability and Its Management, pp 62-68, Williams & Wilkins, Baltimore, 1987.
43. **Moody FG**. Postcholecystectomy syndromes. In: Nyhus LM (ed) Surgery Annual—1987, pp 205-220, Appleton & Lange, Norwalk, CT/Los Altos, CA, 1987.
44. **Moody FG**, Thompson DA. Postoperative jaundice. In: Schiff L, Schiff ER (eds) Diseases of the Liver, pp 1223-1233, J.B. Lippincott Co., Philadelphia, 1987.
45. **Moody FG**. Consultant on Chapter 6, Biliary tract, liver and pancreas. In: Hickey RC (ed) Year Book of Cancer, pp 113-125, Year Book Medical Publishers, Chicago, 1987.
46. **Moody FG**. Comments on Chapter 7, Stomach and duodenum. In: Beahrs, OH, Beart RW Jr (eds) General Surgery, Therapy Update Service, pp 1-4, Harwal Medical Publications, Inc., Media, PA, 1988.
47. **Moody FG**, Roth JA. The esophagus and diaphragmatic hernias. In: Hardy JD (ed) Hardy's Textbook of Surgery ed 2, pp 485-513, J.B. Lippincott Co., Philadelphia, 1988.
48. **Moody FG**. Surgical treatment of cholelithiasis. In: Gitnick G (ed) Principles and Practice of Gastroenterology and Hepatology, pp 950-966, Elsevier, New York, 1988.
49. **Moody FG**. Neoplastic disorders. In: Gitnick G (ed) Principles and Practice of Gastroenterology and Hepatology, pp 998-1009, Elsevier, New York, 1988.

50. **Moody FG**, McGreevy JM, Miller TA. Stomach. In: Schwartz SI, Shires GT, Spencer FC (eds) Principles of Surgery ed 5, pp 1157-1188, McGraw-Hill Book Co., New York, 1988.
51. **Moody FG**. Consultant on Chapter 6, Biliary tract, liver, and pancreas. In: Hickey RC (ed) Year Book of Cancer, pp 111-125, Year Book Medical Publishers, Chicago 1988.
52. **Moody FG**. Postcholecystectomy syndrome. In: Cameron JL (ed) Current Surgical Therapy ed 3, pp 276-280, B.C. Decker Inc., Philadelphia and Toronto, 1989.
53. **Moody FG**, McGreevy JM. Complications of gastric surgery. In: Greenfield LJ (ed) Complications in Surgery and Trauma ed 2, pp 449-470, J.B. Lippincott, Philadelphia, 1990.
54. **Moody FG**. The surgical consultation. In **Moody FG** (ed) Surgical Treatment of Digestive Disease ed 2, pp 53-59, Year Book Medical Publishers, Chicago, 1990.
55. **Moody FG**. The postcholecystectomy syndrome. In: **Moody FG** (ed) Surgical Treatment of Digestive Disease ed 2, pp 298-309, Year Book Medical Publishers, Chicago, 1990.
56. **Moody FG**, Miller TA. Stomach and duodenum. In: Nora PF (ed) Operative Surgery ed 3, pp 487-497, WB Saunders Co, Philadelphia, 1990.
57. **Moody FG**. Modern day treatment of acute cholecystitis. In: Najarian JS, Delaney JP (eds) Progress in Hepatic, Biliary, and Pancreatic Surgery pp 124-129, Year Book Medical Publishers, Inc., Chicago, 1990.
58. **Moody FG**. Pancreas divisum and other surgical anomalies of the pancreatic ducts. In: Najarian JS, Delaney JP (eds) Progress in Hepatic, Biliary and Pancreatic Surgery pp 260-268, Year Book Medical Publishers, Inc., Chicago, 1990.
59. **Moody FG**. Pós-Colecistevctomia. In: Coelho JCU (ed) Aparelho Digestivo Clínica e Cirurgia vol II, pp 1069-1072, MEDSI Editora Medica e Cientifica Ltda, Rio de Janiero, 1990.
60. Weisbrodt NW, Li YF, **Moody FG**, Haley-Russell D, Myers SI. Cholesterol feeding and gallbladder muscle contractility. In: Snape WJ Jr, Collins SM (eds) Effects of Immune Cells and

Inflammation on Smooth Muscle and Enteric Nerves, pp 25-33, CRC Press, Inc., Boca Raton, 1991.

61. Calabuig R, **Moody FG**. Abdominal cavity: Anatomy and structural anomalies. In: Yamada T, Alpers DH, Owyang C, Powell DW, Silverstein FE (eds) Textbook of Gastroenterology pp 2045-2055, J.B. Lippincott, Philadelphia, 1991.
62. Thompson DA, **Moody FG**. Intra-abdominal abscesses and fistulas. In: Yamada T, Alpers DH, Owyang C, Powell DW, Silverstein FE (eds) Textbook of Gastroenterology pp 2057-2065, J.B. Lippincott, Philadelphia, 1991.
63. Li YF, **Moody FG**. Diseases of the mesentery and omentum. In: Yamada T, Alpers DH, Owyang C, Powell DW, Silverstein FE (eds) Textbook of Gastroenterology pp 2066-2071, J.B. Lippincott, Philadelphia, 1991.
64. Li YF, **Moody FG**. Diseases of the peritoneum. In: Yamada T, Alpers DH, Owyang C, Powell DW, Silverstein FE (eds) Textbook of Gastroenterology pp 2071-2078, J.B. Lippincott, Philadelphia, 1991.
65. Runkel NS, **Moody FG**. Diseases of the retroperitoneum. In: Yamada T, Alpers DH, Owyang C, Powell DW, Silverstein FE (eds) Textbook of Gastroenterology pp 2079-2085, J.B. Lippincott, Philadelphia, 1991.
66. **Moody FG**, Ortega JM. Exploratory laparotomy. In: Yamada T, Alpers DH, Owyang C, Powell DW, Silverstein FE (eds) Textbook of Gastroenterology pp 2662-2668, J.B. Lippincott, Philadelphia, 1991.
67. Becker JM, **Moody FG**. Ulcerative colitis. In: Sabiston DC Jr (ed) Textbook of Surgery, pp 927-940, W.B. Saunders, Philadelphia, 1991.
68. **Moody FG**. Cholecystitis and cholelithiasis. In: Rakel RE (ed) Conn's Current Therapy 1992 pp 411-413, W.B. Saunders, Philadelphia, 1992.
69. Speranza V, **Moody FG**. Common bile duct stones: Therapeutic approach. In: **Moody FG**, Montorsi W, Montorsi M, Zennaro F. Advances in Surgery pp 229-232, Serono Symposia Publications from Raven Press, New York, 1991.

70. **Moody FG**, Ferrarese S. Cholecystectomy and colon cancer. In: **Moody FG**, Montorsi W, Montorsi M, Zennaro F. Advances in Surgery pp 237-239, Serono Symposia Publications from Raven Press, New York, 1991.
71. **Moody FG**, Calabuig R, Thompson DA, Li YF, Runkel NS. Diseases of the peritoneal cavity. In: Yamada T, Albers DH, Owyang C, Powell DW, Silverstein FE (eds) Atlas of Gastroenterology pp 369-378, J.B. Lippincott, Philadelphia, 1992.
72. **Moody FG**: The changing health care economy: Impact on surgical techniques. In: Gelijns AC (ed) Technology and Health Care in an Era of Limits (Medical Innovation at the Crossroads, Vol. III, pp 231-245, Institute of Medicine, Washington, D.C., 1992.
73. Miller TA, Reed RL II, **Moody FG**. Gastrointestinal hemorrhage. In: Barie PS, Shires GT (eds) Surgical Intensive Care, pp 743-765, Little, Brown and Co., Boston, 1993
74. **Moody FG**, Potts JR III. Postoperative Jaundice. In: Schiff L, Schiff ER (eds) Diseases of the Liver ed. 7, pp. 370-376, JB Lippincott, Philadelphia, 1993.
75. **Moody FG**, Miller TA. Stomach. In: Schwartz SI, Shires GT, Spencer FC (eds) Principles of Surgery ed 6, pp 1123-1152, McGraw-Hill, Inc., New York, 1993.
76. **Moody FG**, Potts JR III. Congenital anomalies of the pancreas. In: Trede M, Carter DC (eds) Surgery of the Pancreas, pp 369-379, Churchill Livingstone, Edinburgh, 1993.
77. **Moody FG**. Ch. 7 Stomach and duodenum. In: Beahrs Oh, Beart RW Jr, Pemberton JH (eds) Surgical Consultations, Mosby-Year Book, Inc., St. Louis, pp. 1-19, 1993.
78. **Moody FG**, Potts JR III. Dysfunction of the ampulla of Vater. In: Braasch JW, Tompkins RK (eds) Surgical Disease of the Biliary Tract and Pancreas--Multidisciplinary Management, pp 334-348, Mosby-Year Book, Inc., St. Louis, 1994.
79. **Moody FG**. Surgical Treatment of gallstones. In: Gitnick G (ed) Principles and Practice of Gastroenterology and

Hepatology (ed 2), pp 599-610, Appleton & Lange, Norwalk, CT, 1994.

80. **Moody FG**. Neoplastic disorders. In: Gitnick G (ed) Principles and Practice of Gastroenterology and Hepatology (ed 2), pp 635-642, Appleton & Lange, Norwalk, CT 1994.

81. **Moody FG**, Potts JR III. Overview of surgery. In: Nyhus LM (ed) Surgery Annual 1995, pp 1-27, Appleton & Lange, Norwalk, Ct, 1995.

82. **Moody FG**, Calabuig R. Abdominal cavity: Anatomy, structural anomalies, and hernias. In: Yamada T, Albers DH, Owyang C, Powell DW, Silverstein FE (eds) Textbook of Gastroenterology ed 2, pp 1178-1188, J.B. Lippincott Co., Philadelphia 1995.

83. **Moody FG**, Runkel NF. Diseases of the retroperitoneum. In: Yamada T, Albers DH, Owyang C, Powell DW, Silverstein FE (eds) Textbook of Gastroenterology ed 2, pp 2314-2321, J.B. Lippincott Co., Philadelphia, 1995.

84. **Moody F**, Weisbrodt N. Post-surgical motility disorders. In: Kumar D, Wingate D(eds) An Illustrated Guide to Gastrointestinal Motility (ed 2), pp 673-690, Churchill-Livingstone, London, 1993.

85. **Moody FG.** Síndrome pós-colectistectomia. In: Coelho JCU (ed) Aparelho Digestive (ed 2), pp 1339-1344, Editora Medical Cientifica Ltda., Rio de Janiero, 1996.

86. Li YF, Weisbrodt N, and **Moody FG**. The biliary tract. In: Jensen SL, Gregersen H, Shokouh-Amiri MH, Moody FG. (eds) Essentials of Experimental Surgery: Gastroenterology, pp 41-1-41-10, Harwood Academic Publishers, Amsterdam, 1996.

87. **Moody FG**. Gallstones and biliary tract. In: Bone RC (Series ed), Graham DY, Ertan A (Section Eds) Current Practice of Medicine vol IV, sec 13, pp 20.1-20.5, Churchill Livingstone, New York, 1996.

88. **Moody FG**, Haley-Russell D, Li YF, Weisbrodt NW. Bacterial translocation in experimental acute pancreatitis. In: Faist E, Baue AE, Schildberg FW (eds) The Immune Consequences of

Trauma, Shock and Sepsis—Mechanisms and Therapeutic Approaches pp 887-897, Pabst Science Publishers, Lengerich, Germany, 1996.

89. Becker JM, **Moody FG**. Ulcerative colitis. In: Sabiston DC Jr (ed) Textbook of Surgery ed 15, W.B. Saunders Company, Philadelphia, 1997, pp 1001-1013.

90. **Moody FG**. Tratamiento de los quistes, los cálculos y las estenosis biliares mediante las técnicas más avanzadas. In: González EM, Hidalgo P (eds) Actualización en Cirugía del Aparato Digestivo, Jarpyo Editores, S.A., Madrid, Spain, 1996, pp 391-394.

91. **Moody FG**, Mercer DW, Taylor MB. Intraabdominal abscesses. In Taylor MB (ed) Gastrointestinal Emergencies ed 2, Williams & Wilkins, Baltimore, 1997, pp 725-736.

92. **Moody FG**, Potts JR III. Congenital anomalies of the pancreas. In: Trede M, Carter DC (eds) Surgery Of The Pancreas ed 2. Churchill Livingstone Inc., New York, 1998. pp391-401.

93. **Moody FG.** Postcholecystectomy problems. In: Cameron JL (ed) Current Surgical Therapy ed 6, Mosby, St. Louis, 1998, pp434-438.

94. **Moody FG.** The role of surgical sphincteroplasty. In Beger HG, Warshaw AL, and Buchler MW et al (eds) The Pancreas ed 2, Blackwell Science LTD, Oxford, 1998, pp824-

95. **Moody FG**, Mercer DW. Surgery of the Esophagus and Stomach. In Moody, FG (ed) Atlas of Ambulatory Surgery, WB Saunders Company, Philadelphia, 1999, pp 151-168.

96. **Moody FG**. Lower Extremity Procedures. In Moody, FG (ed) Atlas of Ambulatory Surgery, WB Saunders Company, Philadelphia, 1999, pp 277-290.

97. **Moody FG,** Calabuig R. Abdominal Cavity: Anatomy, Structural Anomalies and Hernias. In: Gastroenterology, 2nd Ed. Lippincott Williams and Wilkins, Philadelphia, 1999, pp 2355-2365.

98. **Moody FG,** Kwong, Karen. Biliary: Benign. In: The Practice of General Surgery, WB Saunders Company, Philadelphia, 2002, pp 653-658.
99. **Moody FG,** Sphincterotoby/Sphincteroplasty for Papillary Dysfunction: Stenosing Papllitis. In: Atals of Gastrointestinal and HepatoPancreato- Biliary Surgery. 2007, pp 811-818.
100. **Moody FG**. Postcholecystectomy Syndrome. In: General Surgery: Principles and International Practice. Ed. Bland KI, Büchler MW, Csendes A, Garden OJ, Sarr MG, Wong J. Vol 2, Part 10:2008, pp 1029-1034.

BOOKS

1. Baron JH, **Moody FG** (co-eds). Foregut, 324 pp, Butterworth Publishers, London, 1981.
2. **Moody FG** (ed-in-chief). Advances in Diagnosis and Surgical Treatment of Biliary Tract Disease, 167 pp, Masson Publishing USA, 1983.
3. Greenberger NG, **Moody FG** (co-eds). The Year Book of Digestive Diseases 1984, 455 pp, Year Book Medical Publishers, Chicago, 1984.
4. Greenberger NG, **Moody FG** (co-eds). The Year Book of Digestive Diseases 1985, 495 pp, Year Book Medical Publishers, Chicago, 1985.
5. Baron JH, **Moody FG** (co-eds). Esofago y Estomago, El Manual Moderno, 320 pp, S.A. de C.V., Mexico, D.F., 1985.
6. Baron JH, **Moody FG** (co-eds). Foregut, Russian edition, 303 pp, 1985.
7. **Moody FG** (ed-in-chief). Surgical Treatment of Digestive Disease, ed 1, 847 pp, Year Book Medical Publishers, Chicago, 1986.
8. Greenberger NG, **Moody FG** (co-eds). The Year Book of Digestive Diseases 1986, 479 pp, Year Book Medical Publishers, Chicago, 1986.
9. Greenberger NG, **Moody FG** (co-eds). The Year Book of Digestive Diseases 1987, 487 pp, Year Book Medical Publishers, Chicago, 1987.
10. Greenberger NG, **Moody FG** (co-eds). The Year Book of Digestive Diseases 1988, 475 pp, Year Book Medical Publishers, Chicago, 1988.
11. Greenberger NG, **Moody FG** (co-eds). The Year Book of Digestive Diseases 1989, 459 pp, Year Book Medical Publishers, Chicago, 1989.
12. **Moody FG** (ed-in-chief). Surgical Treatment of Digestive Disease, ed 2, 940 pp, Year Book Medical Publishers, Chicago, 1990.

13. Greenberger NG, **Moody FG** (co-eds). The Year Book of Digestive Diseases 1990, 454 pp, Mosby-Year Book, Chiicago, 1990.
14. Greenberger NG, **Moody FG** (co-eds). The Year Book of Digestive Diseases 1991, 467 pp, Mosby-Year Book, Chicago, 1991.
15. Gitnick G (ed), LaBrecque DR, **Moody FG** (co-eds). Diseases of the Liver and Biliary Tract, 677 pp, Mosby-Year Book, Chicago, 1992.
16. **Moody FG**, Montorsi W, Montorsi M, Zennaro F (eds). Advances in Surgery, 465 pp, Serono Symposia Publications from Raven Press, Vol 84, New York, 1991.
17. Greenberger NG, **Moody FG** (co-eds). The Year Book of Digestive Diseases 1992, 460 pp, Mosby-Year Book, Chicago, 1992.
18. Greenberger NG, **Moody FG** (co-eds). The Year Book of Digestive Diseases 1993, 510 pp, Mosby-Year Book, Chicago, 1993.
19. Gitnick G, LaBrecque DR, **Moody FG** (eds). Malottie del Figato Edelle vie Biliari, Edizone italiana 573 pp, 1993, a cura di Ezio Ventura, McGraw-Hill Libre Itlia srl, Milano.
20. Greenberger NG, **Moody** FG (co-eds). The Year Book of Digestive Diseases 1994, 522 pp, Mosby-Year Book, Chicago, 1994.
21. Greenberger NG, **Moody FG** (co-eds). The Year Book of Digestive Diseases 1995, 552 pp, Mosby-Year Book, Chicago, 1995.
22. Jensen SL, Gregersen H, Shokouh-Amiri MH, **Moody FG** (co-eds). Essentials of Experimental Surgery: Gastroenterology, 725 pp, Harwood Academic Publishers, Amsterdam, 1996.
23. Greenberger NG, **Moody FG** (co-eds). The Year Book of Digestive Disease 1996, 536 pp, Mosby-Year Book, Chicago, 1996.
24. Greenberger NG, **Moody FG** (co-eds). The Year Book of Digestive Disease 1997, pp, Mosby, St. Louis, 1997.